W9-AET-249

SPENSER STUDIES

I

SPENSER STUDIES
A Renaissance
Poetry Annual

I

EDITED BY

Patrick Cullen AND *Thomas P. Roche, Jr.*

UNIVERSITY OF PITTSBURGH PRESS

SPENSER STUDIES:
A RENAISSANCE POETRY ANNUAL
edited by Patrick Cullen and Thomas P. Roche, Jr.

is published annually by the University of Pittsburgh Press as a forum for Spenser scholarship and criticism and related Renaissance subjects. Manuscripts ordinarily should be from 3,000 to 10,000 words in length, should conform to the *MLA Style Sheet,* and should be submitted *in duplicate.* They will be returned only if sufficient postage is enclosed (overseas contributors enclose international reply coupons). Manuscripts and editorial correspondence should be addressed to Thomas P. Roche, Jr., Department of English, Princeton University, Princeton, N.J. 08540.

Within the United States, *Spenser Studies* may be ordered from the University of Pittsburgh Press, Pittsburgh, Pa. 15260.

Overseas orders should be addressed to Feffer and Simons, Inc., 100 Park Avenue, New York, N.Y. 10017, U.S.A.

Published by the University of Pittsburgh Press, Pittsburgh, Pa., 15260
Feffer and Simon, Inc., London
Manufactured in the United States of America

ISSN 0195-9468
ISBN 0-8229-3408-6

For
Leicester Bradner
and
John E. Hankins

Contents

3

"Quietnesse of Minde":
A Theatre for Worldlings as a Protestant Poetics
CARL J. RASMUSSEN

Jan Van Der Noot's *A Theatre for Worldlings* (1569), the poems for which were translated by an adolescent Edmund Spenser, has been generally ignored by Spenserians. However, the prose commentary that accompanies this work is a remarkable piece of rhetoric that teaches us how to read the poems of *A Theatre* and in so doing suggests the lineaments of a poetics rooted in Van Der Noot's Reformed Protestantism. Van Der Noot states that his intention is to move the reader from vanity to spiritual knowledge. This concern with dispositions of the will encourages the reader to consider the speakers of the poems in the *Theatre*. In other words, the poems are dramatic monologues which explore spiritual states. The speakers of the Petrarch "Epigrams" and the Du Bellay "Sonets" (the first two groups of poems) are worldlings ensnared in illusion. The speaker of the four apocalyptic "Sonets" on the other hand, is the Christian visionary, St. John, whose visions are an allegory of conversion. Van Der Noot's extensive commentary on these final four sonnets is notorious for its virulent antipapal polemic, but this polemic has been misunderstood. For Van Der Noot, Rome is a metonymy for a spiritual condition: Rome is his allegory of vanity, and vanity is overcome not with violence (though Van Der Noot does not necessarily eschew violence) but with the Word, which engenders faith and "quietnesse of minde" in the faithful.

29

The Allusive Presentation of *The Shepheardes Calender*
RUTH SAMSON LUBORSKY

Two aspects of the first edition of *The Shepheardes Calender* have been noticed in the critical literature: The apparatus is said to imitate that of the newly edited classic, and this imitation is cited as an example of Renaissance self-consciousness. The research reported here extends the range of these observations by analyzing the entire presentation and by asking who directed it. What emerges as the result of a complex comparative method is that the first edition presents a unique appearance; it does not resemble the printer's other products nor any other single book of its time. The book looks the way it does for three reasons: its presentation (1) incorporates features from other books whose authors are referred to explicitly in the text or into whose genre the *Calender* fits, including chiefly Marot, the newly edited Vergil, the calender/almanac, and the illustrated fable book; (2) imitates the manuscript and early printed book by the way in which some of the decorative initials are placed; and (3) seems to imitate the annotated emblem book by means of the arrangement of the eclogue unit. Because of the originality of the idea of an allusive presentation as well as the complexity of the references, it is argued that we can infer authorial direction—that Spenser, "the newe poet," created a new book.

69
On Reading *The Shepheardes Calender*
BRUCE R. SMITH

For most twentieth-century readers *The Shepheardes Calender* is a less accessible work than *The Faerie Queene,* mainly because it draws on three distinct literary genres more familiar to sixteenth-century readers: classical eclogue, medieval moral almanac, Renaissance pastoral romance. These three genres share a pastoral scenario, but they differ markedly in formal structure, in the nature of the hero, in perceptions of time, in the sense of an ending, and, most importantly, in the intellectual and emotional responses they demand from a reader. The demands they make are, in fact, contradictory. A reader of the work is made to arrive at a reconciliation by working through three conflicting roles. The delicate poise of responses experienced at the end—sympathy for Colin Clout's passion and yet a detached awareness of the larger issues that Colin's career entails—reproduces exactly the artistic irony that Spenser the epic poet has achieved toward Spenser the amorous versifier. A reader finishes *The Shepheardes Calender* possessed of the special skills needed to read *The Faerie Queene.*

95
The Final Emblem of *The Shepheardes Calender*
JUDITH M. KENNEDY

The emblems of *The Shepheardes Calender* are of the kind of *impresa* or device known as the *mot.* These devices are characterized by enigmatic ambiguity and by personal application to the individual's inner intentions. The two words opposed in the final emblem, "Merce non mercede," have a common ancestor (*merx, mercis:* "reward") and in the Renaissance could to some extent be considered synonymous. The distinctions made by the contrasting negative in the final emblem are potentially enigmatic and require that the reader scrupulously meditate the kinds of reward being sought or rejected. The final emblem is unlike the other emblems of the *Calender* in that it is not attached to an eclogue or assigned to a character. In its place at the close of the poem the emblem invites meditation on its application to the amorous, poetic, and religious themes of the *Calender* as a whole. Because

Spenser introduces it as the envoy to his book, we are invited to read it as referring to the author and as explaining his name, Immerito.

107

The Drama of *Amoretti*

ALEXANDER DUNLOP

This reading of *Amoretti* is an attempt to synthesize the insights of traditionalists and numerologists by focusing on the psychology of the lover as poet-narrator. I suggest that we may profitably read *Amoretti* as a dramatization of the process of learning to love. The lover-poet in *Amoretti* progresses from a state of normal human ignorance to a state of relative wisdom concerning love. Because the lover, through his human limitations, is imperfect in his understanding of love, we cannot take his assertions at face value; hence, much of his ranting and complaining shows mainly the inadequacy of his understanding. The lover's education proceeds in three stages, relating to the religious framework of the sequence. The first is the long period of trial and preparation, which corresponds to Lent. The second state is that of revelation through Christ's example of perfect love. The third stage is that of the temporary physical separation of the lovers corresponding to the physical separation of man from God. Recognition of the limitations of the poet-lover enables us to see the important element of irony in *Amoretti*. The irony of the drama results from his inability to relate his personal experience to the larger context of religious values embodied in the symbolic framework that the reader can see, but that the lover cannot. The article includes also new insights into several of the problematical details of the sequence, such as the superscription over sonnet 58, the placement of 62 and the repetition of 35.

121

Babbling Will in *Shake-speares Sonnets* 127 to 154

MARGRETA DE GRAZIA

In this group of sonnets, language takes on the reductional or annihilative tendencies of the speaker's will. Its formal aspects mirror his murky desire to commit acts of darkness with a dark mistress. Common and proper nouns lose their affirmative value so that "fair" becomes "black" and "Will" is reduced to "nothing." Figurative language derives from privative states of absence, want, poverty, sickness. Syntax favors negative constructions even when making affirmations. Logic consists of fallacies rather than proofs so that assertions verge on nonsense. The speaker's discourse should be seen as Shakespeare's poetic rendition of nonlanguage, confused speech, or babble. Tradition taught Elizabethans that Pentecost held out hope of resolving Babylonic linguistic confusion, both that incurred by Nimrod and that made current by contemporary babblers. Reformation of language could be possible if accompanied by conversion of heart or will. The nature of this speaker's passion, however, rules out this possibility. He has given voice not simply to harlotry but to idolatry. His worship of black, flesh, and nothingness both parodies and, more grievously, denies God's Word. His language resists positive, affirmative formulation because it is based on an irrevocable denunciation of creation and Creator. The speaker's will and language are destructive and suicidal, but both remain desperately beyond repair.

135
The "carelesse heauens":
A Study of Revenge and Atonement in *The Faerie Queene*
HUGH MacLACHLAN

If man exists in a world in which there is no system of divine retribution, he is forced to bear responsibility for justice himself. And those who are capable of extracting justice must do so both for themselves and for others who are the victims of evil but too weak to retaliate themselves. This is the situation Spenser explores in the first eight cantos of Book II of *The Faerie Queene*. These cantos can be read as a study of the nature of blood vengeance as understood by Guyon, first from a pagan and classical perspective, and then from the perspective of Christian reconciliation—a movement from personal revenge to divine vengeance and ultimately to divine forgiveness in the figure of Prince Arthur. In the Book of Temperance, Spenser presents us with an anatomy of vengeance as both an ethical and a theological problem for man. And Guyon, a man who is ostensibly a Christian, though one who conceives the world in a classical and essentially pagan manner, must confront the spiritual and psychological problems inherent in a system of personal justice (and injustice), ultimately acknowledging both his own sinfulness and in Arthur a divine mediator upon whom God's wrathful vengeance against all mankind (including Guyon) is justly imposed.

Though wrath and vengeance can be controlled (to a large extent) by human temperance, and classical magnanimity (Guyon) can offer the best of men a paradigm of mercy to live by, in the end this view forgets that *all* men, including the best, need forgiveness. The Mystery of the Redemption, which Spenser questions at the beginning of canto viii, is solved with an understanding of divine magnanimity: grace freely given, not as just reward for the good man's goodness (for it would go to Pyrochles too, if only he would take it), but as an act of divine mercy in the face of human evil. And even divine vengeance in the end will be abated, if man will choose to accept in its stead divine love.

163
The Art of Veiling in the Bower of Bliss
ANTOINETTE B. DAUBER

While recognizing its moral corruption, generations of readers have been distressed when Guyon destroys the Bower of Bliss without a twinge of regret. We cannot wholeheartedly applaud the triumph of an unimaginative, limited virtue over a work of art of compelling beauty. But while Guyon awkwardly defends temperance at all costs, Spenser, almost mysteriously, champions his own visionary poetry, exposing the bad faith of Acrasia's art and setting his knight's virtue in its proper place. The enchantress's art exploits the powerful suggestiveness of veils in order to deceive the viewer. Crystalline fountain and splashing damsels, both multiply veiled, hold out the promise of a divine vision. Guyon, the innocent, yields and is ensnared. While the knight fights back in a release of violence, Spenser, in two images unmistakably his own, traces gossamer nets and restores intimations of divinity to them. Following on the Bower's destruction, humbled by the ease with which art may be misused, the poet examines the relationship between mediator and vision in the proem to Book III. To the one-sided idea of veil as accommodation enunciated in the proem to Guyon's book, he incorporates new insights. The veil covering his divine queen is both a sign of separateness and a vehicle of union, the transitional zone in which self and other may dissolve. Boldly repudiating Guyon's vigilant restraint, the poet joyously succumbs to the seduction of a heavenly art: "My senses lulled are in slomber of delight."

177
Canto Structure in Tasso and Spenser
MAREN-SOFIE RØSTVIG

The new analytical approach illustrated here has its theoretical basis in Augustine's structural concept of unity. Unity is found in a symmetrical or graded arrangement of parts, and the linking between parts is supported by a conscious manipulation of the verbal texture. Both Tasso and Spenser employ significant patterns of verbal repetition to underline thematic or narrative developments (in the epic as a whole, in a single canto, or in a segment). Good examples of the compositional technique are found in the narrative segments on Corceca's house (*FQ* I.iii.10–21) and the escape from the Castle of Pride (*FQ* I.v.45–53). While there are many formal and thematic similarities between Tasso's *Gerusalemme liberata* 15 and *FQ* II.x, in Spenser's chronicle of Briton kings the textual patterns are more elaborate, at the same time that they have the important function of revealing the presence of a unified pattern which flatly contradicts the impression that the course of history is chaotic. Especially noteworthy is the linking, by means of verbal repetition, of stanzas II.x.9 (on the arrival of Brutus in England) and II.x.50 (on the incarnation), a linking which turns this forty-two-stanza sequence into a British analogue to sacred history.

SPENSER STUDIES

I

CARL J. RASMUSSEN

"Quietnesse of Minde":
A Theatre for Worldlings
as a Protestant Poetics

*I*N 1567, fleeing Spanish repression in the Netherlands along with thousands of his countrymen, a Flemish patrician and Protestant named Jan Van Der Noot left Antwerp for London. There he published in 1568 a book called *Het Theatre oft Toon-neel.* A French version, *Le Theatre,* appeared in the same year, and in 1569 there appeared an English version commonly known as *A Theatre for Worldlings. A Theatre* contains three groups of emblematic visionary sonnets. The first group, called "Epigrams," is a translation of Petrarch's *Rime* 323, a sequence of allegorical visions concerning the death of Laura. The second group, called "Sonets," is a translation of eleven visions of the fall of Rome from Joachim Du Bellay's *Songe,* a sonnet sequence inspired by Petrarch's *Rime* 323 and appended to *Les Antiquitez de Rome.* The third group, also called "Sonets," consists of translations of four sonnets written by Van Der Noot himself based on St. John's visions in the Book of Revelation. The sonnets are accompanied by illustrations, and the whole work concludes with a massive 214-page prose commentary, "A Briefe Declaration of the Author vpon his visions."[1]

A Theatre is significant for a number of reasons. It has been called the first English emblem book, and it could be called the first English sonnet sequence.[2] More importantly, however, the poems of *A Theatre* were translated from the French by a teenaged Edmund Spenser. As Spenserian juvenilia, *A Theatre* both serves as a cultural link between Spenser and the Continent in the late 1560s and, in the words of J. A. Van Dorsten, "marks the transition from a period in which 'England, the mother of excellent minds,' had grown 'so hard a stepmother to poets,' to the great flowering of humanist-inspired vernacular experiments in the late-seventies."[3]

Despite its importance, however, *A Theatre* has not been given serious treatment by English-speaking scholars.[4] The crude nature of the edition, with Spenser's juvenile translations and its woodcuts as opposed to the rather elegant copperplates of the Dutch and French editions, has not encouraged English-speaking scholars to consider it as art.[5] More serious objections center on the prose commentary, which is generally dismissed as a stock expression of world-contempt and antipapal propaganda. Though some interesting recent scholarship has tended to correct neglect of the prose commentary, *A Theatre* as an aesthetic entity remains largely misunderstood.[6] This neglect is not justifiable, for though superficially distasteful, the prose commentary is a subtle and complex piece of rhetoric and a rare scholarly resource. It serves as a lens through which we can read the poems of *A Theatre* as they were intended to be read, and it suggests the lineaments of a poetics—a poetics rooted in Van Der Noot's Reformed Protestantism. The existence of such a poetics has wide-ranging implications. The commentary not only contributes to our understanding of the poems in *A Theatre,* but also sheds light on the still murky literary contexts of the mid–sixteenth century. We should not forget that *A Theatre* was perhaps a formative influence on one of the major, though still enigmatic, poets of the English Renaissance, Edmund Spenser.

Like a good Renaissance poet, Van Der Noot presumes to teach. This intention is apparent both in the dedicatory epistle to Queen Elizabeth and in the opening of the prose commentary. I quote at length from both passages, respectively:

> I haue among other my trauayles bene occupied aboute thys little Treatyse, wherin is sette forth the vilenesse and basenesse of worldely things, whiche commonly withdrawe vs from heauenly and spirituall matters. To the end that vnderstanding the vanitie and baseness of the same, and therewithall consideryng the miserable calamities that ensue therupon, we might be moued the rather to forsake them, and gyue oure selues to the knowledge of Heauenly and eternall things, whence all true happinesse and felicitie doth procede.
> (Sigs. A₃–A₃v)

> I haue thought it good, so compendiously as possibly I may, to shewe how vaine, transitorie, deceitfull, vnprofitable, and vncertain worldly things be, and that heauenly things only are euerlasting, immortal, excellent, good, and most to be desired, euen as God him self is the fountain of all goodnesse, and perfecte in all things which can be desired, yea more a greate deale than oure vnderstandyng is able to vtter or to comprehende: to this ende and purpose, that men conuertyng vnto the Lorde, in hym only seeking their whole salua-

tion and perfect blysse, myght leade their life paciently with a good conscience in all quietnesse of minde and spirite, and so to enioy the true christian libertie and spirituall gladnesse here in thys worlde, that in the worlde to come they might be inheritours (by grace) of the euerlasting ioyes in eternall glorie, purchased thorough the bloud of oure Sauioure Jesus Christ.   (Sigs. E₁–E₁v)

It is clear from these passages that Van Der Noot's prose commentary is rooted in two concepts: the vanity of worldly things and the knowledge of "Heauenly and eternall things." If we are to understand the *Theatre* we must take care fully to grasp these concepts. By the knowledge of "Heauenly and eternall things" Van Der Noot does not at all refer to comprehension: God is "more a great deale than oure vnderstandyng is able to vtter or to comprehende." Clearly the spiritual knowledge of which Van Der Noot speaks is *faith*. For Protestants of the time faith was indeed a mode of knowledge. Calvin, for example, defines faith as "a firm and sure knowledge of the divine favour toward us, founded on the truth of a free promise in Christ, and revealed to our minds, and sealed on our hearts, by the Holy Spirit" (*Institutes* 3.2.7).[7] So that there might be no doubt, Calvin elaborates on what he means by knowledge:

By knowledge we do not mean comprehension, such as that which we have of things falling under human sense. For that knowledge is so much superior, that the human mind must far surpass and go beyond itself in order to reach it. Nor even when it has reached it does it comprehend what it feels, but persuaded of what it comprehends not, it understands more from mere certainty of persuasion that it could discern of any human matter by its own capacity.

(*Institutes* 3.2.14)

For Van Der Noot, as for Calvin, spiritual knowledge, or faith, is a kind of visionary knowledge of transcendent things which manifests itself in a spiritual condition of calm and beatitude. Given this concept of knowledge, Van Der Noot cannot be interested in a rote didacticism. He cannot teach propositions because the transcendent God is not to be contained in propositions. Instead, Van Der Noot seeks to convert the reader "vnto the Lorde," that is, to illumine the reader with the visionary knowledge of faith and thereby instill in the reader the beatitude of "quietnesse of minde and spirite."[8]

To understand better what Van Der Noot means by knowledge of "Heauenly and eternall things," we must also grasp what he means by the vanity of worldly things. Since Van Der Noot intends to move the reader "to enioy the true christian libertie and spirituall gladnesse *here in thys worlde*" (my italics), it would be inconsistent for him to preach world-contempt. [9] Quite to the contrary, Van Der Noot affirms the goodness of the world in a caveat at the beginning of the prose commentary:

> But before we enter any farther to speake of the vanities of worldly and transitorie Richèsse, I wil warne thee (gentle Reader) that when I speake of substance, riches, estates, bodily health, of wife and children, and other like, whiche all are the good giftes of God, I mean not in respect of the thing it selfe, nor yet the good vse of the same (for in it is no suche default,) but onely I meane the great abuse whiche commonly is seene in the vnnatural and vnbrideled desire, whervnto rich and worldly men ar inclined. (Sig. E₁v)

The things of this world are in themselves good. Vanity cannot inhere in the objective world, "in respect of the thing it selfe." Rather, vanity is the abuse of the objective world by the "vnnatural and vnbrideled desire" of the human will. In other words, the vanity of worldly things is an aspect of the self: It resides in the concupiscent will of fallen man. This psychologizing of vanity, which implies a direct rejection of the medieval tendency to world-contempt, is a hallmark of Protestant thought. [10]

It is now apparent that Van Der Noot's fundamental concepts, worldly vanity and spiritual knowledge, refer to spiritual states or tendencies of the human will. Because of his interest in the will, or what we might call the self, Van Der Noot is what the Protestant philosopher Paul Tillich would call an "Existential thinker":

> The Existential thinker cannot have pupils in the ordinary sense. He cannot communicate any ideas, because *they* are just *not* the truth he wants to teach. He can only create in his pupil by indirect communication that "Existential state" or personal experience out of which the pupil may think and act. Kierkegaard carries out this interpretation for Socrates. But all Existential philosophers have made similar statements—naturally, for if the approach to Existence is through personal experience, the only possibility of educating is to bring the pupil by indirect methods to a personal experience of his own Existence. [11]

Van Der Noot is precisely such a teacher. Poetry (or, in the case of the prose commentary, rhetoric) is his "indirect method" for confronting the "Existential state" of the reader. The concern with existential states instead of with the world of objects is indicative of a kind of mysticism:

> There is more of the Protestant than the Catholic heritage in this kind of "mysticism"; but it *is* mysticism in trying to transcend the estranged "objectivity" as well as the empty "subjectivity" of the present epoch. Historically speaking, the Existential philosophy attempts to return to a pre-Cartesian attitude in which the sharp gulf between the subjective and the objective "realms" had not yet been created, and the essence of objectivity could be found in the depth of subjectivity—in which God could be best approached through the soul.[12]

To understand Van Der Noot's Protestant poetics, we must first understand his "pre-Cartesian attitude."

As we have seen, Van Der Noot intends to move the reader to spiritual knowledge by confronting him with worldly vanity. Since, however, vanity inheres in the will, it cannot be fully evoked by mere images from the "objective" world.[13] Worldly vanity is to be *experienced* as a set of human responses to the world. Similarly, faith is not an intellectual apprehension of the objective world but a visionary knowledge which transcends the merely objective. In this light the poems of *A Theatre* emerge not as simple emblems but as a series of dramatic monologues which explore the soul in its relation to God and his creation: *A Theatre* evokes worldly vanity and spiritual knowledge in and through the personae of the poems as these personae respond to emblematic representations of reality. The emblems themselves are not objective. They are subjective transformations of the objective world which serve to reflect the existential states of the personae. In effect, Van Der Noot's Protestant mysticism generates dramatis personae who are the characters in his *Theatre*.

The fact that *A Theatre* is indeed a theater is suggested by the title which alludes to the *topos*, prevalent in the Renaissance, of the *theatrum mundi*, the theater of the world. The *theatrum mundi* is essentially a Neoplatonic metaphor which cogently illustrates the insubstantial nature of the phenomenal world. However, insofar as the *topos* can be made to focus on the perversity of the human will, that is, to illustrate the confused and concupiscent responses of the will to the phenomenal world, it can serve the Protestant mysticism which informs Van Der Noot's thought. Plotinus, a traditional source for the *topos*, at times seems to employ the *theatrum mundi* to illustrate the vanity of the will in its embrace of the phenomenal world:

Murders, death in all its guises, the reduction and sacking of cities, all must be to us just such a spectacle as the changing scenes of a play; all is but the varied incident of a plot, costume on and off, acted grief and lament. For on earth, in all the succession of life, it is not the Soul within but the Shadow outside of the authentic man, that grieves and complains and acts out the plot on this world stage which men have dotted with stages of their own constructing. All this is the doing of man knowing no more than to live the lower and outer life, and never perceiving that, in his weeping and in his graver doings alike, he is but at play. . . . We must remember, too, that we cannot take tears and laments as proofs that anything is wrong; children cry and whimper where there is nothing amiss.[14]

In this passage Plotinus does not disparage the phenomenal world as such. Rather, he disparages the human will which so passionately participates in it. Plotinus implies that the *theatrum mundi* is indeed the creation of human folly. Such a use of the *topos* is entirely consistent with Van Der Noot's Protestant mysticism. Though he was not necessarily a Neoplatonist, Van Der Noot employs a Neoplatonic *topos* for his own ends.[15]

In the light of Van Der Noot's Protestant mysticism and use of the *theatrum mundi,* the title of *A Theatre* reveals its full significance:

A THEATRE
wherein be repre-
sented as wel the miseries & calamities that follow the voluptuous Worldlings,
As also the greate ioyes and
plesures which the faith-
full do enioy.
An Argument both profitable and
delectable, to all that sincerely
loue the word of God.   (Sig. A₁)

The reader may expect to encounter the "voluptuous Worldlings" and "the faithful" in the personae of the poems of *A Theatre* and to experience their respective spiritual states from within, through the medium of lyric poetry. By thus empathizing freely with a series of narrators who embody the spiritual spectrum from vanity to faith, the reader is to be led on a spiritual journey. Because the poems of *A Theatre* are in this large sense rhetorical, the prose commentary cannot "objectively" comment upon them.

Instead, the prose commentary itself mimics the lyric flow of the poems and thereby becomes a kind of record of the intended effect of the poems on the reader.

Having stated his intention to lead the reader to "quietnesse of minde," Van Der Noot begins with a diagnosis of the disease which he intends to cure. This diagnosis amounts to a seventeen-page explication of 1 John 2. 15–17, verses which serve as one of the important thematic loci in *A Theatre:*[16]

> Loue not the worlde, neyther the thyngs that are in the worlde: If any man loue the worlde, the loue of the Father is not in hym. For all that (sayth he) whych is in the worlde, is the luste of the eyes, and the pride of lyfe, is not of the father, but of the worlde, and the worlde passeth away, and the lustes therof, but he that fulfylleth the wyll of God abydeth for euer.   (Sig. F₂)

(Van Der Noot inexplicably omits the lust of the flesh, but he develops the theme in his commentary.) The verse reinforces Van Der Noot's suggestion that worldly vanity is the result of human lust, and he expands upon this theme in the explication. With a host of examples, he argues that lust, through its perversion of the phenomenal world, generates the illusions of the *theatrum mundi:*

> Earthy & transitorie things are like vnto a cloude painted on a wall, whiche seemeth to be some thing, where as it is nothyng: as a foole foloweth the shadow of a cādle, thynking it to be some body, euen so doth the carnall and voluptuous man folow and pursue the earthly trashe in stede of heauenly treasures.   (Sig. E₇)

This nexus of lust and illusion is the spiritual condition of worldly vanity.

The lengthy explication of the verse from 1 John, while establishing certain terms important for the whole commentary, serves as a prelude to the commentary on the epigrams from Petrarch which constitute the first sequence of sonnets in *A Theatre.* For example, Van Der Noot's discussion of "Loue" establishes the perspective from which the reader is to view Petrarch's love for Laura; it is an ominous perspective:

> Plato sayth, that Loue at the beginning, giueth some sweetenesse, but in the ende engendreth one mischiefe vpon an other. . . . And these things followyng, proceede from carnal loue, to wete, care, sorrowes and griefes, weaknesse of the braynes, curiousnesse in ap-

parell, madnesse, dreames, thoughts and sighyng, calamities, er-
rours, anguish, vnquietnesse, trouble, foolishnesse, vncomlynesse,
wantonnesse, mystrustfulnesse, iealousie, and other lyke. . . . Loue
maketh a man oute of hys wyttes, and cleane besyde hym selfe, it
casteth hym backwarde, and seduceth hym thorough sweetenesse
and flatterie, it counselleth nothyng accordyng vnto reason and
equitie, but leadeth vnto al enormities.   (Sigs. F₁–F₁v)

We should recall that Van Der Noot does not condemn sexuality in itself.
As we have seen, he calls wife and children "good giftes of God." However, his attitudes about "Loue" should give us pause: His epigrams are
translations of love poems by one of the most famous lovers in Italian
literature.

  The commentary on the epigrams begins with a brief biography of
Petrarch—Van Der Noot is ever conscious of persona:

Of which oure visions the learned Poete *M. Francisce Petrarche* Gentleman of *Florence,* did inuent and write in *Tuscan* the six firste, after
such tyme as hee had loued honestly the space of .xxi. yeares a faire,
gracious, and a noble Damosell, named *Laurette,* or (as it plesed him
best) *Laura,* borne of *Auinion,* who afterward hapned to die, he being
in *Italy,* for whose death (to shewe his greate grief) he mourned ten
yeares togyther, and amongest many of his songs and sorowfull lam-
entations, deuised and made a Ballade or song, containyng the sayd
visions, which bicause they serue wel to our purpose, I haue out of
the *Brabants* speache, turned them into the Englishe tongue.

                                        (Sigs. F₃–F₃v)[17]

This sketch is sympathetic to Petrarch. The story of "honest" love is wist-
fully sad. But, as we have seen, the story is placed in a context which
views "Loue" in a sterner way. There is a clear inconsistency here: In one
instance Van Der Noot speaks of "Loue" as blatant folly and in another
instance proceeds to tell the story of Petrarch's love for Laura. The inconsistency, however, is purposeful. It reveals a rhetorical intention. If we
read the biographical sketch of Petrarch from the perspective of the commentary on 1 John, we are aware that the Petrarch of the epigrams, however sympathetically treated, is a worldling and that the epigrams are the
vain "dreames" brought forth by "weaknesse of the braynes." In effect,
Van Der Noot has subtly prepared us to view Petrarch from an ironic distance, but this preparation has not been so obvious or harsh as to destroy
our natural empathy for the situation or our susceptibility to the lyric

power of the poetry. The prose commentary directs us to view the Petrarch persona both critically and sympathetically or, in literary terms, with fear and pity: We are moved to view the Petrarch persona as a tragic hero.

The six epigrams follow a common pattern in which the persona contemplates the destruction of something beautiful or magnificent and laments its passing. These "visions" are followed by a four-line envoy (sig. B₇v) in which the persona, overcome with melancholy, expresses a desire to die. Van Der Noot reads the first three epigrams as allegories of the death of Laura.[18] He then skims over the final three and presents this conclusion:

> And thus as he hadde passed ouer many a yeare in greate and vn-
> fayned loue towardes hir (duryng hir life time) what with flatterie
> and what in commendyng of hir beautie, caused him vpon a sodaine
> chaunge after hir departure (as it is sayde) so long a time to mourne
> and to lamente, but considering with him self, that there was no
> comfort, hope or saluation in worldely loue to be loked for, turned
> himselfe to Godwarde, lamenting and sorowing the rest of hys lyfe,
> and repented hym of his former life so ydlely and vndecently spent.
>
> (Sigs. F₄–F₄v)

Van Der Noot's interest in Petrarch's change of heart (which perhaps refers to Petrarch's *Secretum*)[19] serves to intensify the ironic distance between the persona and the reader. Here it becomes explicit that Petrarch's love for Laura is in fact the expression of a "life . . . ydlely and vndecently spent." This gentle invocation of the sterner perspective established by the commentary on 1 John encourages the reader to see the persona's melancholy—which is evident in all the poems and particularly so in the request for death in the envoy—as sinful despair. Laura's death should not evoke despair at all. Petrarch himself says in the tenth line of the last epigram that "well assurde she mounted vp to ioy" (sig. B₆v). The persona's despair is the mark of his vanity. His love for Laura immerses him in the particularity and apparent randomness of phenomenal events. He is lost in the *theatrum mundi*.

The Petrarch persona's response should be faith. Faith apprehends the providential plan which infuses the world and thereby dispels despair. Calvin speaks thus of the force of the awareness of Providence:

> But Christ declares that, provided we had eyes clear enough, we
> should perceive that in this spectacle the glory of his Father is brightly
> displayed. . . . When the sky is overcast with dense clouds, and a

violent tempest arises, the darkness which is presented to our eyes, and the thunder which strikes our ears, and stupifies all our senses with terror, make us imagine that everything is thrown into confusion, though in the firmament itself all continues quiet and serene. In the same way, when the tumultuous aspect of human affairs unfits us for judging, we should still hold that God, in the pure light of his justice and wisdom, keeps all these commotions in due subordination, and conducts them to their proper end.   (*Institutes* 1.17.1)

The Petrarch persona does not have eyes clear enough to see the providential plan. He is therefore a worldling, but because of his grand passion and because of his lyric power (if we overlook Spenser's feeble translation) the reader has been moved to see him feelingly. The intensity of Petrarch's "honest" love for Laura excites the reader's empathy, and the consequences of that love evoke the reader's commiseration. The fact that we have been rhetorically encouraged by the prose commentary initially to empathize with the Petrarch persona suggests that we are not merely to judge him for his faithlessness. Our empathy compels us to experience, with Aristotelian fear and pity, his sin. From Van Der Noot's Protestant perspective, the Petrarchan "Epigrams" constitute a tragedy.

The second group of poems in *A Theatre* consists of eleven sonnets from Du Bellay's *Songe*. The commentary on specific poems is very brief, serving only to indicate that the emblems represent the ruins of Rome. However, the commentary on the whole group proceeds to suggest that the ruins of Rome are evidence of God's hand in history. Van Der Noot sketches the history of Rome: how it from "a base and low estate was lifted vp, and become very hie" (sigs. F_5–F_5v); how, because of lust, the Romans sought to attain empire; and how, for this lust, the Romans "haue bene iustly plagued, receyuing according to their desertes, such measure as they had measured to others" (sig. F_6v). Thus, Rome was overrun and destroyed, and "This is shewed vnto vs by these visions and sonets" (sig. F_7). The ruins of Rome, rather than a melancholy waste, are an affirmation of God's providence:

So *Rome* neuer obtained the like estimation since, as it had before being in his floure, as it is to be seene yet by some auncient monuments, buildings columnes, & walles, which appere there as yet to beare witnesse of Gods vengeance which came vpon them for their sin and wickednesse, to the ende that all godly and well disposed persons mighte perceiue, that God can and will perfourme his promises, the which he hath thretned in his worde.   (Sig. F_7)

All the visions in *A Theatre* reveal the workings of Providence. Petrarch should recognize God's providential hand in nature: Though Laura dies, she is saved. Du Bellay should recognize God's providential hand in Roman history: The ruins of Rome suggest that God punishes the wicked.[20] But Providence is not apparent to worldlings. Petrarch despairs at his visions. The Du Bellay persona expresses a numinous wonder—even, perhaps, a kind of faith as is apparent in his first sonnet: "So I knowing the worldes vnstedfastnesse, / Sith onely God surmountes the force of tyme. / In God alone do stay my confidence" (sig. B_8), but his "faith" is incomplete. He never comes to realize the full religious significance of the things he sees. He is overcome with wonder and awe at the magnificence of Rome and even laments its ruin.

Though Van Der Noot does not make as much of Du Bellay's spiritual career as he does of Petrarch's, a clue to his view of the Du Bellay persona is supplied by the four poems from the *Songe* which he omitted from the "Sonets." Of the four, at least two (8 and 14) allude to the Book of Revelation. In other words, the work itself, though in a veiled way, interprets the ruins of Rome in terms of the Christian Apocalypse.[21] By omitting the sonnets which most explicitly suggest this interpretation, Van Der Noot left the Du Bellay persona without scriptural moorings. The persona, though possessed of a religious consciousness, is spiritually adrift. Scripture is an essential guide for the faithful, and Calvin expresses this fact with a vivid metaphor—the metaphor of Scripture as spectacles:

> For as the aged, or those whose sight is defective, when any book, however fair, is set before them, though they perceive that there is something written, are scarcely able to make out two consecutive words, but, when aided by glasses, begin to read distinctly, so Scripture, gathering together the impressions of Deity, which, till then, lay confused in their minds, dissipates the darkness, and shows us the true God clearly. (*Institutes* 1.6.1)

The Du Bellay persona cannot read in the book of nature (or, rather, of history) because he lacks the spectacles of Scripture. He thus falls short of the knowledge of "Heauenly and eternall things."

There is one possible exception to the lack of scriptural allusion in the Du Bellay "Sonets," however. In the last one (sig. D_1v) the persona sees "Typhaeus sister," with a hundred vanquished kings at her feet, struck down by the heavens. In the woodcut she is dressed like Roma Victrix. As Gilbert Gadoffre has pointed out (speaking of the *Songe*) "la soeur du grand Typhée" has much in common with the whore of Babylon. Like the whore (in Revelation 17.18) she reigns over the kings of the earth, and she is attacked by the heavens and destroyed.[22] Van Der Noot himself suggests the relationship because he identifies Rome both with "Typhaeus sister" (sig. F_5) and with the whore of Babylon (sig. K_5). But they are not exactly identical. Both are images for Rome, but at different historical periods. In Van Der Noot's interpretation, "Typhaeus sister" represents imperial Rome; the whore, papal Rome. "Typhaeus sister" is a pagan mythical image that darkly prefigures the biblical whore of Babylon. The important thing to understand, however, is that the two are typologically related.[23] Once this relationship is understood, the Du Bellay "Sonets" reveal their own meaning: The ruins of Rome represent Christ's victory. The scriptural allusion, however, is abstruse enough to be beyond the persona. Because he lacks scriptural perspective (due to Van Der Noot's selected omissions) the Du Bellay persona is, in Calvin's terms, confused in darkness.

The relative importance of the final sonnet sequence, the four apocalyptic sonnets, is suggested by the fact that nearly three-fourths of the prose commentary is dedicated to it.[24] As the richly allusive visions of a divinely inspired persona, they are the gem for which the entire sequence serves as setting. The apocalyptic sonnets are grouped with and arise out of the Du Bellay sonnets because, on one level, they are about Rome:

> *Daniel* and *Paule* they haue foretold that *Antechrist* shoulde be borne of the subuersion of the Empire, and desolation of *Rome*. And to the ende we myght speake more at large of the thing, I haue taken foure visions out of the reuelation of S. John, where as the holy ghost by S. John setteth him out in his colours. (Sig. G_2v)

Antichrist in the guise of the beast of the Apocalypse is the image dominating St. John's first two visions, and Van Der Noot devotes his commentary to assisting his visionary persona by explicating Antichrist, by setting him out "in his colours." Van Der Noot's interpretation of Antichrist is complex. On one level (as the passage above suggests) he identifies Antichrist with the Roman church. This level is reinforced by Van Der Noot's spelling, "Antechrist," which suggests a vague eschatological anticipation of the collapse of the Roman church. On another level, however, Van Der Noot identifies Antichrist with worldly vanity. As a spiritual condition, Antichrist cannot be isolated as an objective historical entity and thus transcends identification with any human institution. The setting out of Antichrist "in his colours," therefore, involves both vigorous antipapal polemic and anatomy of spiritual states. For Van Der Noot, however, these processes are not separate. By attacking Rome, Van Der Noot attacks the vanity by which it is possessed.

The first apocalyptic sonnet is about the rise of the beast of the Apocalypse. The beast (i.e., Antichrist) signifies "the congregation of the wicked and proude hypocrites . . . whelpes and generations of the deuyll" (sig. G₂v). Later Van Der Noot calls the beast the "cursed generation of *Antechrist,* his [Satan's] beastly membres" (sig. G₆v). Van Der Noot here, as elsewhere, parodies St. Paul's metaphor of the mystical body of Christ (1 Corinthians 12.12–27). The beast is a spiritual entity: the mystical body of Satan. Van Der Noot's polemic further presumes that the mystical body of Satan is at war with the mystical body of Christ and that all mankind is divided between them. There is no middle ground. These two cosmic images thus form the metaphorical framework for the commentary on the first three sonnets. Onto this spiritual framework Van Der Noot weaves the antipapal polemic by identifying the beast, the "membres" of Satan, with the Roman hierarchy. The Roman hierarchy is Satan's bureaucracy:

This beast is that great Antechrist (of whom we haue spoken right now) or rather the bodie of the diuel, containyng within him the Pope, Cardinals, patriarkes, legates, bishops, doctors, abbots, priours, chanons, Monkes, friers prebendaries, priests, indulgences, bulles, Nonnes [etc.]. (Sig. K₁v)

In the second sonnet, which is about the whore of Babylon and her fall, Van Der Noot finds an allegory about the Roman church: The whore is papal Rome, and her fall is a prophecy of the success of the Reformation and the ultimate collapse of the papacy (sigs. K₃–K₇).

The task of explicating Antichrist is not so simple, however. Antichrist is ultimately a spiritual condition, and to explicate it fully, Van Der Noot cannot simply rail at Rome. However, he has fully (if implicitly) explicated the condition of vanity in the Petrarch and Du Bellay poems and their commentary, and further explication would be repetitive. Nonetheless, he must incorporate the theme of vanity into his explication of Antichrist. He does so by returning to the theme of illusion. The Roman church is a medium of carnal illusion—it codifies as dogma the tissue of illusion generated by lust:

Sathan is only of abilitie and power to blowe into their eares the thyng whiche they with violence, and by force maintayne: where as he is but able by fansies and inspiration, there are these his meete instruments to perfourme it & put in execution by violence, and

power, by menaces and compulsion. . . . When he hath only en-
gendred and foūd out any error or false doctrine, they with al dili-
gence, as an infallible truth, allow, confirme and stablishe it, and
make of it a necessarie article to beleue on. . . . As he hath founde
out any lye (as he is the father of all lies, and hath ben since the beginning) so may they holde it for a perfecte written veritie, makyng
it of good authoritie and might, as experience may testifie, they haue
done. (Sigs. G₃–G₃v)

On the surface, this is simply more polemic, but it establishes a crucial
point. The Roman church is not in itself vain. Rather, it is the medium or
the locus of vanity. Vanity is what Van Der Noot seeks to overcome, for
vanity—not the Roman church as such—keeps the worldlings in bondage:

As the holy ghost and the sprite of Christ openeth the misteries of
the truth in his elect euen so on the other side hath the spirit of er-
roure, since the death and reuelation of Christ, darkned truth and
set forth the secretes of his malice in the ennimies of Christ.
(Sig. G₇v)

I do not mean to suggest that Van Der Noot does not viciously attack the
Roman church. I do mean to suggest that Rome is not the focus of his at-
tack. Viewed with spiritual understanding, the Roman church for Van
Der Noot is merely a metonymy, a palpable embodiment, of the Anti-
christ of worldly vanity. In other words, the Roman church becomes Van
Der Noot's allegory of vanity.

Having shown Antichrist "in his colours" in the commentary on the
first two apocalyptic sonnets, Van Der Noot proceeds to explicate the
overcoming of Antichrist in his commentary on the third. In part, he
looks to the dissolution of the Roman church, and he views the confiscation of religious houses in England and Germany as prophetic occurrences.[25]
But this historical level is subordinate to a larger, spiritual sense: Antichrist must be overcome in the souls of men. Therefore, the commentary
on the final two sonnets turns away from polemic and concerns itself with
the spiritual Antichrist. Worldly vanity is to be overcome by an act of en-
lightenment. Indeed, Van Der Noot's own weapon in the great cosmic
battle of his times is his *Theatre,* which seeks to lead its reader to "quietnesse of minde."

At the beginning of the commentary on the third apocalyptic sonnet
Van Der Noot at last unveils the source of the knowledge of "Heauenly
and eternall things":

A Theatre for Worldlings as a Protestant Poetics

I saw the heauens open: that is to say. The misteries of God were shewed me, and his secretes were fully declared and expoūded vnto me, I perceiue that through faith and humblenesse, great knowledge of the misteries of God were obtained. For the heauens are opened when Gods word is freely preached, and are shut vp when it is not preached, or not regarded, but in the stead of it, men are fedde with dreames and lies.   (Sig. M₅v)

Scripture is the medium of God's "misteries." Indeed Van Der Noot interprets St. John's esoteric, visionary experience as an allegory of the simple act of reading (or hearing) Scripture.[26] The commentary here for the first time opens the possibility of a purely mystical—one is tempted to call it anagogical—reading of all four apocalyptic sonnets. They can now be seen as a mirror of the soul's journey from vanity to faith; the experience of the divinely inspired persona, St. John, is an allegory of Christian conversion. The first two sonnets, mystically interpreted, are about the Babylonian captivity of the flesh: In this sense the biblical image of Antichrist is a mirror of vanity in the human soul. The third sonnet, as we shall see, is about the victory of Christ, the Logos or divine wisdom, over vanity in the souls of the faithful; the fourth, about the spiritual liberty won through this victory. Taken together, the four sonnets constitute the Gospel message in miniature. It should be noted that for Calvin, as for other Reformers, the Gospel is the effectual element in Scripture and all Scripture can be subsumed in the Gospel.[27] Therefore the apocalyptic "Sonets" can be said to contain the whole of Scripture.

At the heart of Scripture is Christ. St. John encounters Christ in the image of the faithful man who overcomes the beast in the third apocalyptic sonnet. This image has several different but interrelated significances for Van Der Noot. It evokes Christ's passion.[28] It is also a prophecy of the victory of the Reformers over the Roman church.[29] Most importantly, however, in a spiritual sense, the image is an allegory of Christ's victory over vanity in the souls of the faithful. Above all, Christ is the Word, the image of the invisible God:

And his name was called the word of God. Christ Jesu the sonne of god, is that eternall and euerlasting word of God, which was from the beginning by God, by whom also heauen and earth are made, and all that in them is, the verye Image of his substance in whom the father is represented, wherby also we vnderstand and know the wil of the father, for the word of God is a true guid of conscience. The word was made flesh: that is, became mā for our sakes, sauing, justifying, and glorifying all those that beleeue on him.   (Sig. M₈)

Christ in his role as the "verye Image of his substance in whom the father is represented" is the cosmic Christ, the Logos upon whom the cosmos is structured and by whom man is able to know the transcendent God. This is the Christ of Colossians,

> Who is the image of the inuisible God, the first borne of euerie creature. For by him were all things created, which are in heauen, and which are in earth, things visible and inuisible: whether *they be* Thrones, or Dominions, or Principalities, or Powers, all things were created by him and for him, And he is before all things, and in him all things consist. And he is the head of the bodie of the Church: he is the beginning, & the first borne of the dead, that in all things he might haue the preeminence. For it pleased *the Father,* that in him shulde all fulnes dwell, And by him to reconcile all things vnto him self, and to set at peace through the blood of his crosse bothe the things in earth, and the things in heauen.
>
> (Colossians 1.15–20, Geneva edition)[30]

In the sense that Christ is the only possible object of spiritual knowledge and is known not merely intellectually but through the transcendent process of faith, Christ is the Truth:

> This is the onely and true sonne of God which is called faithfull, iust, and true, bicause he is founde faithfull, and vnfallible in hys promises and woorde, for the Lord (saith the Psalmist) is very righteous in all his wayes, true in his sayings, perfect in all his doings. He cannot but teach a right, and speake a trouth, for he is the truthe him selfe, No more cannot those which are indued in his spirite, who leadeth and conducteth them in all truthe.   (Sig. M₆)

As Truth, the cosmic Christ breaks the nexus of lust and illusion in the souls of the faithful. Thus the third apocalyptic sonnet allegorically represents the process of spiritual liberation: St. John sees a vision which represents the breaking of the bonds of sin. This spiritual victory is the necessary condition for the overcoming of the historical Antichrist. The sword with which the faithful man destroys the beast is the Scripture, which has the power to liberate the faithful and to condemn the wicked (sigs. M$_8$v–N$_1$ and O$_2$v–O$_3$). The liberating force of Christ dispels the vanity which Van Der Noot finds in the Roman church. For Van Der Noot, the historical struggle with Rome is finally an outward manifestation and result of the invisible battle waged by the Word in the souls of the faithful.

In the fourth apocalyptic sonnet St. John contemplates the New Jerusalem. The New Jerusalem is both a heavenly city and an allegory of the spiritual condition of faith:

> *I saw* (sayth S. John) *a newe heauen, and a new earth.* S. Peter sayth also, that euery thing (going before the iudge) shalbe clensed and purified, and not consumed, for al things must be changed and made cleane of all corruptiblenesse. He meaneth not (sayeth *Aretes*) that the creatures shoulde consume away, and be no more, but onely ỹ they seruing to a better vse, shoulde be renued, so the godly and chosen shall be deliuered two maner of wayes, that is to say: Here in this worlde from sin, & hereafter of death & damnation, & so shall be led & conducted vnto the true libertie & ioyfull inheritance of ỹ children of God. (Sigs. O₃v–O₄)

Van Der Noot in the remainder of the commentary considers the mystical level exclusively. He explicates the New Jerusalem as a spiritual state to be experienced *in this world*. For example, the foundation stones of the New Jerusalem—which Van Der Noot discusses in great detail (sigs. P₂v–P₅v)—signify the gifts and graces of the Holy Spirit. The "Chrisophrasius,"[31] the tenth stone garnishing the foundations of the New Jerusalem, represents visionary poets:

> *The tenth of a Chrisophrasius,* whose nature is to shine like gold, and yet greenish in the sight. Such are those, who hauing receiued good knowledge & perfect wisdom of God, distribute vnto others according vnto the talent which god hath deliuered vnto thē. Therby to awake the sluggish and dreaming people, and bring to heauenly meditations. Amongst those, may Ezechiel wel be coūted, which in his time did see maruellous things, and wonderful straunge Reuelations. (Sig. P₄v)

This discussion of those who have received the "talent" to "distribute good knowledge" may suggest Van Der Noot's conception of his own poetry. Perhaps through his poetry, a gift of the Holy Spirit (doubly so since his apocalyptic "Sonets" were inspired by Scripture), he would be a second Ezekiel to wake the people from their carnal dreams. The New Jerusalem—the experience of faith—is in part structured on a foundation of such visionary poets.

In the middle of the New Jerusalem, St. John finds the sources of spiritual knowledge and the tranquility which they engender. An angel leads him into the city to the River of the Water of Life, the doctrine of Christ which "maketh whole, and gyueth saluation to oure soules" (sigs. P_6–P_6v). The river is the two testaments of Scripture (sigs. P_6v–P_7). The angel also leads St. John to the tree of life, "namely Christ Jesus the mediatour and pastour, the sauiour and redeemer of the worlde" (sig. P_7). Its fruits signify the fruits of the Holy Spirit which adorn the world (sig. P_7): "All they which are thys Congregation & people haue continually so long as they lyue, greate Consolation in all their assaultes and trialles, and in all kinde of aduersitie both spirituall and temporall" (sigs. P_7–P_7v). Even in the tribulation of this world, the faithful enjoy the fruits of the New Jerusalem. Like Rome, the New Jerusalem is an allegorical image of a spiritual condition. Rome, the carnal city of man, is the image of worldly vanity. The New Jerusalem, the city of God, is the image of the knowledge of "Heauenly and eternall things." The concepts on which Van Der Noot's prose commentary is structured are figured forth in the images of the Augustinian earthly and heavenly cities. The Augustinian cast of Van Der Noot's Protestant thought tends to dissolve his antipapal polemic in mystical allegory.

St. John, whose visions are multiply allusive and complex, is not as prominent a narrator as are Petrarch and Du Bellay. In the woodcut accompanying the final sonnet (sig. D_6), St. John is portrayed on the mount of contemplation, directed by the angel to view the New Jerusalem, the outward image of his spiritual condition. His general lack of prominence is, however, fitting. His visions do not arise as the result of his own concupiscent desires or misguided musings. He is not properly a character wrapped in the illusions of the *theatrum mundi*. On the contrary, his visions are scriptural images which convey revealed knowledge to the faithful. In this sense, St. John is almost passive. His only activity is reading Scripture, the source of spiritual knowledge. As the Christian visionary who plumbs the scriptural mysteries, St. John overcomes the illusions of the *theatrum mundi* and experiences the "quietnesse of minde" represented by the New Jerusalem.

As if to remind us of its true function, the prose commentary ends with a call to faith:

Therefore bridle thy lust, and refraine thy heart from al worldly, carnal, and transitorie riches, and be lifted vp in mynde and spirite to heauenly and vncorruptible treasures: so shalte thou be regenerate of the holy ghoste, and being confirmed by the worde of God, may well be called *Microcosme,* that is, the whole worlde vppon the little foote.   (Sigs. R_8v–S_1)

The use of the word "Microcosme" here is interesting and significant. The term, of course, was a commonplace referring to man as a model or epitome of the universe, but Van Der Noot uses the term in a specifically Protestant sense. In this sense, to be a "Microcosme" is to participate in divinity, as Calvin indicates: "Hence certain of the philosophers have not improperly called man a *microcosm (miniature world),* as being a rare specimen of divine power, wisdom, and goodness, and containing within himself wonders sufficient to occupy our minds, if we are willing so to employ them" (*Institutes* 1.5.3). Man has claims to being a "Microcosme" only if he be regenerated through Christ:

We now see how Christ is the most perfect image of God, into which we are so renewed as to bear the image of God in knowledge, purity, righteousness, and true holiness. . . . Therefore, as the image of God constitutes the entire excellence of human nature, as it shone in Adam before the fall, but was afterwards vitiated and almost destroyed, nothing remaining but a ruin, confused, mutilated, and tainted with impurity, so it is now partly seen in the elect in so far as they are regenerated by the Spirit.   (*Institutes* 1.15.4)

To effect this process of regeneration by setting out the "perfect image of God" in the midst of the labyrinthine theater of the world, *A Theatre for Worldlings* was written.

University of Wisconsin, Madison

Notes

This paper, in a slightly different form, was discussed at the Special Session on Netherlandic and Flemish Influences on the English Renaissance at the Modern Language Association Convention in Chicago, December 1977. Special thanks are due to those present at this session, particularly Professors Jan Van Dorsten, Paul Sellin, Frank Warnke, Joan Weatherly, and Stanley Wiersma, for gracious criticism, advice, and encouragement.

1. All citations from *A Theatre* in my text are to the Scholars' Facsimiles & Reprints facsimile edition (New York, n.d.). Except for the substitution of *s* for its variant ſ, I retain the original spelling.

2. Louis S. Friedland, in his influential introduction to the Scholars' Facsimiles & Reprints edition of *A Theatre* (New York, 1939), p. iii, calls *A Theatre* "the first Renaissance emblem-book printed in England in the English language." This suggestion is not uncommon among *Theatre* scholars; see, for example, Harold Stein, *Studies in Spenser's Complaints*

(New York: Oxford University Press, 1934), p. 111. Not everyone agrees with *Theatre* scholars, however. Rosemary Freeman, in *English Emblem Books* (London: Chatto & Windus, 1948), p. 32, and John L. Lievsay in the entry "Emblem" in the *Princeton Encyclopedia of Poetry and Poetics,* ed. Alex Preminger (Princeton: Princeton University Press, 1965), p. 217, both cite Whitney's *A Choice of Emblemes* (1586) as the first English emblem book. Freeman and Lievsay, it seems, rely on Alciati's *Emblematum liber* as the necessary paradigm. The format of *A Theatre* is different from that of *Emblematum liber,* but, nonetheless, *A Theatre* is a book of emblems in English and it does antedate Whitney. Though it has been considered by some an emblem book, *A Theatre* has not been considered a sonnet sequence. The title of the first sonnet sequence in English is usually reserved for Sidney's *Astrophil and Stella.* (See, for example, Lawrence J. Zillman's entry "Sonnet Cycle" in the *Princeton Encyclopedia,* p. 784.) However, as I argue in this paper, *A Theatre* is indeed a sonnet sequence, and, though the extent of its influence was probably not large, it does antedate *Astrophil and Stella.* It should also be noted here that the Dutch edition, *Het Theatre,* is considered a pioneer work of Renaissance literature in the Dutch language; see Leonard Forster, *Janus Gruter's English Years: Studies in the Continuity of Dutch Literature in Exile in Elizabethan England,* (published for the Sir Thomas Browne Institute; Leiden: Leiden University Press, 1967), pp. 49–50.

    3. J. A. Van Dorsten, *The Radical Arts: First Decade of an Elizabethan Renaissance* (published for the Sir Thomas Browne Institute; Leiden: Leiden University Press, 1970), p. 84.

    4. *Theatre* scholarship has traditionally tended to focus on other than literary issues, e.g., bibliography and Spenser's role as translator. See, for example: W. J. B. Pienaar, "Edmund Spenser and Jonker Jan van der Noot," *ES* 8 (1926), 33–44, 67–76; Stein, *Studies in Spenser's Complaints,* pp. 109–41, 172–75; Louis S. Friedland, introduction to the Scholars' Facsimiles & Reprints edition, pp. iii–xvii, and "The Illustrations in *The Theatre for Worldlings,*" *HLQ* 19 (1955–56), 107–20; and Leonard Forster, "The Translator of the *Theatre for Worldlings,*" *ES* 48 (1967), 27–34. Other studies—usually by Dutch-speaking scholars—have begun the task of looking at the *Theatre* as a coherent piece of literature. Important in this regard are W. A. P. Smit's facsimile edition, *Het Bosken en Het Theatre* (Amsterdam: Wereldbibliotheek "Onze Oud Lettern," 1953), which is rich in notes and commentary; S. F. Witstein's source study, *De verzencommentaar in "Het Theatre" van Jan Van Der Noot* (Utrecht: Instituut voor Vergelijkend Literatuuronderzoek, 1965); J. A. Van Dorsten's chapter, "Spenser's *Theatre* Translation," in *The Radical Arts,* pp. 75–85; and Charles R. Davis's chapter on *A Theatre* in "Petrarch's *Rime* 323 and Its Tradition Through Spenser" (Ph. D. diss., Princeton University, 1973), pp. 106–59. Davis's chapters on Petrarch and Du Bellay are also helpful.

    5. Stein, *Studies in Spenser's Complaints,* pp. 111–13, hypothesizes that unlike the elegant Dutch and French editions which were "largely or wholly for presentation purposes," the English edition "seems to be an ordinary trade book." Alfred W. Satterthwaite in *Spenser, Ronsard, and Du Bellay* (1960; rpt. Port Washington, N. Y.: Kennikat Press, 1972), pp. 28–29, compares the English and French versions: "This addition of woodcuts in the English version, reiterating with crude simultaneity the message of the words, gives the English an air of constructed propaganda, which apparently is just what Van der Noot intended, while the French, artificial though it may sound as a whole, still has the mien of literature." The French edition, of course, has the advantages of Du Bellay's *Songe* in the original and Clement Marot's translation of the Petrarch.

    6. The most important study in this regard is Van Dorsten, "Spenser's *Theatre* Translation." Also of significance are the studies by Witstein and Davis. I have profited particularly from these three studies. It seems as though Dutch-speaking scholars have been more

willing to view the *Theatre* as a unified sequence than have English-speaking scholars. They tend (correctly, in my view) to view the sequences from Petrarch and Du Bellay from the specifically religious perspective of the Apocalyptic *Sonets*. For example, Van Dorsten, p. 76, suggests that "the entire sequence reaches both its climax and its solution in the four apocalyptic visions." Similarly, Witstein in her chapter "De verzen in *Het Theatre,*" pp. 9–19, argues that the sequences from Petrarch and Du Bellay are examples of a medieval *vanitas* tradition which become expressions of *avaritia* in the light of the religious and ethical orientation of the four apocalyptic sonnets. Though I have differences with Van Dorsten and Witstein, I agree with their emphasis on the apocalyptic sonnets: The prose commentary, with its immense concentration on these sonnets, encourages this emphasis.

7. In my text I quote from the Henry Beveridge translation of Calvin's *Institutes*, 2 vols. (1845; rpt. Grand Rapids: William B. Eerdmans, 1972). Like *A Theatre*, Calvin's *Institutes* are structured on the question of the knowledge of God. See, for example, Edward A. Dowey, *The Knowledge of God in Calvin's Theology* (New York: Columbia University Press, 1952); and T. H. L. Parker, *Calvin's Doctrine of the Knowledge of God* (Grand Rapids: William B. Eerdmans, 1959). Since *A Theatre* and the *Institutes* are structured on the same question, the *Institutes* are an especially apt example of the intellectual context. By employing Calvin as a frame of reference, as I do throughout the paper, I do not mean to suggest that Van Der Noot was exclusively a Calvinist. For a long time, it was simply assumed that the prose commentary is a Calvinist tract. Recently, however, scholars have argued that the *Theatre* is *not* a Calvinist work. This trend has its origins in S. F. Witstein's monograph. Witstein argues that the two main sources for Van Der Noot's commentary on the apocalyptic sonnets were Dutch translations of John Bale's *The Image of bothe Churches* and Heinrich Bullinger's *In Apocalypsin conciones centum*. These findings are important, but Witstein misuses them. In her chapter "Excurs. Jan Van Der Noot en die Bullingeriaanse theologie" (*De verzencommentaar*, pp. 35–41) she suggests that Bullinger, probably Van Der Noot's main theological influence, emphasized ethics at the expense of the Reformed doctrine of predestination. Van Dorsten, in *The Radical Arts*, while properly correcting Witstein's ethical emphasis by suggesting that the *Theatre* is (p. 80) "religiously revelatory in intent—not purely moralistic," argues on pp. 77–78 that the *Theatre* "is not a Puritan tract. . . . paradoxically, the militant Van Der Noot's ultimate message is one of unity and peace. The most explicit part of his compilation, the long prose commentary borrowed largely from Bale and Bullinger and essentially un-Genevan in theological content, culminates in an elaborate anthology of scriptural places. Their keyword is 'charity'." Van Dorsten goes on to link Van Der Noot with the Family of Love and refers to him as "the *quondam*-Calvinist Familist-inclined Fleming" (p. 80). I agree that Van Der Noot's message is "religiously revelatory in intent" and that it has to do with unity, peace, and charity—but such a message is not necessarily "un-Genevan in theological content." Witstein is most likely correct that Bullinger was Van Der Noot's main theological influence, but Bullinger's thought was not particularly "un-Genevan." In 1566 Bullinger issued the *Second Helvetic Confession* (*Confessio Helvitica posterior*), which became the standard confession for the Reformed Protestant churches on the Continent—including Geneva. Though they did have subtle differences, Bullinger and Calvin were in basic agreement on the Reformed doctrines of predestination and reprobation; on this question see G. C. Berkouwer, *Divine Election* (Grand Rapids: William B. Eerdmans, 1968), pp. 192–94. Van Der Noot himself makes no fine distinctions among theologians. He praises all the major Reformers—including Lutherans (sigs. K_7–K_7v): "Cal to remembraunce what God hath wrought by his seruants, *Iohn Wicliffe, Iohn Hus, Martine Luther, Oecolampadie, Zwinglie, Melancton, Capito, Bucer, Caluin, Theodore de Beza, Viret, Peter Martyr, Bullinger, Alasco, Brenti[us] Regius,* and other

moe." Given that Van Der Noot was demonstrably influenced by Bale and Bullinger, the most that can be said with precision about his theology is that he was a Reformed Protestant. Therefore, the most thorough and systematic expression of his intellectual context is Calvin's *Institutes*. Philip Schaff in *The Creeds of Christendom* (1919; rpt. Grand Rapids: Baker Book House, n.d.), vol. 1., pp. 448–49, has written of the importance of the *Institutes:* "The 'Institutes' are by far the clearest and ablest systematic and scientific exposition and vindication of the ideas of the Reformation in their vernal freshness and pentecostal fire. . . . It [i.e., the *Institutes*] overshadowed all previous attempts at a systematic treatment of Protestant doctrines, not only those of Zwingli and Farel, but even Melanchthon's *Loci theologici*, although Calvin generously edited them twice in a French translation with a complimentary preface (1546)."

8. In this regard Van Der Noot's poetics differs significantly from that of Sir Philip Sidney. For Sidney, poetry should delight, teach, and move the reader to virtuous action "with the end of well-doing and not of well-knowing only" (*A Defence of Poetry* in *Miscellaneous Prose of Sir Philip Sidney*, ed. Katherine Duncan-Jones and Jan Van Dorsten [Oxford: The Clarendon Press, 1973], p. 83). Sidney proceeds to argue "that moving is of a higher degree than teaching, it may by this appear, that it is well nigh both the cause and effect of teaching. For who will be taught, if he be not moved with desire to be taught? And what so much good doth that teaching bring forth (I speak still of moral doctrine) as that it moveth one to do that which it doth teach? For, as Aristotle saith, it is not γνῶσις [gnosis] but πρᾶξις [praxis] must be the fruit. And how πρᾶξις can be, without being moved to practise, it is no hard matter to consider" (p. 91). For Sidney human corruption can be counteracted by poetry which through delighting the imagination bypasses the degenerate senses and intellect and moves the will. Insofar as it eschews gnosis in favor of praxis and avoids the issue of faith, Sidney's poetics is quite different from Van Der Noot's revelatory poetics. For further discussion of Sidney as a Protestant theoretician, see Andrew D. Weiner, "Moving and Teaching: Sidney's *Defence of Poesie* as a Protestant Poetic," *JMRS* 2 (1972), 259–78; see also Weiner's *Sir Philip Sidney and the Poetics of Protestantism* (Minneapolis: University of Minnesota Press, 1978).

9. For example, Friedland, *A Theatre*, p. xiii: "In setting forth the purpose of 'thys little Treatyse' (Aiii and verso) Van der Noot strikes an authentic note in the gamut of Renaissance themes: the insufficiency of earthly things and the nostalgia for heavenly and eternal bliss. Enamored of the medieval contempt for the world, many a Renaissance poet forgot now and again that their own contemporaries were discovering and laying the foundations of the new, other world on this very earth. A wise contempt, for the 20th century was to discover that the new earthly 'paradise' was even less satisfactory than the old."

10. Luther's commentary on Ecclesiastes is entirely devoted to setting forth the Protestant view of worldly vanity. I quote briefly from an English edition printed by John Day, printer of the Dutch and French editions of the *Theatre;* Martine Luther, *An Exposition of Salomons Booke, Called Ecclesiastes or the Preacher* (London, 1573), sigs. A₇v–A₈: "These naughty affections (I say) and enterprises of men doth Salomon in thys booke condemne, and not the creatures themselues: For touching the vse of these creatures, he himself sayeth hereafter: *There is no thyng better then to be meary in thys life, and to eate and drinke, and man to reigne in his labour. &c.* Where he shoulde be founde vtterly against hymselfe, if he should condemne the thynges, and not rather the abuse of them, which is onely in our affections. Certayne foolish men, not perceiuyng these thyngs, haue taught us absurde opinions about the contempt and forsakyng of the worlde, and haue themselues cōmitted many absurde thynges, as we read in the liues of the fathers."

11. Paul Tillich, "Existential Philosophy," *JHI* 5 (1944), 55. On Calvin as an existential thinker, see Dowey, *The Knowledge of God*, pp. 24–31.

12. Tillich, "Existential Philosophy," p. 67.

13. It is true that allegorical images can represent spiritual states. The emblems in *A Theatre* often—though not always—function this way. For example, the ruins of Rome in the Du Bellay *Sonets* by association represent human vanity (lust for empire, pride, worldliness, etc.). Nonetheless, to evoke the experience of vanity in the reader other devices are required.

14. Plotinus, *Ennead* 3.2.15. I have used the translation by Stephen Mackenna (London: Philip Lee Warner, 1921), vol. 2, pp. 29–30.

15. Roy Battenhouse in "The Doctrine of Man in Calvin and in Renaissance Platonism," *JHI* 9 (1948), 447–71, argues for an underlying similarity between Calvin's thought and Renaissance Neoplatonism. On this question see also Charles Trinkaus, "Renaissance Problems in Calvin's Theology," *SRen* 1 (1954), 59–80. The catalogues of the British Museum and the Bibliothèque Nationale indicate that four editions of Plotinus in Marsilio Ficino's Latin translation were published in Protestant Basel in the sixteenth century: 1540, 1559, 1562, and 1580.

16. The seventeen-page explication (sigs. E_2–F_2) precedes the quotation of the verse. Van Der Noot introduces the explication on sig. E_2: "Also I will speake of the loue, confidence and inordinat lust, and of the chasyng and puttyng away of vertue and godlynesse, & the going astray from God, dependyng vpon his creatures, yea vpon vanitie it selfe." This introduces the themes treated in the verse from 1 John.

17. The assertion here that "I [either Van Der Noot or Roest, the translator of the prose] haue out of the *Brabants* speache, turned them into the English tongue" has received much attention. Of course, Spenser translated the poems from the French. On this complex question see, particularly, Pienaar, "Spenser and van der Noot," and Forster, "Translator."

18. Van Der Noot's commentary on these poems relies on Petrarch's sixteenth-century Italian commentators: Vellutello, Gesualdo, and Bembo (see Witstein, *De verzencommentaar,* pp. 21–23). Charles R. Davis in his chapter on *A Theatre* (in "Petrarch's *Rime* 323") conveniently provides English translations of their commentaries on Petrarch's *Rime* 323. The Italian commentators interpret Petrarch's despair as the rejection of a corrupt world. For Van Der Noot the world is not corrupt—the human will is.

19. For an assessment of the *Secretum* and its place in Petrarch's spiritual development, see Hans Baron, "Petrarch: His Inner Struggles and the Humanistic Discovery of Man's Nature," in *Florilegium Historiale: Essays Presented to Wallace K. Ferguson,* ed. J. G. Rowe and W. H. Stockdale (Toronto: University of Toronto Press, 1971), pp. 18–51.

20. History is an aspect of the total creation, as Calvin makes clear, *Institutes* 1.5.7: "In the second class of God's works, namely those which are above the ordinary course of nature, the evidence of his perfections are in every respect equally clear. For in conducting the affairs of men, he so arranges the course of providence, as daily to declare, by the clearest manifestations, that though all are in innumerable ways the partakers of his bounty, the righteous are special objects of his favor, the wicked and profane the special objects of his severity."

21. For an interesting reading of the *Songe* along these lines, see Gilbert Gadoffre, "Structures des mythes de Du Bellay," *Bibliothèque d'humanisme et renaissance* 36 (1974), 273–89, and "Histoire et destin dans les *Antiquités de Rome*," *Zeitschrift für Französische Sprache und Literatur* 85 (1975), 289–304. These essays along with new material are included in Gadoffre's *Du Bellay et le sacré* (Paris: Gallimard, 1978).

22. Gadoffre, "Structures," p. 281.

23. The last of the Du Bellay "Sonets" is very similar to the second apocalyptic sonnet, which is about the fall of the whore of Babylon. The two poems are indeed typologically related. They differ in two ways, however. The second apocalyptic sonnet is about *the*

whore of Babylon, papal Rome. Typhaeus' sister, imperial Rome, is only a predecessor. In addition, St. John, the persona of the apocalyptic "Sonets," sees reality as it is—through the scriptural type. The Du Bellay persona, on the other hand, has no way of knowing that what he sees is in any way related to a scriptural type. What he sees is veiled and abstruse.

24. About 68 pages of the commentary are devoted to introduction, conclusion, and commentary on the "Epigrams" and Du Bellay "Sonets." About 146 pages are devoted to commentary on the four apocalyptic "Sonets," becoming in places a commentary on the Book of Revelation.

25. Van Der Noot says the following about the confiscation of religious houses (sig. L_1v): "Now in this our time, she [i.e., the whore] shal haue a more sharper and seuere iudgement through the publishing & preaching of gods word, to the comfort of all beleeuers. Which although it be somewhat as it were deferred, yet let them be as well assured of this hir iudgement to come, as we know and certainly beleeue the other to be come. Cal to remembrāce, and compare this place with the haling & plucking downe of Abbays, Frieries, and other religious houses (as they cal them) in *Germanie, England,* and in other places, and make your accompts, that more and more sorowes shal happen, and surely fal vpon hir shortly." It is important to recognize that Van Der Noot associates the political collapse of Rome with the dissemination of Scripture.

26. Cf. Calvin, *Institutes* 3.2.6: "The true knowledge of Christ consists in receiving him as he is offered by the Father—namely, as invested with his Gospel. For, as he is appointed as the end of our faith, so we cannot directly tend towards him except under the guidance of the Gospel. Therein are certainly unfolded to us treasures of grace. Did these continue shut, Christ would profit us but little. . . . We are not here discussing whether, in order to propagate the word of God by which faith is engendered, the ministry of man is necessary (this will be considered elsewhere); but we say that the word itself, whatever be the way in which it is conveyed to us, is a kind of mirror in which faith beholds God. In this, therefore, whether God uses the agency of man, or works immediately by his own power, it is always by his word that he manifests himself to those whom he designs to draw to himself."

27. *Institutes* 2.9.2: "By the Gospel, I understand the clear manifestation of the mystery of Christ. I confess, indeed, that inasmuch as the term Gospel is applied by Paul to the doctrine of faith (2 Tim. iv. 10), it includes all the promises by which God reconciles men to himself, and which occur all throughout the Law." However, a certain discrepancy of necessity exists, and this is an unresolved tension in Calvin's theology. For a discussion of this issue see Dowey, *The Knowledge of God,* pp. 155–64, and Parker, *Calvin's Doctrine,* pp. 93–99.

28. Sig. M_6: "He hath done according to iustice and equitie in condemning that wicked and abhominable whoore, in destroying that filthie sinagoge of Sathan, in deliuering and exalting his poore afflicted Churche. First of all he did fight in his owne persone, as a worthy Champion against the deuill, hel, and damnation, whom he hath ouercome, conquered and vanquished by his owne death, and glorious passion."

29. Sigs. M_6–M_6v: "And now doth he ouerthrow the Deuill, and all his adherēts, by the meanes of his faithful seruants, distributers of his holy woord and mysteries, which he nowe graciusly sendeth vnder the figure of the white horse." The warriors who follow the faithful man are Christ's ministers (sigs. M_8–M_8v), and the battle between the faithful man and the beast is the ongoing battle between the faithful and tyrants. The Reformation is part of this battle, and Van Der Noot includes a history of the Reformation from the time of Wycliffe and Hus (sigs. N_4–N_7). This history leads into a vehement defense of marriage (sigs. N_8–O_2), the relevance of which is not precisely clear.

30. Cf. Calvin, "Commentary on Colossians," 1.15 (quoted in Dowey, *The Knowledge of God,* p. 15): "the term image is not related to essence, but has a relation to us. For Christ is called the image of God on this ground, that he makes God in a manner visible to us. . . . The sum is this—that God in himself, that is, in his naked majesty, is invisible, and that not to the eyes of the body only, but also to the minds of men, and that he is revealed in Christ alone, that we may behold him as in a mirror."

31. The *OED* says the following about "Chrysoprase": "The ancient name of a golden-green precious stone, now generally believed to have been a variety of the beryl, or to have included that among other stones of similar appearance. It was one of the stones to which in the Middle Ages was attributed the faculty of shining in the dark."

RUTH   SAMSON   LUBORSKY

The Allusive Presentation
of *The Shepheardes Calender*

*One must recognize that the reading of a text in such different forms as a
"modern" French print, an early English black letter with woodcuts, or a fifteenth century manuscript with illuminations, makes correspondingly different impressions; the variation in form almost constitutes a variation in the
text itself.*[1]

*T*HE FIRST edition of *The Shepheardes Calender*, printed by Hugh Singleton in 1579, is a visual statement of the newness E. K. claimed for its author. The physical book does not look like any other single book of its
time. It is a unique combination of many books and functions as an analogue to the literal work, directing its readers to the models and traditions
of the text. What they saw makes fair claim to being the first printed
book of English poetry whose presentation was planned deliberately to be
allusive.

Such self-conscious allusiveness makes the *Calender* important in the history of the printed book. But if we are able reasonably to suppose that it
was Spenser who planned this allusiveness, then the presentation becomes
important also as a unit of the poem's meaning. One of the results of the
following analysis of the presentation is that such a supposition does seem
to be likely; that what we see in the physical appearance of the first edition
of the *Calender* represents, in its unconventional parts, authorial intention.

This is the first analysis of the entire presentation. That there is a problem worth investigating emerges only when we track down the references
given in the single previous extended mention of the presentation,
William Nelson's. He isolates two parts: what he calls the "form," and
the illustrations. The form "was intended to impress the reader with a
sense of the importance of the work. This collection of English poems by
an unknown author was equipped with apparatus proper to an edition of a
Latin classic: an introduction pointing out the singular merits of the
poem, a disquisition on the nature and history of its genre, a glossary and
notes. No English poet had ever been announced so pretentiously." The

illustrations are mentioned later in the context of the influence of the *Calendar & Compost of Shepherds,* the titular ancestor of Spenser's poem, which "gave Spenser the idea of illustrating each of his eclogues with a woodcut labeled with the astrological sign appropriate to the month." A note tells us that the cuts are said to resemble those in certain editions of Vergil's *Bucolics.*[2]

Nelson's conclusion is not overstated; in fact, the presentation of the *Calender* is pretentious in even more ways than he describes, its referential range wider and more complicated. The "apparatus," for example, turns out to allude to more than the newly edited Latin classic. However, the illustrations are not copies of, nor do they even look like any previous Vergilian ones. Were this so, the *Calender* would resemble an early continental illustrated Vergil.[3] Instead the cuts turn out to be original, depictive, and to quote from a variety of sources.

It may seem ordinary to use the words "woodcut," "depictive," and "original" in describing illustrations made for new poetry in the England of 1579. It is extraordinary. No new poetry had been so illustrated in England, as far as I have been able to discover, within at least two decades and would not be for at least two centuries. The *Calender*'s cuts represent the end of a line: The woodcut technique was being supplanted by copper engraving; and the depictive mode by both the decorative and the newest kind of illustration, the emblematic, which required expertise from readers who had to unravel the symbolic meaning, a process opposite to any easy and explicit relating of illustration to text.[4]

In almost every way the *Calender*'s cuts carry an archaic aura. Not only are they out-of-date in method and technique, but their style is crude, even for a time hardly noted in England for superior woodcuts. Vaguely reminiscent of the labor-of-the-month cut the reader saw at the top of his almanac, the style leaves an impression quite like that made by certain aspects of Spenser's language—old-fashioned and, at times, rude.

To describe the *Calender* as a book containing old-fashioned depictive woodcuts giving a rustic or homely impression is a corrective to describing it as impressive and alluding to the Latin classic. Both descriptions fit, and they mirror a similar combination in the text. But that is not the whole story. What the reader saw was more than a hybrid formed by the conjunction of two traditions, the humanist—represented by the imitation of a freshly edited classical text—and the folk, or traditional—insisted on both by the book's title and by its old-fashioned depictive illustrations cut in a calendrical style. The reader saw a book containing an unusually plain title page for its time, an introductory section whose units seem out of the conventional order, and a main section of twelve eclogues, whose layout is printed with two major peculiarities: a gloss subsequent to, rather than marginal with, the main poem; and oddly set decorative initials. In what follows the meaning of this presentation is investigated through the discovery of the models for it.

I

Every presentation, of course, has a meaning, but if the format is appropriate to the kind of book and in the fashion of the time, the effect is conventional; the meaning is that the presentation is not to be remarked. "Apart from special devices to meet special problems, there are well-established conventions for most features of any book, and designers tend to work within these conventions. Books are expected to 'look like that,' and only an eccentric or an innovating genius can burst through the barriers of convention."[5] It is not hard to demonstrate that the total presentation of the *Calender* is remarkable; what is difficult is to show how much of what seems remarkable is intentional.

To do this I have used a comparative method, examining each element and the sequential combination of elements, the layout, within three contexts. (1) The examples set by Singleton's previously printed books. The purpose was to determine house style, which naturally changed over the years. A Singleton product of the 1550s looks in many ways like books from other houses printed then, while a Singleton product of the 1570s resembles books from other printers issued at the same time more than it does those printed by Singleton in the 1550s.[6] (2) The changes made in the subsequent four quarto editions containing the original illustrations and published within the century by John Harrison.[7] The purpose was to determine which formal features were carried on as a part of the book's tradition. In the absence of specific instructions, workmen tend to normalize or conventionalize, a process which has been documented for the spelling in successive editions of the *Calender*.[8] This is why the changes in presentation in the four subsequent editions are interesting; they suggest which features of the first edition were sensed as being somehow inappropriate, not fitting, not "looking like that," and so were automatically corrected. But how can we be sure these changes were made for fashionable rather than for economic reasons? We are reasonably sure because each of the four editions has the same number of gatherings as the first does and therefore uses the same amount of paper (although none is an exact page-for-page setting throughout).[9] Since paper, the printer's main expense, is a constant, the changes may be supposed to have been made not for economic but for normalizing reasons. (3) The examples of other relevant books. The purpose was to determine both the conventions of the time and models.[10]

Let us look at the 1579 quarto edition, first describing its presentation and then isolating each element more closely, noting what is unusual, what might have been expected to appear but does not, and suggesting models for these units and for the book.

The introductory matter is contained within the first gathering. (1) [π1ʳ] The title page is organized in three units; the second concludes with a device of three dots; the last, the imprint, is separated from the first two by a small printer's ornament. (2) [π1ᵛ] Immerito's poem, "To His Booke," is so printed as to fill the entire page and is preceded by an ornamental bar. (3) [π2ʳ–3ᵛ] E. K.'s "Epistle to Harvey." The title is arranged in the same way, printed with the same fonts, and followed by the same device as are the units on the title page. (4) [π4ʳ–4ᵛ] "The generall argument" by E. K.

The rest of the book is printed in fourteen gatherings, [A–N⁴] consisting of twelve units, one for each month; and following the last month is a poem which is referred to as the "Envoy" in the critical literature but is not so labeled in the text. The colophon takes up the last page [N4ᵛ].

Each monthly unit consists, in order, of a running head (the name of the month), an original illustrative woodcut within a border unusually heavy for the time, the eclogue number (e.g., "Aegloga Quinta"), a prose "Argument," a long poem ending with one to three "Emblemes" (so labeled), and followed by a "Glosse" by E. K. which serves at the same time as a commentary, and is also called a "scholion" in the epistle. Horizontal bars of printer's ornaments separate the "Embleme" from "Glosse" throughout. Otherwise, decorative initials and ornamental and figurative head and tail pieces occur erratically. The "Envoy" is separated from the final "Glosse" by an ornamental bar.

Three fonts are used: black letter, italic, and roman, all of which are combined on the title page. The text is printed in 83 textura (English black letter); the individual arguments, the envoy, proper names within the text, and marginalia in "August" in 80 italic; "To His Booke," the running heads, and eclogue number, in 142 italic; and the epistle, general argument, and glosses, in 68 roman. The signatures are noted sometimes in arabic, sometimes in roman numerals.[11]

The oddness of the introductory units consists of two things: a title page which seems inappropriately bare for the kind of book it announces, when judged by contemporary standards; and an unexpected order for the following two units—"To His Booke," and E. K.'s epistle.

The title page would look conventional if it had a border, the only "purely Renaissance trait of book appearance" according to one scholar of the printed book.[12] Every other element is unremarkable: the three fonts, triadic arrangement, printer's ornament and device are all characteristic of many English books of the time and typical of Singleton's house style. But his practice did include the use of borders (e.g., I:2, 13) as well as larger ornaments (e.g., I:9, shown in fig. 1). Had either of these been employed, the title page of the first edition would seem unexceptional, as the title pages of subsequent editions do, where the spareness of the title page of the first edition is "corrected." The next three editions have ornamental or figural borders (fig. 2); the fourth, a large printer's device.[13] Title page borders appear on most of the books of Spenser's acquaintance; on the works of contemporary English poets, such as Gascoigne, whose works were printed in the 1570s; on Spenser's other books; and on the Vergil (see fig. 3) and the Chaucer used by Spenser.[14] In fact, most English books of any pretention at the time announced themselves by a filled and imposing title page, as shown in figure 4 (e.g., II: 18, 19, 21, 42, 43, 50, 52, 53, 59, 67). For this reason, the disparity between the modesty of the title page to the first edition of the *Calender* and the illustrated, overdecorated pages that follow is glaring.[15]

The nearest pertinent resemblance I have been able to find to the spare title page of the *Calender* is the example of title pages in certain editions of Marot and Ronsard. The resemblance is not close because the English use of three fonts is uncharacteristic of French books of the time. Many French title pages seem quite plain when compared with their English contemporaries. A 1549 Lyon edition of Marot (II:35) shows five lines of print in a V shape, a printer's device, and imprint; we see the same layout in a 1553 Paris Ronsard (II:45).[16]

The argument that Marot, in particular, may be one of the primary models for the title page in the *Calender* takes on force when that title page is looked at as a unit with the poem printed on its verso, "To His Booke."[17] The English reader would not have expected the author's address to his work to come after the title page; he would have looked for the dedication, as is explained below. While the French reader would have expected to see the privilege for the printer on the verso of the title page, the French custom does not seem to have been as rigid as the English. We see a significant exception in certain editions of Marot's original and in his collected works (although not in his translations when published separately). In these editions, the author's poem to his book ("L'autheur à son livre") and the poem ("A sa dame") are printed on the verso of the title page described above and are followed by Marot's motto, "La Mort ny Mord," which Spenser adopts as Colin's "embleme" in "November."[18]

The example of these editions of Marot seems closest to what we see in

A
Reply with the occasion thereof, to a late
rayling, lying, reprochful and blasphemous libel, of the
Papists, set vpon postes, and also in Paules church
in London: against god, his truth, his annointed, the
whole state, and vniuersall church of Christ, with a
cattolog, of the vile termes there-
in conteined.
(*.*)

ALSO, A BRIEFE REPREHENSION, OF
a most vile facte, (more lately) which though more
priuate, yet little lesse contemptious, and don
also, in S. Paules church London.

PSALME. 16. 10.
I beleeued, therefore did I speake,
for I was sore troubled.

FIGURE 1. *A reply with the occasion thereof to a late rayling, lying, reprochful and blas-phemous libel of the Papists.* London: Hugh Singleton, 1579. (By permission of the Folger Shakespeare Library.)

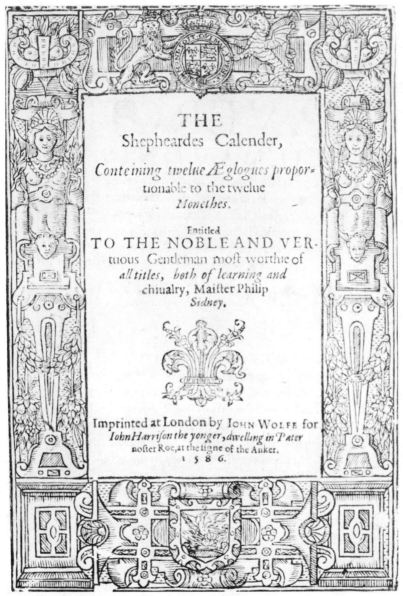

THE
Shepheardes Calender,

Conteining twelue Æglogues propor-
tionable to the twelue
Monethes.

Entitled
TO THE NOBLE AND VER-
tuous Gentleman most worthie of
all titles, both of learning and
chiualry, Maister Philip
Sidney.

Imprinted at London by IOHN WOLFE for
Iohn Harrison the yonger, dwelling in Pater
noster Roe, at the signe of the Anker.
1586.

FIGURE 2. *The Shepheardes Calender.* London: Thomas East for John Harrison, 1586. (By permission of the Folger Shakespeare Library.)

P. VERGI-
LII MARONIS

Opera, doctiſſimis Phil. Melanch. ſcholiis,
& Eobani Heſſi annotationib., quinetiam
ex Eraſmi Chiliad. Adagiis paſſim ad-
notatu, illuſtrata: caſtigatiuſque
quàm hactenus impreſſa.
ANN. M.D.
XLII.

VERGIL. DE SEIPSO.
Mellifluum quiſquis Romanū neſcit Homerū,
Me legat, & lectum credat utrunq; ſibi.
Illius immenſos miratur Græcia campos:
At minor eſt nobis, ſed bene cultus ager.
Non miles, paſtor, curuus non deſit arator.
Hæc Grais conſtant ſingula, trina mihi.

FIGURE 3. Vergil. *Opera.* Antwerp: Dumaeus, 1542. (Princeton University Library.)

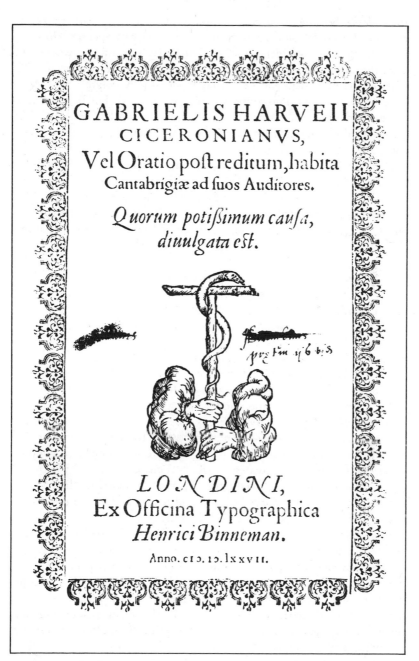

FIGURE 4. Gabriel Harvey. G. *Harveii Ciceronianus.* London: Henry Bynneman, 1577. (By permission of the Folger Shakespeare Library.)

the *Calender* because of the conjunction of placement, appearance, the author's address to his work, and the motto used later by Spenser. However, it is not the only pertinent citation; Du Bellay's work also was printed with the author's address to his work on the verso of the title page.[19] The texts of Marot's poem and Du Bellay's poems ("A sa lyre" and "A son livre") repeat conventions found also in Spenser's "To His Booke." In all three poems the author sends his books into the world ("A sa lyre" begins: "Va doncques maintenant my Lyre"), all three invoke a royal audience, and "A sa lyre" mentions envy.

In contradistinction to the French example, we hardly ever find "To His Booke" placed immediately after the title page in English books of the time.[20] The *Variorum* (7.235) refers to Caxton's edition of *The Moral Proverbes of Crystyne* (1478), and to Skelton, several books of Lydgate's, and Chaucer's *Troilus*. Of these, one is embedded in the text (Chaucer), the others are printed at its end (Lydgate and Skelton), or as colophon (Caxton).

In content these English poems share many of the same topoi with the French, and both are just as close (in the same and different ways) to Spenser's poem.[21] But "To His Booke" and the French poems appear on the verso of the title page, while the English do not. For these reasons I would argue that Spenser alludes to Marot (and perhaps Du Bellay) as well as to the older English poets, but has given the French the pride of place.

Were "To His Booke" a dedication, however, it would be in its expected place because "before the death of Henry the Eighth the customary order of title page, dedication and epistle to the reader is established in more pretentious books." By 1579 this order seems unvarying for the first two elements.[22] Is Spenser's poem, in addition to being the author's address to his work, a dedication? If so, what are we to make of the prose letter that follows it immediately, E. K.'s "Epistle to Harvey"? Although it is commonly called the "Dedicatory Epistle" in the critical literature, it is not so labeled in the *Calender* itself, and it is placed where the English reader would have expected the epistle to the reader.

Answers emerge by examining the traits of the Elizabethan dedicatory epistle and comparing them, in turn, with "To His Booke" and E. K.'s epistle.[23] By definition, the dedicatory epistle is a formal inscription in which the poet sends his book to the world in general, and to a dedicatee in particular. Usually humble in tone, the epistle's necessary content is flattery. It has three traits relevant here: the statement of source (genre); the defense of a given poetic theory; and mystification, often suggested by anonymity.

When we examine the text of "To His Booke" we find that the poem has many of the qualities of a dedication.

TO HIS BOOKE.

> Goe little booke: thy selfe present,
> As child whose parent is vnkent:
> To him that is the president
> Of noblesse and of cheualree,
> And if that Enuie barke at thee,
> As sure it will, for succoure flee
> Vnder the shadow of his wing,
> And asked, who thee forth did bring,
> A shepheards swaine saye did thee sing,
> All as his straying flocke he fedde:
> And when his honor has thee redde,
> Craue pardon for my hardyhedde.
>   But if that any aske thy name,
> Say thou wert base begot with blame:
> For thy thereof thou takest shame.
> And when thou art past ieopardee,
> Come tell me, what was sayd of mee:
> And I will send more after thee.
>   Immeritô.

The author releases his book to the world, in humility and with flattery to a dedicatee and asks for his protection. "A shepheards swain" suggests genre (source) and mystery which is intensified by the final verse and the signature.

Spenser's poem differs in two ways from the general description of the convention. The dedicatee is not named, and the dedication comes in the form of a poem, not an epistle. The first qualification can be answered if we accept William Ringler's plausible argument that "his honor" refers to the earl of Leicester.[24] If he were the dedicatee who was named originally on the title page, the word "honor" would have served as an explicit reference to him (as it now serves as clue). The second qualification is that "To His Booke" is not an epistle, it is a poem. But surely this does not rule out its functioning as a dedication.[25] The placement and contents suggest that it is a dedicatory poem and the author's address to his work.

If the poem is dedicatory in part, what then is E. K.'s so-called Dedicatory Epistle? It is in the position of the conventional explicatory letter to the reader and takes on the tasks of such a letter: praise of the author and his work. It serves also as a critical and editorial preface. But it is something else, too, something I have found no precedent for. It seems to be a letter asking Harvey to be joint patron with Sidney of the entire work.

There are three major references to Harvey in the epistle. The first is in the title: "To the most excellent and learned both / orator and poete, Mayster Gabriell Haruey, his / verie special and singular good frend E. K. commen- / deth the good lyking of this his labour / and the patronage of the / new Poete." The second occurs at the end of the letter proper:

These my present paynes if to any they be pleasurable or profitable, be you iudge, mine own good Maister Haruey, to whom I have both in respect of your worthinesse generally, and otherwyse vpon some particular and special considerations voued this my labour, and the maydenhead of this our commen frends Poetrie, himselfe hauing already in the beginning dedicated it to the Noble and worthy Gentleman, the right worshipfull Ma. Phi. Sidney, a special fauourer and maintainer of all kind of learning. Whose cause I pray you Sir, yf Enuie shall stur vp any wrongful accusasion, defend with your mighty Rhetorick and other your rare gifts of learning, as you can, and shield with your good wil, as you ought, against the malice and outrage of so many enemies, as I know wilbe set on fire with the sparks of his kindled glory. And thus recommending the Author vnto you, as vnto his most special good frend, and my selfe vnto you both, as one making singuler account of two so very good and so choise frends, I bid you both most hartely farwel, and commit you and your most commendable studies to the tuicion of the greatest.

The third is in the postscript, where E. K. praises Harvey's English poems, begging him to publish them as he has his "Latine Poemes, which in my opinion both for inuention and Elocution are very delicate, and superexcellent."

On the face of it E. K., with flattery, dedicates his own work to a named dedicatee, Harvey; refers to the friendly relationship between them; and asks for protection. But he does not ask for his own protection; he asks Harvey to be Spenser's patron ("the patronage of the new Poete"). What then is the role of Sidney? The reference to him is ambiguous because it leads nowhere. If the "Whose" of the sentence following the Sidney name refers to Spenser, Harvey is being asked to protect him. This seems to be the most likely reference because "Whose" should refer to a person, since

E. K. writes of "the sparks of his kindled glory." If, as seems less likely, "Whose" applies to "all kind of learning" ("Whose cause") Harvey is being asked to take over a role Sidney would be expected to assume. Whichever interpretation is accepted, the effect is the same: Sidney is impotent as a patron in protecting Spenser (Harvey will have to do that), or Sidney needs Harvey's help.

That this curious circumstance has not been noted before is probably due to the fact that contemporary conventions of format order have not been consulted. Once "To His Booke" is identified as being partially dedicatory, E. K.'s epistle must be redefined. It is complicated because it seems to be three things at once: his own dedicatory epistle which, since it comes immediately after Spenser's dedicatory poem, creates a kind of equality between them; an epistle to the reader; and a request that Harvey be joint patron of the entire work.

The last unit in the introductory matter is not complex in its reference. "The generall argument of the whole booke" is probably patterned after the "General Somme" appearing in many contemporary Vergils (e.g. II:59).

We see that these introductory units, when taken together, form a complex announcement of the new kind of book the reader has in hand. It represents a synapse where disparate models connect: the ordinary English books of the time (typography), the rustic and continuous calendrical tradition (title), Marot (and perhaps Du Bellay), and the Latin classic. It is issued under the patronage of two dedicatees, emphasizing the collaborative nature of the text where Spenser writes the poem and E. K. praises, explains, and comments.

Even more complex in its allusions is the unusual eclogue unit forming the main text of the *Calender*. Only its typeface would have seemed conventional.[26] If the eclogue "looks like that," what is "that"?

Perhaps the most convincing way to answer this general question is to look first at the particular elements which make up the eclogue, suggesting possible models, and then, at the gestalt. The elements are: (1) the woodcut, (2) the individual argument, (3) the long poem ending with one or more "emblemes," and (4) a "glosse" subsequent to the poem which includes the features of a commentary.

Because it contains new illustrative woodcuts, *The Shepheardes Calender*, taken as a book printed in the last third of the sixteenth century in England, is unique among its kind—original, imaginative literature, as we have seen already. This means that the decision to illustrate was not *pro forma*, it must have been taken deliberately. The choice could not have been Singleton's; he had not been connected with an illustrated book since 1558. That the cuts were considered to be integral is shown by their having been carried on in the four subsequent quarto editions (and in the folio editions of 1611 and 1617).[27]

The cuts carry three separate kinds of referential meanings: because of their existing at all, because of where they exist (their position on the page), and because of their style and content. Discussion of their position on the page is postponed until the meaning of the entire eclogue unit is raised; the general meaning of depictive illustration in imaginative literature is raised in the conclusion; the other issues belong here.

To ask why the book is illustrated is to ask, in the context of this investigation, what other kinds of books the reader would have been reminded of, what other books or genres connected with the *Calender* were illustrated, and what precedents Spenser might have had in mind.

The scope is not as large as might be supposed; the field narrows, I judge, to five kinds of illustrated books: imaginative literature, translations of the classics, the emblem book, the fable book, and the calendar-almanac.

The examples of Lydgate, Chaucer, and Barclay are the only relevant ones I have been able to find for the first category, that of imaginative literature printed earlier in the century with woodblocks. Of these, only Barclay is directly influential, because the *Calender*'s cuts contain quotations from elements of two of the three blocks in the *Egloges* of 1515 (II:4). Neither the blocks in the printed Chaucer nor those in Lydgate's translation of the *Troy Book* bear any relation to those in the *Calender*. Instead, it is the fact that Chaucer and Lydgate were illustrated at all that is important, because this precedent might have been in Spenser's mind.[28]

The same supposition applies to the case of the illustrated classic, especially Vergil. While the Dumaeus *Virgil* of 1542 (II:56), which Spenser used, does not contain illustrations, Marot's translation of the first eclogue of the *Bucolics* does.[29] The contemporary reader may not have singled out the precedent of Marot from the mass of illustrated Vergils, but Spenser may very well have done so.[30] However, Marot is one instance among many; illustrated Vergils were common.[31] While some of the cuts find echoes in some of the *Calender* cuts, these relations are found also in other pastoral illustration, so that a one-to-one correspondence cannot be shown.

Distinct from the classic is the third kind of illustrated book, the continental emblem book. Imported into England by the time of Edward VI, increasingly popular, emblem books became the "nouvelle vague" of their era.[32] Through his association with *A Theatre for Worldlings* Spenser had direct contact with this sort of illustration.[33] Although the emblematic style was not chosen for the *Calender*'s illustrations, a reference to an Alciati emblem is among the allusions in the "Januarye" cut. Furthermore, as

I argue below, the layout of a certain kind of illustrated emblem book affects importantly the layout of the eclogue unit in the *Calender*. It is perhaps this overall impression of an emblem-book page which has caused some critics to mislabel the *Calender*'s cuts by calling them emblematic.

The illustrations in the emblem book derive partially, in their nonhieroglyphic aspects, from Continental fable books. They are pertinent here because a few of the cuts in the *Calender* contain elements from these illustrations, no doubt reflecting Spenser's incorporation of fable material in the poem. Because fable books were popular and used in the schools, the reader would have recognized the imitations in the *Calender*'s cuts.[34]

The last kind of illustrated work to be discussed is the most obvious—the calendar itself; of all the books considered here, its illustrative tradition is the oldest, and its effect on the cuts we are considering the most profound.[35] Many of its conventions are quoted throughout the *Calender* cuts —the astrological sign, the labor-of-the-month, the rustic buildings. In addition, specific quotations of elements in the cuts of *Le grant kalendrier* reinforce the allusion of the poem's title.[36] The style of the cuts would have reminded the reader of two earlier kinds of calendar illustrations: those in the *Calendrier historial* (II:7) and those he would have seen at the top of his English almanac (II:3). When the calendar, almanac, and prognostication began to be printed together as an annual publication in England around 1540, the combined result contained labor-of-the-month cuts which were imported from France, used, reused, and copied well into the next century.[37]

The cuts in *The Shepheardes Calender* resemble or contain quotations from the illustrations in each of the books just discussed (with the exception of Chaucer and Lydgate), that is, Barclay, the classic, the emblem book, the fable book and the calendar in all its forms. Of these, the calendrical allusions predominate.

In contrast to the sources for the illustrations, there are surprisingly few models for an argument at the beginning of the individual eclogue. One would have expected that many contemporary Vergils would be so printed, but this is not the case. Only a few of the English Vergils inspected have an individual argument at the beginning of the eclogue unit (e.g., II:64); if found at all, the arguments are usually grouped at the end of the text or are bunched together with the introductory matter. But in a few Continental Vergils the argument is printed at the head of the eclogue. Two kinds of Vergilian format coexisted on the Continent by the 1530s. The earlier is exemplified by a Venice edition of the *Opera* (II:57); this double-columned layout with multiple argument derives from that in the earlier printed book, which in turn is based on that of the manuscript.

Here (fig. 5) we see double columns of commentary surrounding a third, middle column of text. The "Argument" is printed before the illustration preceding each eclogue. Often, more than one argument occurs; in the example shown there are two—one by Ovid, one by Mancinelli. In the newer format, where the text is set in one column, we do not find the individual argument above the eclogue as a matter of course. It does not so appear in the Vergil Spenser used (II:56), shown in figure 6, where we see the end of eclogue 2 and the beginning of 3. However, other Vergils also printed with the commentary of Aelius Eobanus Hessus do contain an argument preceding the eclogue, as we see in figure 7, a Cologne Vergil of 1535 with Hessus' commentary (II:55). The one column layout seems closer to the *Calender*'s, but it does not include the illustration appearing in the older three-column spread. It is likely that either or both of these prototypes occurred to Spenser's readers.[38]

In addition to the Vergilian, we find three other precedents pertinent to the *Calender*. The first is Mantuan, whose eclogues translated by Turberville (II:32) appeared with individual arguments. Next, the argument, not necessarily so labeled, is a conventional element in many contemporary fable books including a collection that contains the original of the tale "The Oak and the Briar," which Spenser uses in "Februarie."[39] Finally, many prose genres were printed with an individual argument (again, not necessarily so labeled) at the beginning of a discrete unit (chapter, story, etc.). One of these is the way-of-life book, a genre in which the *Calender,* by the very meaning of its name, can be placed. In certain contemporary pilgrimage books or way-of-life books, we find the unit of picture, argument, and text, shown in figure 8 from Bateman's *The Trauayled Pylgrime* (II:6).

The next individual element in the eclogue unit, the "glosse," is even more puzzling—not because it exists, but because of where it exists. It is subsequent to the text, and one would have expected it to be marginal. It would be tedious to give many examples of the marginal gloss; marginalia are a standard feature in contemporary books, occurring in many Vergils including the Dumaeus Vergil (II:56; see fig. 6); in other classics (Horace, II:23); in popular literature (Foxe, II:16; Chaucer, II:8; Bateman, II:6). Many of Singleton's books are printed with marginalia (I:1, 9, 12, 14). But, it could be objected, the gloss in the *Calender* is extensive; might it not be too cumbersome to print as marginalia? While other examples of long marginalia might be given (they run for as much as fourteen lines in the Horace just cited) the best is in one of Singleton's own books (I:9), where two marginal glosses run beside the text, the inner one being extensive (fig. 9).

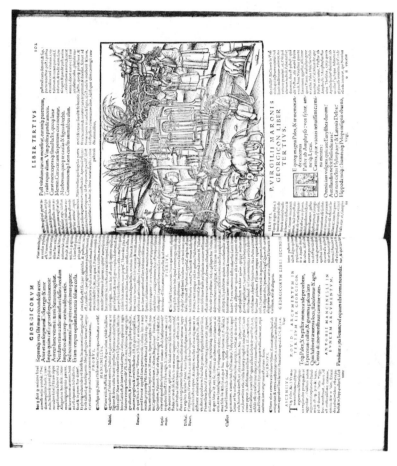

FIGURE 5. Vergil. *Opera*. Venice: Giunta, 1552. (By permission of the Folger Shakespeare Library.)

PALAEMON

ači uestři int   Eheu quid uolui misero mihi : floribus Austrum
telligi, Iolâ   Perditus, & liquidis immisi fontibus apros.
bonů cuiť.   Quem fugis ah demens? habitarût Dii quoq; syluas,
Dardaniusq; Paris. Pallas quas condidit arces
Ipsa colat : nobis placeant ante omnia syluæ.
Rursus hor-   Torua leæna lupum sequitur, lupus ipse capellam,
tať Alexin,   Florentem cytisum sequitur lasciua capella:
ut se redan-   Te Corydon ô Alexi : trahit sua quemque uoluptas.
met, ab ex-   Aspice, aratra iugo referunt suspensa iuuenci,
emplo.   Et Sol crescentes decedens duplicat umbras,
ἐπιφώνημα.   Me tamen urit amor : quis enim modus adsit amori?
Castigatio.   Ah Corydon, Corydon, quæ te dementia cepit?
Semiputata tibi frondosa uitis in ulmo est.
Argumen-   Quin tu aliquid saltem potius, quorum indiget usus,
tat ab utili.   Viminibus, molliq; paras detexere iunco?
Inuenies alium, si te hic fastidit Alexis.

ECLOGA TERTIA,
PALAEMON.

MENALCAS, DAMOETAS. PALAEMON.
MENAL.

ExTheocri-   Dic mihi Damœta, cuium pecus ? an Meliboei?
to sumpta,   DA. Nô, uerû Aegonis : nuper mihi tradidit Aegon.
& ad imita-   ME. Infelix ô semper ouis pecus : ipse Neæram
tionê Gre-   Dum fouet, ac,ne me sibi præferat illa,ueretur
cam scripta   Hic alienus ouis custos bis mulget in hora:
est hæc eclo-   Et succus pecori, & lac subducitur agnis.
ga.   DA. Parcius ista uiris tamen obiicienda memento.
Nouimus & qui te transuersa tuentibus hircis,
Et quo, sed faciles Nymphæ risere, sacello.
ME. Tum crede,cùm me arbustum uidere Myconis,

At

ECLOGA III.   6

Atque mala uites incidere falce nouellas.
DA. Aut hic ad ueteres fagos, cùm Daphnidis arcum
Fregisti, & calamos : quæ tu peruerse Menalca
Et cùm uidisti puero donata, dolebas:
Et si non aliqua nocuisses, mortuus esses.
ME. Quid domini faciant, audent cum talia fures?
Non ego te uidi Damonis pessime caprum
Excipere insidiis, multùm latrante Lycisca?
Et cùm clamarem : Quò nunc se proripit ille?
Tityre cogu pecus : tu post carecta latebas.
DA. An mihi cantando uictum non redderet ille,
Quem mea carminibus meruisset fistula caprum?
Si nescis, meus ille caper fuit, & mihi Damon
Ipse fatebatur : sed reddere posse negabat.
ME. Cantando tu illum ? aut unquam tibi fistula cera
Iuncta fuit ? non tu in triuiis indocte solebas
Stridenti miserum stipula disperdere carmen?
DA. Vis ergo inter nos quid possit uterque uicissim
Experiamur ? ego hanc uitulam (ne forte recuses,
Bis uenit ad mulctram,binos alit ubere fœtus)
Depono : tu dic mecum quo pignore certes.
ME. De grege non ausim quicquam deponere tecum:
Est mihi namq; domi pater, est mihi & nouerca:
Bisq; die numerant ambo pecus, alter & hædos.
Verùm id,quod multò tute ipse fatebere maius,
(Insanire libet quoniam tibi) pocula ponam
Fagina, cælatum diuini opus Alcimedontis,
Lenta quibus torno facili superaddita uitis,
Diffusos hederâ uestit pallente corymbos.
In medio duo signa, Conon, & quis fuit alter,
Descripsit radio totum qui gentibus orbem?

In eos côue-
nit, q aliqd
dicit, quod
nihil ad re
facit.

In eos côue-
nit, Barba-
ros nimirû,
& indoctos
q quicqd fa-
ciunt, inte-
pestiuè a-
gunt.

archimedes

Tem

FIGURE 6. Vergil. *Opera.* Antwerp: Dumaeus, 1542. (Princeton University Library.)

P. VERG. MARO. BVCO.

ARGVMENTVM PRIMAE ECLOGAE.

In prima Ecloga introducuntur Tityrus & Melibœ-
us. Sub Tityro persona Vergilii: sub Melibœo alius, cui
ager erat ademptus. Itaq; Vergilius, quo euidenius for-
tunam suam, atq; adeo Cæsaris beneficia explicaret, ex
diuerso introduxit alium aduersa fortuna, cui ager erat
ademptus, & ipse à patria pulsus.

ECLOGA I. TITYRVS.

MELIBOEVS ET TITYRVS
interlocutores.

Tityre, tu patulæ recubans sub tegmine fagi,
Syluestrem tenui Musam meditaris auena.
Nos patriæ fines, & dulcia linquimus arua:
Nos patriam fugimus, tu Tityre lentus in umbris
Formosam resonare doces Amaryllida syluas. **Tit.**

O Melibœe, Deus nobis hæc otia fecit.
Namq; erit ille mihi semper Deus, illius aram
Sæpe tener nostris ab ouilibus imbuet agnus.
Ille meas errare boues, ut cernis, & ipsum
Ludere, quæ uellem, calamo permisit agresti.
Non equidem inuideo, miror magis undiq; totis **Mœ.**

Vsq; adeo turbatur agris: en ipse capellas
Protinus æger ago: hanc etiam uix Tityre duco.
Hic inter densas corylos modo namq; gemellos,
Spem gregis, ab silice in nuda connixa, reliquit.
Tityre

Marginalia: Auθωπα. Homo hominem dæmonium, ut Deus. Tollit suspicionem. Ratio.

ECLOGA I.

Tityre, tu patulæ, & cætera.) Exordium, quo capiat
beneuolentiam à persona Tityri: & genus carminis ex-
primit, Nos patriæ fines.) Auriben est & interpretario,
adiuncta expositione. Ille meas errare.) Reddit cau-
sam cur sit Cæsarem loco numinis habiturus, beneficii
subtexens, Vsq; adeo turbatur.) Hypotyposis est, & exemplum à sua persona, quo tantarum turbarum uehe-
mentiam ostendit.

Sæpe malum hoc nobis, si mens non læua fuisset,
De cœlo tactas memini prædicere quercus.
Sæpe sinistra caua prædixit ab ilice cornix.
Sed tamen iste Deus qui sit, da Tityre nobis.
Vrbem, quam dicunt Romam, Melibœe putaui **Tit.**
Stultus ego huic nostræ similem, quo sæpe solemus
Pastores ouium teneros depellere fœtus.
Sic canibus catulos similes, sic matribus hædos
Noram, sic paruis componere magna solebam.
Verum hæc tantum alias inter caput extulit urbes,
Quantum lenta solent inter uiburna cupressi. **Mœ.**
Et quæ tanta fuit Romam tibi causa uidendi?
Libertas, quæ sera tamen respexit inertem, **Tit.**
Candidior postquam tondenti barba cadebat,
Respexit tamen, & longo post tempore uenit.
Postquam nos Amaryllis habet, Galatea reliquit.

De cœlo tactas.) Tacta quercus, agri uastationem: de
cœlo, iram Cæsaris significabat. Vrbem, quam dicunt.)
Orditur narrationem à loci descriptione: & est longum
Hyberbaton.
Sic canibus catulos.) Collatio est Bucolica, qua aliquot
dissimilitudinis formulas cogerit, cuiusmodi scilicet te-
studinem Pegalo comparare, & culicem elephanti con-
ferre

Marginalia: Amplificatio est ab omni. Laus urbis Romæ & est com. Mœ. Tit. paratio.

A 4

FIGURE 7. Vergil. *Bucolica.* Cologne, 1535. (The Vatican Library.)

The trauailed Pylgrime

The Author by Reason taketh his iourney, and receyueth the Speare of Regiment.

FIGURE 8. Stephen Bateman. *The Trauayled Pylgrime, bringing newes from all partes of the worlde.* London: H. Denham, 1569. (By permission of the Folger Shakespeare Library.)

¶ A briefe cattileg of the reprochfull and blasphemous termes used in the aftefaye I.pdtl, againft God, his Gofpell, his anoinced, and the whole ftate as followeth,

2.Timo.4. 14.15.

Behold with what villanous and reprochful fpeaches this young vores At R,blafphemeth god,in defiling the hoft of Ifrael, euen Gods Churche England as it were, euen curfeth our DAVID by his gracious NESSE, or other an olderabsa-kasfent from the Romifh SENA-CHERIB, with a mouth full of all manner of villanies and reprochfull blafphemies, againft God, hardigron, the Lords anointed, euen our godly,lawful,and moft gracious NESSE-SIA, with the whole ftate, and fo confequently, againft Chrift Iefus, and his maiestfull Church,a part whereof, our Church of England is.

2.Sap.17. read the cha.

Efa.3.reade the chapt.

¶ Pptimus, marking Marchiulis, verye Atifts and Vethinsate Deniers of God, all our beings hypocrite,aruifers of totes in bigbills, apes hereticas, raylers, perfecuters, conturers, murers of Saintes, hoores, fhamelies impudir,dyke atmurs & pretenders of gittls blounfred, thinking our fouereigne not bleft,but the condition, fynally fuch as Gods curfe will roote out, and dying to a fhame full end.

By which fpeaches of tongue and pen, together with fome practife knowne, (but no in ferrent) we may fee as in a glaffe, (if wee woulde beleue, or experience could teach,) what is in the hearts of all obftinate Papiftes, of whom this infatiate maxime was giuen of late: Papiftes imp,yefto, practife treafon, Papiftes gitting martyre, murther crueltye, Dthwife not euill England, but all lambes when they are, espeer haue bane, or pitifeufe be, feting our felfe: Better therefore fuch in time were iuftice fecured, then Prince and people fhould be gittes murdered.

Luke.19.40.

¶ fo impudent boldres,and reprochfull blafphemies,of fo prouoke & vile a Philif.ine,and fo raylyng: NABASAIN,fhold haue had fome anfwer, God would furely haue caufed ftones to cry,as he hath opened as it were (but the mouth of an Affe) in refpecte of the godly learned, to chide the boldnes of fuch blafphemous Ifalmites and rayling NABASSINS.

Ihey

They fet their mouth againft Deauen,and their tonge walketh through the earth. Pfal.73.9.

They go on amie fro in the euening, they barke like dogges, and goe about the citye: behold they fpaigte in their talke, and fhoopes are in their lippes.

The wicked be ftrangers from the woombe, euen from the bellye haue they erred and fpeake lyes, their poyfon is lyke the poyfon of a Serpent.

A reply to the aboue fayd late rayling, lying libell of the mifking papiftes,fet vyth poftes, who not onlye fame (but flatly fhew) to be in deede non of gods religion, but are the very apes of god, of Chrift, of Iefus, of Gofpell, of Turke and of all heretickes, from whom they haue patched vp as well (in opinion, as ceremonies) they marking monettrp and mingle mangle cum pur, of fublime, ingraffine, ienuliktie and herefie, and haue con firmed the fame with condrinations,magicall artes, falfe miracles, lying woombes, deceauble figures, malitious bruifes, treafonable pradifes,and horrible murders. And that fo manifeft, as their bad the bruill can not without blufhing denye the fame.

Thy cloake thus turned on the right fide.

Some that hath eyther naturall wit, or grace, wil holde of a fewe fuch a religion, but only fuch as becaufe they perceiue not the loue of the truth, that they might be faued, God therefore fended them ftrong delufions that they fhoulde beleeue lyes, that al they might be damned, which beleue not the truth, but had pleafure in vnrigteoufnes.

I hereby of a true chriftian, and therefore of faithful fubiects.

Tume fed thy Pope thou Lucke an ape, and kepe well thy necke I vile thee: Leaft halter ape, &hel die rake, if trayour they doe finde thee. Our Quene her grace, God grant long life, both here (in deede) and euermore: Who feekes your loyaltye and fayth, and not to maiure you therefore,

In

This as true religion alfo bewrifed with Idolatry,hypocrifie, fuperftrution, vaine glory, couetoufnes coltonage, fimony,extortion,bribery,periury forgery, whoredom, adulterye, &c.

This as true of the popifh genercion,as of al mens generation.

You fhall perfoaue both labell and informe the better, if you confer proofs wyth places (in deede) and note to maiure you therefore.

FIGURE 9. A reply with the occasion thereof. London: Hugh Singleton, 1579. (By permission of the Folger Shakespeare Library.)

The placement of the gloss matters not only for the general reason of the importance of prior models which underlies my whole argument, but for the importance Spenser placed on this issue. He wrote, in a postscript to his letter to Harvey of April 1580: "I take it best my *Dreames* shoulde come forth alone, being growen by meanes of the Glosse *(running continually in maner of a Paraphrase)* full as great as my Calendar" (*Var.* 10:18; italics mine). It seems reasonable to conclude that Spenser positioned the gloss in the *Calender* deliberately because so much else in the presentation can only be explained by the assumption of specific instructions having been given (as we have seen and shall see), and because he intended to be deliberate with the placement of the gloss in his *Dreames*. He paid attention to the matter.

Among the books cited so far only a few models for a subsequent gloss can be found. The first two are Vergils; the third, Ronsard; the last, the emblem book. In the 1535 Vergil with Hessus' commentary, the eclogue is set up in the following way: argument, text (with marginal gloss) broken into units, prose commentary after each unit (fig. 7).[40] We see a similar format in Plantin's great 1575 edition of Vergil (II:62), where the units of text (without marginal gloss) are separated by commentary. But the format of neither Vergil corresponds closely to the *Calender*'s, where the text is not broken into units.

A closer visual parallel to the gloss in the *Calender* occurs in certain editions of Ronsard's works, a connection already suggested on a textual basis by W. L. Renwick. He points out that the commentary in the *Calender* "was compiled with Spenser's permission and assistance: that is clear. Ronsard had published his early works in the same fashion, with notes by Antoine Muret; and for the same reason," the demand that the "new learned poetry" be taken seriously in his country.[41] The presentation of a 1553 Paris edition of Ronsard (II:45) includes an unruled, relatively spare title page; a preface by Marc Antoine de Muret "sur les commentaires," with its own dedication; a text arranged so that, with the exception of the last four odes which are glossed together, each poem, printed in italic, is followed by the word "Muret" in roman, after which a gloss/commentary appears. This verbal description makes the correspondence between the Ronsard and the *Calender* closer than it appears to be visually; each Ronsard ode is short, comprising with commentary no more than one page, while each poem in the *Calender* goes on for pages. In addition, the fonts are discriminated in the Ronsard edition. But the major difference between the two formats, aside from illustration, is the appearance of the "embleme" unit between the end of the poem and the gloss in the *Calender*.

The annotated emblem book is the last model to be discussed for the gloss in the *Calender*. To present my reasons for urging the emblem book as the paramount but not exclusive source for the layout of the eclogue unit we must change focus from the individual elements to the entire presentation of the eclogue. The question is, Where do we find, among all the models just discussed, the sequence of illustration, individual argument, text with "embleme(s)", and subsequent gloss? The answer is, nowhere. However, a close parallel does exist in those editions of Alciati and other emblem books in which commentary adds a fourth element to the emblem form, whose essentials derive from the first edition of Alciati in 1531.[42] The emblem is printed in a tripartite structure: (1) the picture (*pictura* or *icon*), (2) motto (*inscriptio* or *lemma*) usually printed above the picture, and (3) explanatory text (*subscriptio* or *epigram*) in verse or prose. In the annotated Alciati the commentary appears after the explanatory text.[43]

Let us compare two pages from a 1577 Alciati with commentary (II:2), shown in figure 10, with the format of the eclogue unit in the *Calender*.[44] In the Alciati (p. 314 shows the end of one emblem, p. 315 the beginning of the next) we see, in order, the motto, the picture, the text, and the commentary/gloss. We see these four elements in the *Calender*, but they occur in a different order because the motto (or "embleme" as Spenser calls it) comes at the end of the text instead of preceding the picture as it does in the emblem book. It would seem, therefore, that by means of visual allusion to the contemporary annotated emblem book, as well as by use of the word "embleme," *The Shepheardes Calender* (in addition to its other identities) emerges as Spenser's emblem book.[45]

The identification is surprising and it is open to serious question. First of all, the woodcuts in the *Calender* are not emblematic, they are depictive. Next, the various elements in the emblem book bear a necessary relation to one another, but they do not do so in the *Calender*.[46] Finally, the "emblemes" do not come from the usual emblematic sources. Few are from previous emblem books, perhaps half are from classical texts, and the rest are from other sources—epigram and proverb collections and Marot.[47]

These arguments, and those cited in the notes, are just, but they are not convincing. After all, it is consistent with everything we know about Spenser—his characteristic qualities of innovativeness and syncretism—to suppose that he would have felt free to concoct his own emblem book, to move the motto to the end and call it "embleme," and not to bother about following set rules, any more than he was to do, for instance, with the form of the sonnet in the *Amoretti*. If we accept this argument we can set aside previous critical disclaimers and are then in a position to ask what the emblem book identification means. It is a question I consider in the concluding portion of the article.

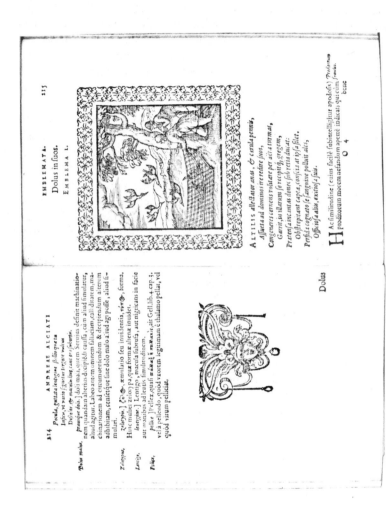

FIGURE 10. Andrea Alciati. *Omnia Emblemata.* Antwerp: Plantin, 1577. (By permission of the Folger Shakespeare Library.)

The Allusive Presentation of *The Shepheardes Calender*

While the identification of the *Calender* with the annotated emblem book is illuminating, it is, of course, partial. I have seen no emblem book, for instance, with an individual argument as part of the emblematic unit. This element in the eclogue is taken perhaps from the relevant editions of Vergil, or Mantuan, or a combination including the other models proposed. In fact, the establishment of an emblem-book allusion does not mean that any of the suggestive models just discussed needs to be discarded; there is no need for exclusivity. Each model feeds into the book as a whole: "Historically, every work of art is a fragment of some larger unit, and every work of art is a bundle of components of different ages, intricately related to many other works of art, both old and new, by a network of incoming and outgoing influences."[48]

Of all the components of the presentation the most curious is the last to be discussed—the decorative initials scattered throughout the main part of the book. (The two decorative initials in the introductory section at the head of the epistle and argument are set normally.) Their use is odd in two ways: They occur inconsistently and they are set peculiarly. Inconsistency means that the initials occur at times at the beginning of an eclogue, at times within an eclogue which does not start with such an initial. Peculiarity of placement means that we do not see what we would expect. Normally, a decorative initial is set so that the text surrounds it on two or three sides (see fig. 5); normally, the initial is aligned with the left-hand margin.

With one exception, and that is partial, none of this is the case in the body of the *Calender*. Decorative initials are set at the start of only four eclogues—"Januarye," "June," "September," and "December." They occur at the beginning of internal sections in two eclogues which do not have such initials at their beginning: in "Aprill," at the start of the lay to Eliza; and twice in "August," at the start of the singing match between Perigot and Willye, and at the start of "Ye wastefull woodes." None of the initials is placed normally on the page, as described above and as seen in the introductory section. Only the eight-line "Januarye" initial is aligned with a left-hand margin, that of the preceding prose argument; this is the exception referred to above, and it is partial because the left-hand margin of the verse into which it is set does not extend beneath the initial so as to surround it. None of the other initials is aligned with any left-hand margin; all jut out into the white page. All except one are set partially into the text on the right; in "December" the six-line initial is set completely to the left of the poem, but to the right of the preceding argument.

No precedent for this placement and use of initials occurs in Singleton's other books.[49] The subsequent editions of the *Calender* "correct" the way in which the decorative initials are printed in the first edition; they are set normally or omitted; all internal initials are dropped.[50]

Why are the initials printed in this way? To answer this, it makes sense to separate inconsistency from peculiarity. It is arguable that inconsistency —the irregular occurrence of the decorative initials—does not reflect Spenserian planning but rather the conditions under which the book was produced.[51] Peculiarity—the unconventional setting—cannot be set aside in the same way. The setting must be deliberate because it cannot be reconciled with normal printing practice. It is much harder to compose an irregular than a regular galley; it is simpler to insert the initial so that it is aligned with the rest of the matter in the galley. To place decorative initials in the way in which we see them in the first edition of the *Calender* is impractical, time-consuming, and uneconomical. The printer would have had to rearrange his form.[52]

The most satisfactory explanation I can arrive at is that the placement of the decorative initials imitates either the early printed book or the manuscript tradition on which it was modeled: "the large and decorative bookinitial and the smaller chapter initials projecting into the margin were an essential feature of the manuscript."[53] If this is the allusion, its effect would be to give the reader a sense of continuity with the way in which the written word was transmitted in the past. Several of the authors mentioned in the *Calender* first appeared in manuscript—Vergil, Langland, Lydgate, and Chaucer. Many calendars, including the book of hours, contained magnificent decorative initials. Any, or all of these, could be alluded to. One cannot say. What is fairly certain is that allusion must be intended, since the curious printing must have been deliberate.

II

Two kinds of investigations have run together in this discussion of the presentation, one reinforcing the other. The first is the assessment of what parts are conventional, what unconventional; the second, their reference. As a specific unit of the presentation emerges as unconventional, as seemingly arbitrary, we naturally ask about why it looks like that. The answer turns out to be that many models have been built on the base formed by the conventions of the typography and house style of the printer's shop. These include calendars—the English almanac and *Le grant kalendrier* with its English descendants; Marot, and, possibly, Ronsard and Du Bellay; the newly edited classic, specifically Vergil in illustrated and unillustrated editions; the illustrated fable and pilgrimage books; Chaucer and the manuscript tradition with possible allusion to the other older English writers

mentioned in the *Calender;* and the emblem book. In addition, the collaborative nature of the *Calender* is announced partially by means of the contemporary conventions of book format. There may be two dedications;
there are certainly two dedicatees—Spenser names Sidney, and may have
named Leicester originally; E. K. names Harvey. Last, we see that because
the *Calender* is an illustrated book with specially commissioned depictive
cuts it is anomalous for its kind in its time.

If we examine these conclusions in the light of previous scholarship on
the *Calender*, we find surprises and shifts of emphasis. The three surprises
comprise the dedication(s), the statement the book makes simply because
it is illustrated in the way it is, and the identification of the annotated emblem book as the primary model for the eclogue unit. The shifts of emphasis concern Marot and the calendar. Of these, only the matter of the two
dedications seems to require no further discussion; one need simply note
that they exist.[54]

This is not so with the illustrated book. A good deal of contemporary
evidence suggests that by the time the *Calender* appeared depictive illustrations were so out-of-date as to be, if not scorned, certainly looked down
on. The sophisticated reader of 1579 hardly needed an illustration to explain the text to him. He took pleasure in unraveling the meaning of emblematic illustration. But the semiliterate audience did need such help, and
it was to this readership that the original *Calender and Compost of Shepherds*
was addressed. If we transpose "semiliterate" to apply to any language we
find that the same need for help explains the existence of the cuts in the
first illustrated *Virgil,* Sebastian Brant's 1502 edition (II:54). They were
put there specifically to help the floundering schoolboy, semiliterate in
Latin. Brant writes at the end of the book: "Let others explain Vergil in
eloquent speech and be pleased to hand him on to boys by pen and by
word of mouth. Brant wished to publish him for the unlearned and rustic
men with simple pictures and drawings."[55] The *Calender*'s readers were
hardly "unlearned and rustic." Why then did Spenser choose to have his
book illustrated in this way? In the absence of primary evidence the best
way to answer the question is to calculate the effect of the cuts on contemporary readers. They would have been reminded of other books that continued to contain such illustrations—the pilgrimage and fable books, the
reprints of the illustrated classic; and of the wider range of books that used
to be illustrated in the first half of the century; and perhaps of the very
early illustrated book. They would have recognized the calendrical references. Readers' reactions were probably ambivalent; while they might have
taken pleasure in recognizing the models and allusion, they might have re-
acted to the out-of-date quality in the way we respond today when a fash-

ion is brought out as new that we associate with our parents' or grandparents' time. Pleasurable or not, this reaction would have contained a sense of the continuity with the past, epitomized by these illustrated books.

It is hardly for the reason of continuity that Spenser stresses Marot. We must ask baldly, Why Marot? Until now critics have assumed the question and answered it by examining Marot's use of pastoral, citing Spenser's past connections with Marot's poems in his translations for *A Theatre for Worldlings,* and assessing the quality and extent of Spenser's imitations. To add to this work, I want to answer the question in another way. First we should review the pervasiveness of the references to Marot. In the text we find the adoption of Marot's nickname "Colin"; his motto, "La Mort ny Mord," which Spenser uses as an "embleme"; and the imitations of his poems in "November" and "December." In the presentation we see that Marot is alluded to by the unit of title page and "To His Booke," and that he may be one of the authors whom Spenser connected with the illustrated book: Marot's translations of the *Bucolics* and of Ovid were illustrated, his translations of the Psalms were printed to be bound with the *Calendrier historial* of 1563, whose style is so reminiscent of the cuts in *The Shepheardes Calender.*

What has not been mentioned is what the title pages of Marot's works proclaim: "Clément Marot, de Cahors, vallet de chambre du Roy."[56] Sophisticated English readers may not have read Marot's pastorals, may not have seen his illustrated translations from the classics, may not have known of the association of the *Calendrier historial* and the *Pseaumes*; but if they had seen any one of Marot's works they would have known from the title page that Marot's patron was his king, François I. A contemporary English reference to Marot shows that he was seen in this way; he is mentioned by Churchyard in an introductory poem to Skelton's works (II:51) that follows the Latin poem on the verso of the title page: "You see howe forrayn realms. / Advance their Poets all: / And ours are drowned in the dust, / Or flong against the wall, / In Fraunce did Marrot raigne." In short, Marot did have what Cuddie wants but does not have, he did "sitt" "in Princes pallace" to transpose the famous line in "October." Of the poets who are named in the *Calender,* the one who is closest chronologically to Spenser and who had royal patronage is Marot. It is arguable that this is among the reasons for his dominant presence in the *Calender.*

If the word "dominant" sums up the allusions to Marot, a much stronger word, "pervasive" perhaps, must be applied to the use of calendrical material. The present research adds two findings to the extensive previous critical work on the connection of the calendar and *The Shepheardes Calender.* First, we see that the illustrations, when they are not directly depictive, are primarily calendrical in style and content. Next, we find that the format of the eclogue unit imitates that in the annotated emblem book. The calendar and emblem book are connected because, looked at historically, the emblem book was the newest instance of a secular form class which included the calendar as well as the fable book and way-of-life literature. They are all guides; they point man's way; the fable, way-of-life, and emblem books show examples. In fact one meaning of the word "calendar" was "example" or "model."[57] Spenser's range is comprehensive both generically and temporally; he includes every kind of calendar in his *Calender*, which ends with "Loe I haue made a Calender for euery yeare."

To call the *Calender* Spenser's emblem book is not to deny that it is a maverick, both because it contains nonemblematic illustrations and because the eclogue unit does not meet the specifications of an emblem. But this is to argue ideologically, and ideology did not control Spenser's way of thinking; the image was dominant. It has been the contention of this article that, in the presentation of *The Shepheardes Calender,* the contemporary reader saw a new book containing the images of its many models.

Drexel University

Appendix I
Books Printed by and for Hugh Singleton Cited in the Text

This list is based on Paul G. Morrison, *Index of Printers, Publishers, and Booksellers in A. W. Pollard and G. R. Redgrave, "A Short Title Catalogue of Books Printed in England, Scotland & Ireland and of English Books Printed Abroad 1475–1640"* (Charlottesville, Va.: Bibliographical Society of the University of Virginia, 1961). Since Morrison's *Index* was published the second volume (I–Z) of the projected three volume new *STC* has been printed. The third volume, comprising an index of printers, may list additional relevant Singleton publications, now unattributed.

This appendix and the one following are amalgams. They rely on the new *STC* for dating and other bibliographical information when this is possible alphabetically; otherwise they reflect the older dating and citations from the catalogue of the library owning the book or the older *STC*.

1. 1558 Cranmer, Thomas. *A confutation of unwritten verities, both bi the holye scriptures and moste auncient autors.* Trans. E. P.
2. 1574 [Another edition]. Werdmueller, Otto. *The Hope of the fayful.* [Trans. M. Coverdale]. J. Allde for H. Singleton.
3. 1576 *A Breefe catechisme.*

4. 1576 Lloyd, Lodowick. *An epitaph vpon the death of Syr Edward Saunders the .19. of November, 1576.* H. S[ingleton]. for H. Disle.
5. 1577 Luther, Martin. *An Exposition upon the CXXX psalme.* Trans. Thomas Potter.
6. 1578 Bèze, Théodore de. *A little catechisme.*
7. 1578 [Another edition]. *A dyall of dayly contemplacion.* [Revised by R. Robinson].
8. 1579 [Another edition of no. 6].
9. 1579 *A reply with the occasion thereof to a late rayling, lying, reprochful and blasphemous libel of the Papists.*
10. 1579 Regius Urbanus. [Another edition]. *A Necessary Instruccyon of the christian faith and hope.* Newly recognized by J. F(oxe).
11. 1579 Spenser, Edmund. *The Shepheardes Calender.*
12. 1579 Stubbs, John. *The discouerie of a gaping gulf whereinto England is like to be swallowed by an other French mariage.* [Anon].
13. 1579 [Another edition of no. 3].
14. 1582 [Another edition of no. 3].

APPENDIX II
Other Books Cited

In this appendix, editions are cited chronologically.

1. Alciati, Andrea. *Emblematum.* Libri II. In eadem succincta commentariola, nunc multo, quam antea, castigatoria. Sebastiano Stockhomero Germano, autore. Antwerp: Plantin, 1566.
2. _____. *Omnia Emblemata, cum commentariis, quibus emblematum omnium aperta origine, mens auctoris explicatur.* Per Claudium Minoem. Antwerp: Plantin, 1577.
3. *An Almanack and prognostication (by J. Hubrighe) for 1569, whereunto is annexed a rule to knowe the ebbes and fluddes along the coast of Englande and Normandie. Also all the principall faires and martes, etc.* London, [1569].
4. Barclay, Alexander. *Here Begynneth the Egloges of Alexander Barclay Prest whereof the fyrst thre conteyneth the myseryes of courters a. courtes.* London: [W. de Worde? c. 1515].
5. Bateman, Stephen. *The Doome warning all men to the judgemente.* London: R. Newberry, 1581.
6. _____. *The Trauayled Pylgrime, bringing newes from all partes of the worlde.* London: H. Denham, 1569.
7. *Calendrier historial.* Lyon: Jean de Tournes, 1563.
8. [Another edition]. *The Workes of Geffray Chaucer.* London: J. Kyngston for J. Wight, 1561.
9. Churchyard, Thomas. *A Discourse of the Queenes Maiesties Entertainement in Suffolk and Norffolk.* London: Henry Bynneman (1578).
10. Cicero. *Opera omnia.* Lutetia apud Bernardum Turrisanum sub Aldino Bibliotheca, 1566.
11. Du Bellay, J. *Recueil de poésie.* Paris: Frederic Morel, 1568.
12. _____. *Les regrets et autre oeuvres poétiques de I. du Bellay.* Paris: Frederic Morel, 1568.
13. _____. *Le sympose de Platon, ou de l'amour et de beauté.* Traduit de Grec en Fran-

çois, avec trois livres de commentaire mis en vers François, par I. du Bellay. Paris: Pour Vincent Sertenas, 1559 [i.e., 1558].

14. Faerno, Gabriele. *Centum fabulae ex antiquis.* Antwerp: Plantin, 1567.

15. Farmer, W. *The common Almanacke for 1587 also a Prognostication.* London: R. Watkins and James Roberts, 1587.

16. Foxe, John. *Actes and Monuments.* London: John Day, 1563.

17. Gascoigne, George. *A Hundreth Sundrie Flowres bounde vp in one small posie.* London: Henry Bynneman for Richard Smith [1573].

18. _____. *The Steele Glas.* London: Henry Bynneman for R. Smith, 1576.

19. Googe, Barnabe, trans. Palingenius, Marcellus. *The Zodiake of Life wherein are twelve bookes.* London: H. Denham for R. Newberye, 1565.

20. Grafton, Richard. [Another edition]. *A Chronicle at large to the first yere of Q. Elizabeth.* London: H. Denham for R. Tottle and H. Toye, 1569.

21. Harvey, Gabriel. *G. Harveii Ciceronianus.* London: Henry Bynneman, 1577.

22. Harvey, John. *An astrologicall addition to the late discourse upon the coniunction of Saturne and Iupiter.* London: R. Watkins, 1583.

23. Horace. *Q. Horatii Flacci poemata omnia doctissimis scholiis illustrata. Iunii Iuuenalis satyrae [Aulie Persii satyrae].* London: G. Norton, 1574.

24. _____. *Horace his arte of poetrie, pistles, a. satyrs Englished and to the Earle of Ormounte by T. Drant addressed.* London: T. Marshe, 1567.

25. Kendall, Timothy, trans. *Flowers of Epigrammes, out of sundrie the moste singular authours.* London: [J. Kingston for] J. Shepperd, 1577.

26. Langland, William. *The Vision of Pierce Plowman.* London: [R. Grafton for] (R. Crowley, 1550).

27. Lavater, Ludwig. *Of ghostes and spirites walking by nyght.* Trans. R. H[arrison]. London: H. Bynneman for R. Watkyns, 1572.

28. Luther, Martin. *A Prophesie out of the nienth chapter of Esaie.* London: Henry Bynneman for G. Seton, 1578.

29. Lydgate, John. *The puerbes of Lydgate.* London: (W. de Worde), [1510?].

30. _____. trans. *The hystorye sege and dystruccyon of Troye.* [By] Guido della Colonna. London: R. Pynson, 1513.

31. Lyly, John. *Euphues, the anatomy of wyt.* London: [T. East] for G. Cawood [1578].

32. Mantuan. *The Eglogs of the poet B. Mantuan Carmelitan, turned into English verse, by G. Turberuille gent.* London: Henry Bynneman, 1567.

33. Marot, Clément. *L'Adolescence Clementine (Oeuvres).* Antwerp: Guil Mantanus voor J. Steels, 1539.

34. _____. *Les Oeuvres de Clément Marot, de Cahors, vallet de chambre du Roy.* Paris: Guillaume Le Bret, 1547.

35. _____. *Les Oeuvres.* Lyon: Jean de Tournes, 1549.

36. _____. *Oeuvres.* Paris: J. Longis, 1554.

37. _____. *Les oeuvres de Clément Marot.* Paris: Jean Rouille, 1571.

38. _____. and Théodore de Bèze. *Les Pseaumes en rime françoise.* Lyon: Jean de Tournes for Antoine Vincent, 1563.

39. _____. *Les traductions de Clément Marot.* Lyon: Jean de Tournes, 1579.

40. _____. *Trois premiers livres de la Métamorphose d'Ovide.* Lyon: Rouille, 1556.

41. Mulcaster, Richard. *The first part of the Elementarie which entreateth of right writing of our English tung.* London: Thomas Vautroullier, 1582.

42. Noot, Jan van der. *A Theatre, wherein be represented as wel the miseries and calamities that follow the voluptuous worldlings.* London: Henry Bynneman, 1569.

43. Peacham, Henry. *The Garden of Eloquence, conteyning the figures of grammar a. Rhetorick.* London: A. Jackson, 1577.
44. Ronsard, Pierre. *Les amours de P. de Ronsard Vandemoys.* Paris, 1552.
45. _____. *Les amours de P. de Ronsard, Vandomois.* Nouvellement augmentées par lui, et commentées par Marc Antoine de Muret. Paris: Chez la veuve Maurice de la Porte, 1553.
46. _____. *Les odes de P. de Ronsard gentilhomme Vandemois.* Paris: Buon, 1571. (Second of six volumes of third collected edition.)
47. _____. *Les Oeuvres.* 2 vols. Paris: Buon, 1567.
48. Seneca [De beneficiis]. *The woorke of the excellent philosopher Annaeus Seneca concerning benefyting.* Trans. A. Golding. London: [J. Kingston for] John Day, 1578.
49. *Les sept saiges de Romae.* Lyon: Jean d'Ogerolles, 1577.
50. Skelton, John. [Another edition]. *Here after foloweth a lytell boke called Collyn Clout.* London: A. Kyston, 1565.
51. _____. *Pithy, pleasaunt and profitable workes.* London: Thomas Marshe, 1568.
52. Spenser, Edmund. *Colin Clovts Come home againe.* London: (T. C[reede].) for William Ponsonbie, 1595.
53. *Three proper, and wittie, familiar letters: lately passed betwene two vniuersitie men.* London: Henry Bynneman, 1580. (Harvey-Spenser correspondence.)
54. Vergilius, Maro Publius. *Opera.* Ed. Sebastian Brant. Strassburg: Grüninger, 1502.
55. _____. *Bucolica.* Acceserunt adnotationes H. Eobani Hessi Poetae. Scholia item quibus artificium Rhetoricum explicatur. Cologne: Leonardo Kullmani, 1535.
56. _____. *Opera.* Doctissimis Phil. Melanch. scholiis, et Eobani Hessi annotationi, quinetiam ex Erasmi Chiliad. Antwerp: Dumaeus, 1542.
57. _____. *Opera.* Venice: Giunta, 1552.
58. _____. *Bucolica.* Venice: Aldine, 1561.
59. _____. *The nyne fyrst bookes of the Eneidos.* Converted in Englishe vearse by T. Phaer. London: R. Hall for N. England, 1562.
60. _____. *Opera.* Antwerp: Plantin, 1564.
61. _____. *Opera.* Antwerp: Plantin, 1572.
62. _____. *Opera.* Antwerp: Plantin, 1575.
63. _____. *Opera.* Venice: Aldum, 1576.
64. Virgil. *The Bucolikes of Publius Virgilius Maro, with alphabeticall annotations.* Drawne into Englishe by A. Fleming. London: J. Charlewood for T. Woodcocke, 1575.
65. _____. [Another edition]. *Thee first foore bookes of Virgil his Aeneis tr. intoo English heroical verse by R. Stanyhurst, wyth oother poetical diuises theretoo annexed.* London: Henry Bynneman, 1583.
66. Veron, Jean. *A moste necessary treatise of free wil, not onlye against the papistes, but also against the anabaptistes.* London: (J. Tisdale), [1561].
67. Whitney, Geffrey. *A Choice of Emblemes and other Devises.* Leyden: Plantin, 1586.

Notes

Some of the research reported here was done at the Plantin-Moretus Museum in Antwerp, the Bibliothèque Royale in Brussels, and the Bibliothèque Nationale in Paris. For the traveling scholarship which made this part of the research possible I thank the American Friends of the Plantin-Moretus Museum.

The Allusive Presentation of *The Shepheardes Calender*

The reader will find it convenient to consult a facsimile of the first edition of the *Calender* (London: The Scolar Press, 1973) throughout the following discussion. I have relied on this facsimile, but my observations have been checked by inspection of the first edition owned by the Carl Pforzheimer Library in New York City.

1. Rosemond Tuve, "Spenser and Some Pictorial Conventions," *SP* 37 (1940), 149.

2. *The Poetry of Edmund Spenser: A Study* (1963; rpt. New York: Columbia University Press, 1965), pp. 32–33, 36, 318, n. 5. It might seem as if the "apparatus" belongs to an investigation of the text rather than the presentation. In fact, it belongs to both: to the text, because it is part of it; to the presentation, because of the unconventional way in which units of the "apparatus" are laid out.

3. "Early," because by the 1550s new Vergilian illustration was no longer depictive but decorative. See Theodore K. Rabb, "Sebastian Brant and the First Illustrated Edition of Vergil," *Princeton University Library Chronicle* 21 (1960), 187–99.

4. What one finds when looking through English illustrated books of the time is so well evoked by Pollard that his description merits quotation at length: "Woodcuts did not cease to be used after this date [1580]. They will be found in herbals (but these were mainly foreign blocks), military works, and all books for which diagrams were needed. They continued fashionable for some time for the architectural or other forms of borders to title pages . . . also for the coats of arms of great men to whom books were dedicated. They are found also at haphazard in the sixpenny and fourpenny quartos of plays and romances, and many of the old blocks gradually drifted into the hands of the printers of ballads and chapbooks, and appear in incongruous surroundings after a century of service. But I cannot myself call to mind any important English book after 1580 for which a publisher thought it worth his while to commission a new set of imaginative pictures cut on wood and that means that woodcut illustration as a vital force in the making of books had ceased to exist." *Fine Books* (1903; rpt. New York: Cooper Square Publishers, 1964), p. 266.

5. M. H. Black, "The Evolution of a Book-Form: The Octavo Bible from Manuscript to the Geneva Version," *The Library*, 5th ser. 16 (1961), 15.

6. The relevant books for comparison with the *Calender* are those listed in Appendix I as numbers 2, 3, 4, 6, 9, 10, 12, 13. Future references to books listed in the appendices are given in the text.

7. Singleton assigned the rights to the *Calender* to John Harrison the younger on 29 October 1580. See *A Transcript of the Registers of the Company of Stationers of London, 1554–1640*, ed. Edward Arber (London, 1875), vol. 2, p. 380. The four editions printed for Harrison were: 1581, Thomas East; 1586, John Wolye; 1591, John Windet; and 1597, Thomas Creede.

8. See the discussion in *Spenser's Minor Poems*, ed. Ernest de Selincourt (1910; rpt. Oxford: The Clarendon Press, 1960), pp. v–xv.

9. In the second edition (1581) the poems are reprinted page-for-page, the glosses are not; the third edition (1586) is not page-for-page; the fourth (1591) is page-for-page from the third; the fifth (1597) is not page-for-page. See Francis R. Johnson, *A Critical Bibliography of the Works of Edmund Spenser Printed Before 1700* (Baltimore: The Johns Hopkins Press, 1933).

10. The large category of relevant books (some of which are listed in Appendix II) includes the textual sources for and influences on the *Calender;* books by people in Spenser's friendship and reference groups; books considered famous at the time; books produced by other printers with whom Spenser had a known contact (e.g., Henry Bynneman, Harvey's printer and the printer of *A Theatre for Worldlings*); those praised by book historians and

bibliographers; and finally, any English books of the time said to contain illustrations, as well as a great many illustrated books printed in France and the Low Countries. Books were inspected in facsimile when the original was not available.

Of course, no bibliographical search can be considered complete. I think of the one reported here as a beginning, open to and requiring further additions. This is needed particularly because, while some aspects of the printed book have been the subject of considerable scholarly investigation (e.g., typography, title-page borders, ornamentation), some have not (e.g., the gloss, the changing book format).

11. The description of font and type size follows that in Frank Isaac, *English Printers' Types of the Sixteenth Century* (London: Oxford University Press, 1936). The account is detailed deliberately so that readers who do not have a facsimile can follow the discussion. It differs from the customary bibliographical description, although it incorporates some of its features, because the aim is different. If the reader refers to such a description he will see that it does not include any notation for "Envoy," "Embleme," capitalization, illustration border, or ornamentation other than that on the title page and colophon. Nor is E. K.'s role defined exactly; while he is identified as the author of the "Dedicatory Epistle," he is not named as author of the "Argument" or the glosses. See Johnson, *A Critical Bibliography*, pp. 2–3.

12. Professor Rudolph Hirsch in a personal communication. The point is made in most discussions of the history of the title page. See A. F. Johnson, *One Hundred Title-Pages, 1500–1800* (London: John Lane, The Bodley Head, 1928), and the discussion in R. B. McKerrow, *An Introduction to Bibliography for Literary Students* (1928; rpt. Oxford: The Clarendon Press, 1972), pp. 93–94. For examples of title pages additional to those shown in Johnson, see *Art of the Printed Book: 1455–1955* (New York: The Pierpont Morgan Library, 1973), and "The Book Trade in the Sixteenth Century," in P. M. Handover, *Printing in London from 1476 to Modern Times* (London: George Allen and Unwin, 1960).

13. The ornament on the title page of the *Calender* is ³/₄″ square. Had Singleton used the ornament he placed on the title page of I:9 which measures 1 ³/₈″ square, the effect would have been within a normal range. The edition of 1581 has a border of printer's ornaments, those of 1586 and 1591, *TPB* no. 198 (R. B. McKerrow and F. S. Ferguson, *Title-Page Borders Used in England and Scotland, 1486–1640* [London: Printed for the Bibliographical Society at Oxford University Press, 1932]).

14. A copy of the Vergil is in the Junius Morgan Collection of the Firestone Library at Princeton University. For the reasons we know this was the version Spenser used, see Henry Lotspeich, "Spenser's Virgils Gnat," *ELH* 2 (1935), 235–41.

The generalization about Chaucer holds whether we accept Miskimin's arguments that Spenser's Chaucer was the Stowe folio of 1561; or Hieatt's, that it was one of the Thynne editions of 1532–1561. See Alice S. Miskimin, *The Renaissance Chaucer* (New Haven: Yale University Press, 1975), pp. 247–50; and A. Kent Hieatt, *Chaucer, Spenser, Milton: Mythopoeic Continuities and Transformations* (Montreal: McGill-Queen's University Press, 1975), pp. 19–28.

15. Such a disparity does not exist in the exceptions I have discovered to the points made here. For example, Singleton uses an even smaller device than that on the *Calender*'s title page on the title page to Luther's *Exposition of the CXXX psalme* (I:5) but the decoration of the book as a whole does not contrast with the title page. The same observation holds for some English translations of the classics, such as Drant's translation of Horace (II:24).

16. See the reproduction of the title page of the *Oeuvres* of 1547 in C. A. Mayer, *Bibliographie des éditions de Clément Marot publiées au XVIe siècle* (Paris: A. G. Nizet, 1975),

p. 61, no. 156. For the imitation and influence of Marot and the effect of the Pléiade on the *Calender* and Spenser, see Merritt Y. Hughes, *Virgil and Spenser,* University of California Publications in English 2, no. 3 (1929), 263–418; W. L. Renwick, ed., *The Shepherd's Calendar* (London: The Scholartis Press, 1930); discussion and references in Anne Lake Prescott, *French Poets and the English Renaissance: Studies in Fame and Transformation* (New Haven: Yale University Press, 1978); and the citations in *The Works of Edmund Spenser: A Variorum Edition,* ed. Edwin Greenlaw et al., 11 vols. (Baltimore: The Johns Hopkins Press, 1932–57), vol. 7, part 1. Hereafter cited as *Var.*

17. "To His Booke" is set up so as to appear almost grandiose in comparison with the effect of the title page. The type is large, the spaces leaded; an ornamental bar precedes the poem. This imposing impression contrasts also with the humility expressed in the poem itself. Subsequent editions of the *Calender* consistently reverse the effect; the title page assumes potency, as we have just seen, while "To His Booke" is drastically reduced in size. All the editions have ornamental bars except that of 1581. However, the large setting of the poem in the first edition probably reflects nothing more than Singleton house style. We find exactly the same use of leaded 80 italic between or preceding sections of closely set type in, for example, I:3. Nor is the practice a Singletonian idiosyncrasy. Introductory matter is often set up in large leaded italic; for instance, the dedicatory epistle in Bateman (II:5).

18. The combination occurs, for example, in the Lyons *Oeuvres* of 1549 (II:35) and in the Paris *Oeuvres* of 1554 (II:36). It does not occur in the other editions of original poetry listed in Appendix II. In some editions the title page is ruled (II:33), or has a border (II:37). In some editions the printer has interposed his own material between the title page and "A son livre," etc. For instance in the Paris edition of 1547 (II:34) the title page is followed by "L'imprimeur au lecteur" after which we find "A son livre." Similarly in the 1571 edition cited above (II:37) we find the following: the verso of the title page is blank, the recto of the next page contains "L'ordre des oeuvres de Clément Marot," its verso contains "A son livre," etc.

However, it is arguable that even in these seeming exceptions the first authorial material remains "A son livre." Whether or not this point is acceptable, the main argument remains. Spenser cannot be presumed to have made a bibliographical survey of the editions of Marot. It is sufficient to show that several contemporary editions did contain the specific combination described above.

19. In a single book combining several volumes of Du Bellay's work (II:12) we find "A sa lyre" on the verso of the title page of volume 1, and "A son livre" on the verso of the title page of volume 5. An untitled poem by Du Bellay is printed on the verso of the title page of his translation of Plato's *Symposium* (II:13).

Chosen because of their known influence on Spenser, Du Bellay, Baïf, and Ronsard are the three members of the Pléiade whose books I inspected. None of the Ronsards seen contains the author's poem to his work on the verso of the title page.

20. The English convention can be illustrated by the order of the introductory matter in Mulcaster's *Elementarie* (II:41): (1) title page, (2) dedicatory epistle, (3) "autoris ipsius ad librum suum," (4) table of contents, (5) peroration. Similarly, among Singleton's books we find, (e.g. in I:10): (1) title page, (2) dedicatory epistle, (3) "Preface to the booke."

A few exceptions to the generalization: (1) John Harvey's *An astrologicall addition* (II:22) contains two Latin poems on the verso of the title page. The first is a prayer for the health and long life of Queen Elizabeth; the second is an address to the patron of the work, explaining what Harvey is doing (translation), its legality, function and audience. (2) Thomas Drant's *Horace, his arte* (II:24) has the Latin poem "De Seipso" on the verso of the title page. Written by Drant, the poem consists of tags taken from the Augustan poets, and chiefly, Vergil's *Georgics*—the youth of the poet, his modesty and uncertainty, the goad of his wish for fame, and the mention of patronage (I thank Dr. Matthew Dickie of the Department of Classics, The University of Illinois, Chicago Circle, for his translation of this poem and explanation of its traditions). (3) In Farmer's *Almanacke* of 1587 (II:15) a poem printed on the verso of the title page apologizes for using agricultural analogies, and for the inadequacy of the work.

21. The shared formulas include the sending of the book into the world, the mention of envy, the prominence of the recipient, and speculation about the book's reception. But it is only in one of Lydgate's poems that the reader is reminded of the second line of "To His Booke:" "As child whose parent is vnkent." The first line of the last verse of Lydgate's *Proverbes* (II:29) reads: "Go lytell bull without tytle or date." Even though Lydgate names himself later, the sense of his first line, like Spenser's second, is the nakedness or defenselessness of the book.

22. Franklin B. Williams, Jr., *Index of Dedications and Commendatory Verses in English Books Before 1641* (London: The Bibliographical Society, 1962), p. x. There are two kinds of exceptions to the generalization. In the first, the epistle to the reader is not the third item. We find this, for example, in (1) Gascoigne (II:18): (a) dedicatory epistle, (b), (c), (d), commendatory poems, (e) author to reader, (f) table of faults; (2) Harvey (II:21): (a) Harvey's dedication to Lewin, (b) Lewin's letter to "Printer and to Students of Eloquence." In these instances the dedication remains the second element. But in the second kind of exception it does not. Here, the English printer has interposed guides for the reader between the standard parts (just as the French printer did for Marot, as note 18 suggests). To cite a few examples, among many, we find that the epistle is preceded by a list of authors printed on the verso of the title page in Kendall (II:25): the same is true in Grafton's *Chronicle* (II:20); and, finally, in the 1561 edition of Chaucer (II:8) the order is: (a) title page, (b) contents of the book, (c) the printer to the reader, (d) Thomas Sackeyville in commendation of the work to the reader, (e) the epistle.

23. The discussion is based on Clara Gebert, "An Anthology of Elizabethan Dedications and Prefaces," Ph.D. diss., University of Pennsylvania, 1933.

24. "Spenser, Shakespeare, Honor, and Worship," *Renaissance News* 14 (1961), 159–61. Ringler argues that Spenser changed the dedication of the *Calender* from the earl of Leicester to Sir Philip Sidney after the middle of October 1579, but neglected to remove a key word, "honor." Ringler shows that Spenser typically discriminated "honor" from "worship," using the first when referring to a nobleman or "person of equivalent dignity," and reserving the second for a knight or gentleman. When he changed the dedication Spenser also changed the appropriate words in E. K.'s epistle but neglected to change "honor" in "To His Booke."

25. An anonymous dedicatory poem in Latin is printed on the verso of the title page to John Marshe's 1568 edition of Skelton (II:51).

26. A noted bibliographer claims the opposite. McKerrow notes the typeface of the *Calender* in the context of describing the shift that occurred in the sixteenth century from black letter to roman type: "early in the reign of Elizabeth roman began to be more popular, and by about 1580 the use of black letter in plays and higher kinds of English verse, as well as in Latin books, had almost ceased, and there seems to have been a tendency to abandon it in scientific and theological literature also." A note reads: "I suspect that the use of black letter in the *Shepherd's Calendar* was an intentional bit of antiquarianism" (*An Introduction to Bibliography,* p. 297, and n. 2).

While the trend McKerrow describes is undeniable, it turns out that black letter was not as anomalous by 1579 in the kinds of books instanced as he says. For example, the texts of the following books from Appendix II are printed in black letter: 17, 19, 25, 28, 31, 43,

The Allusive Presentation of *The Shepheardes Calender*

48, 53, 64, 65. This list has no pretensions to completeness. Its only function is to give examples which challenge McKerrow's statement; its only purpose to determine whether his suspicion about the use of black letter in the *Calender* is correct. The list includes most of the kinds of books he describes, except plays, and goes up to 1583 (65).

27. The point may seem obvious, but it is not. Renwick's otherwise excellent edition of the *Calender* contains no illustrations.

28. The *Troy Book* (II:30) is profusely illustrated with both two-column and one-column depictive cuts placed inconsistently on the page. The 1561 edition of Chaucer (II:8) contains copies of older blocks. These are not depictive, but decorative; they are printed at the point on the double-columned page where a new Prologue begins, and are set three-quarters of the way across the page beginning at one margin or another, thus covering one column and a half of the second.

29. The Marot cuts seem to be copies of the first Vergilian ones of 1502 (II:54). They are reproduced in "Le première eclogue des bucoliques de Virgile," in *Les oeuvres de Clément Marot de Cahors en Quercy* . . . (Paris: J. Schemit, n.d.). For the illustrative traditions in sixteenth-century Vergils see the discussion in Rabb, "Sebastian Brant."

30. The same argument was made above, although in a different context, in the case of the illustrated Chaucer and Lydgate; it holds as well for the illustrated Ovid, whose connection with the *Calender* might not otherwise be immediately apparent.

Vergil and Ovid, the two classical authors whose works were illustrated most frequently earlier in the sixteenth century, were both translated by Marot, and these translations appeared in illustrated versions. The first illustrated edition of Marot's translation of Ovid in the *Oeuvres* of 1549 (II:35) includes twenty-two original woodcuts. See the reproduction of one of these cuts and the discussion in Ruth Mortimer, *French Sixteenth Century Books*, Harvard College Library Department of Printing and Graphic Arts, Catalogue of Books and Manuscripts, part 1 (Cambridge, Mass.: Harvard University Press, 1964), vol. 2, p. 465.

31. Spenser could have seen them in the libraries of Bishop Young, the earl of Leicester, or at Cambridge, whose libraries held illustrated Vergils while Spenser was there. See the list in Herbert Adams, *Catalogue of Books Printed on the Continent of Europe, 1501–1600, in Cambridge Libraries*, vol. 2 (Cambridge: Cambridge University Press, 1967), pp. 318–19, where several contemporary editions with woodcuts are listed.

32. A copy of an *Alciati* (Lyon, 1549) bearing the signature of Edward VI is in the British Museum (Samuel Chew, *The Pilgrimage of Life* [New Haven: Yale University Press, 1962], p. 396, n. 2). Harvey is the source for the statement that in his time at Cambridge students were neglecting Aristotle and the schoolmen for Castiglione, Jovius, and Paradin —the last two are authors of emblem books (E. N. Thompson, *Literary Bypaths of the Renaissance* [New Haven: Yale University Press, 1924], p. 63).

33. Spenser's translations from the French poems of Marot and Du Bellay appear in Bynneman's 1569 edition of Jan Van der Noot's *A Theatre for Worldlings* (II:42). This edition contains woodblock copies of the copper engravings contained in the French and Dutch editions of 1568; they bear no similarity to the *Calender*'s cuts.

34. The most direct quotation of fable illustrations occurs in the "Maye" cut where the depiction of the fox and kid imitates those found, for instance, in *Die Warachtighe Fabulen der Dieren* (Bruges: 1567), and Corrozet's translation of *Aesop* (Paris: D. Janot, 1542).

35. See D. Levi, "The Allegories of the Months in Classical Art," *AB* 23 (1941), 251–91.

36. *The Calendar of Shepherds*, first published under the title *Le grant kalendrier et compost de bergiers* in Paris by Guy Marchant in 1491, appeared in later editions published by Antoine Vérard. Of the many editions printed in England from 1506 on, some had blocks borrowed from Vérard, some poorer copies. See A. M. Hind, "Studies in English Engraving.

RUTH SAMSON LUBORSKY

II: Hans Holbein and English Woodcut in the Sixteenth Century," *The Connoisseur* 91 (April 1933), 223. For a discussion and comparison of the various translations and editions, see H. Oskar Sommer, ed., *The Kalender of Shepherdes* (London: Kegan Paul, Trench, Trübner, 1892).

37. Marot's work is directly connected with the 1563 *Calendrier historial* and many other editions all printed to accompany the Marot–de Bèze *Pseaumes* (II:38). See the discussion and bibliography in Eugénie Droz, "Le Calendrier Lyonnais," *Chemins de l'hérésie* (Geneva: Slatkine, 1974), vol. 3, pp. 2–28.

For the history of the combined form see Carroll Camden, Jr., "Elizabethan Almanacs and Prognostications," *The Library,* 4th ser. (1932), 83–108, 194–207.

38. My discussion of the format of Vergil editions has been supplemented by the valuable advice and assistance of Professor Georg Knauer of the classics department, University of Pennsylvania, who told me of the way in which some Vergils with commentary by Hessus are set up.

Of the seventy-five editions of Vergil I inspected first-hand, ranging in time from 1481 to 1583, I found only a few instances where the individual argument is so printed. Among these are: Venice, 1561 (II:58), Antwerp, 1564 (II:60), Antwerp, 1572 (II:61), London, 1575 (II:64), and Venice, 1576 (II:63).

39. Warren Roberts shows that this tale comes from an old collection, *The Seven Sages of Rome.* In a contemporary French edition, *Les sept saiges de Romae* (II:49), the argument is printed at the beginning of the fable. See "Spenser's Fable of the Oak and the Briar," *Southern Folklore Quarterly* 14 (1950), 150–54.

40. The layout is not limited to Vergils. An edition of Cicero, for instance, has the same arrangement, but without marginal gloss. The text is presented in sections, with commentary after each section (II:10).

41. See his edition of the *Shepherd's Calendar,* p. 172.

42. According to Mario Praz the first prose commentary to accompany an *Alciati* occurs in an edition of 1571 printed in Paris by Dion à Prato with notes by Claude Mignault, or, as he sometimes signed himself, Minos *(Studies in Seventeenth-Century Imagery,* 2nd, rev. ed. [Rome: Beneventana, 1964], p. 39). However, an earlier *Alciati* with commentary was printed by Plantin in 1566 (II:1). A copy is in the Plantin-Moretus collection; its format is the same as that in the 1577 *Alciati* discussed above and shown in figure 10.

43. This layout is close to the format we see also in Faerno's *Centum Fabulae* (II:14). The individual unit consists of title, illustration, poem, emblem, prose description of the picture which illustrates the fable. However, I take the emblem book with commentary to be closer to what we see in the *Calender* because its commentary concerns the text.

44. In this *Alciati*, marginalia identify the characters. However, in an edition of 1566 (II:1) there are no marginalia.

45. The argument is reinforced by the strong likelihood that an *Alciati* emblem is among the allusions of the first cut in the *Calender.* For a suggestive precedent see the analysis of the layout of *A Theatre for Worldlings,* where the editors show that the format is modeled on Alciati's *Emblemata.* Jan van der Noot, *Het Bosken en Het Theatre,* ed. W. A. P. Smit (Amsterdam and Antwerp: W. Vermeer, 1953).

46. "The three parts have a set relationship to one another, for the picture (*res picta*) represents hidden meanings and significance which the text wants to interpret and reveal (*res significans*). The emblem as an entire unit wants to say more than merely what is obvious in the picture; it wants to instruct. The traditional terminology of the interrelationship is that the picture is the body, and the text is the soul; together they produce the *significatio*" (Henri Stegemeier, rev. of *Emblemata, Sinnbildkunst des XVI und XVII Jahrhunderts,* by Arthur Henkel and Albrecht Schöne, *JEGP* 67 [1968], 657).

The Allusive Presentation of *The Shepheardes Calender*

47. Although a good deal of scholarly attention has gone to discovering the texts of Spenser's "emblemes," very little has been focussed on why he uses the word "embleme." Renwick, in his edition of the *Calendar*, mentions the issue only to pass it over: "In *The Shepheardes Calender* Spenser gives for each of the months what he calls 'an emblem': a motto or device . . . forming a moral to each eclogue. There is no connexion between the tenor of the emblems and the woodcuts which illustrate each month" (p. 214).

Rosemary Freeman makes a similar point: "These are not emblems in the same sense [as in the emblem book] . . . they are tags in Latin, Greek, or Italian, which sum up the moral of the whole Eclogue or the arguments of each of the shepherds. E. K., who interprets them in his Glosse, calls them Poesies; they are in effect, what in an emblem proper was generally termed the Motto. . . . Apart from this use of mottoes *The Shepheardes Calender* is not particularly emblematic except when fables are introduced" (*English Emblem Books* [1948; rpt. New York: Octagon Books, 1970], p. 102).

John Bender agrees with Freeman in *Spenser and Literary Pictorialism* (Princeton: Princeton University Press, 1972), p. 155. It is interesting that Freeman, despite her disclaimer, equates the emblem with the motto, as I do for different reasons.

48. George Kubler, "Style and the Representation of Historical Time," *Annals of the New York Academy of Sciences* 133 (1967), 849–50.

49. Two comparisons: One example of the unconventional setting is the *Y* with which "Ye daynte Nymphs" in "Aprill" begins. A *V* taken from the same font is set conventionally at the beginning of E. K.'s epistle. Next, an *H* from the same font is set conventionally in another book Singleton printed in 1579, *A Necessary instruccyon* (I:10). A fragment is at the Bodleian.

50. The practice of setting off these internal sections is continued in subsequent editions by means of a two- or three-line book initial which would have been printed at the same time as the rest of the page.

51. This is the best sense I can make of what seems otherwise to be inexplicable. The production of the book will be discussed in another article.

52. One expert on the printed book in the Renaissance thinks there are only two explanations for so odd a printing—either the work was done by amateurs or it was specifically commissioned, so that the printer did not have to bear the cost of the additional time (Dr. Leon Voet, Director of the Plantin-Moretus Museum, personal communication).

53. Black, "Evolution of a Book-Form," p. 18.

54. Further discussion belongs properly to an investigation of the patronage of the *Calender* and not to the meaning of its presentation.

55. Rabb, "Sebastian Brant," p. 189, and n. 6.

56. The description occurs on most Marot title pages, including the ones described above as "spare." For reproductions, see note 16.

57. "Guide" or "example" is the third meaning given for "Calendar" in the *OED*, which cites Osric's description of Laertes: "He is the card or calendar of gentry" (*Ham.* V. ii. 114).

While the basis of this generic classification is literary, it is false to omit the fact that these different forms also share characteristics of illustration and format. Although these traits do not correspond in a point-to-point way with each other, they do make up, by the sixteenth century, the composite of a family resemblance. An instance of this likeness is noticed by a scholar of English illustrations, who writes that the combination of the woodcuts for Bateman's *The Trauayled Pylgrime* (II:6) with the accompanying interpretation (see fig. 8) are an "anticipation" of the emblem book. Edward Hodnett, *Francis Barlow: First Master of English Book Illustration* (London: The Scolar Press, 1978), p. 43.

BRUCE R. SMITH

On Reading *The Shepheardes Calender*

T**HE SHEPHEARDES CALENDER** has proved such a difficult
book for twentieth-century readers partly because it is an amalgam of
three distinct literary genres—classical eclogue, medieval almanac, and
Renaissance pastoral romance—none of which has been cultivated in English since at least the early nineteenth century. The dramatic mode and
thematic traditions of pastoral eclogue have attracted no major English
poets since Shelley and his *Adonais* (1821); *The Kalender of Shepherdes* was
last published in 1611; and prose romance in a pastoral setting with an
amorous hero may have eventually merged with the novel, but not in a
form that helps us immediately in reading the career of Colin Clout. The
one thing these three genres share, the one thing that made it possible for
Spenser to bring them together in *The Shepheardes Calender,* is the pastoral
scenario: All of them confront the reader with shepherds speaking in a
landscape. Beyond this superficial similarity, however, there are profound
differences among these three genres in such matters as the nature of the
hero, the experience of time, the principle that dictates structure, the
sense of the ending. The hero of pastoral romance, for example, is a lan-
guishing lover like Sincero in Jacopo Sannazaro's prose-and-verse *Arcadia,*
an emotionally intense hero whose complicated narrative past gives him
the illusion of fully rounded character. The speakers in Vergil's *Bucolica*
and in the Renaissance works it inspired, on the other hand, are not per-
sonalities but personae. When the poet summons them to speak for a single viewpoint in a philosophical debate, they leave their narrative past
behind them. The implicit hero of *The Kalender of Shepherdes,* with its didactic prologue and illustrated homilies on virtue and vice, is Mankind as
a moral creature. Passionate poet, philosophical disputant, Mankind who
chooses wrong—Spenser manages to combine all three kinds of hero in
Colin Clout, just as he contrives that the *Calender* incorporates three
structural principles at once: the linear narrative of pastoral romance in
Colin's career, the geometrical symmetry of classical eclogues in the *Calender*'s "three formes or ranckes," and the cyclical continuity of an almanac in the disposition of the poems by months.[1] Indeed, it is just such interplay among seemingly contradictory elements that accounts for the
complexity and richness of *The Shepheardes Calender.*

In one crucial matter, however, the three genres brought together in *The Shepheardes Calender* would seem to be irreconcilably at odds: Eclogue, almanac, and pastoral romance ask a reader to approach the text in fundamentally different ways. In this essay I have attempted to trace Spenser's designs on the reader in his first major published work. I consider first the role of the reader in each of the three genres Spenser brings together, then the solution he plots in *The Shepheardes Calender,* before turning finally to the thematic importance of the reader's choice of strategies in the design of the whole.

I

Pastoral romance and medieval calendar cast the reader in simple if contradictory roles. With its fully rounded, emotionally compelling hero and its wistful escape from the city to the country, pastoral romance woos a disarmed and sympathetic reader. When the hero appears as his own narrator and speaks in first person, as he does in Sannazaro's *Arcadia,* the effect is to give the reader not only an account of events but a consciousness with which to look at them. The consciousness that emerges from Sincero is as ingenuous as it is passionate. Sincero's name tells his story. At the precocious age of eight (Dante was nine when he first saw Beatrice) Sincero first feels the pangs of love and settles his desires on a little girl of noble birth. When in the course of years she fails to return his passion, he takes refuge in the solitude and wildness of Arcadia. "A pilgrim of Love" he describes himself in the epilogue.[2] Through the waxing and waning of seven days and nights his companions are not the savants and courtiers he has known in Naples but humble shepherds whose rude existence does not prevent them from singing and declaiming the elegant verses that regularly interrupt Sannazaro's narrative. It is only about halfway through that the shepherds turn to the narrating persona and ask him to give an account of himself. The story of his unhappy love explains why he finds Arcadia such a sympathetic place: As with Colin in the January fields, the landscape of Arcadia everywhere reflects Sincero's state of mind:

> I cannot catch sight of mountain or wood that I am not wholly convinced that I ought to find her there, though it seem impossible when I think of it. Not a beast, not a bird, not a branch do I sense in motion that I do not wheel about fearfully to see whether it be she, come into these regions to learn what wretched life I lead because of her. Likewise no other thing can I see here that is not primarily the cause of my remembering her with greater fervor and solicitude; and

it seems to me that the hollow caves, the springs, the valleys, the mountains, with all the forests summon her, and the tall trees constantly repeat her name. When sometimes I find myself among those trees, and look upon the leafy elms encircled with the tendrils of the vine, it runs bitterly through my mind with insupportable anguish how far my state is different from that of the insensate trees which, beloved of their dear vines, dwell with them continually in delightful embraces; and I, kept far apart from my desire by so much broad expanse of heaven, by such longinquity of earth, by so many incursions of the sea, consume myself in continual sorrow and tears.

(Pp. 72–73)

No less than his images, Sincero's expansive periods reflect his surges of intense feeling. The sestina with which he finally favors his interlocutors articulates precisely the relationship between poet and landscape glanced at in his story. Repetitions of the six end-words *terra* ("earth"), *piagge* ("shores"), *sole* ("sun"), *sera* ("evening"), *foschi* ("gloomy"), and *sonno* ("sleep") define a vivid metaphor for Sincero's emotional state. The response of one of the shepherds to this bravura performance defines what an indulgent (and self-indulgent) reader of the *Arcadia* must feel: "Heavy are your sorrows, my Sincero, and truly not to be heard without the utmost sympathy" (p. 74).

A reader of *The Kalender of Shepherdes,* on the other hand, would learn to take a decidedly different view of love—and of the text itself. The thousands of English readers who bought up copies of *The Kalender of Shepherdes* in its almost annual editions from 1506 to 1611 got their money's worth: In addition to the usual month-by-month information of an almanac they got a disquisition on "the tre of vyces with the peynes of hell"; a contrasting lesson in "the waye of helthe of man, the tre of vertues"; advice on "fesseke and governoure of helthe"; and a learned dissertation on "astrology fysnomy," the relationship of the human body to the cosmos.[3] Throughout the book, but especially in the "pains of hell" section, vigorously direct woodcuts help *The Kalender of Shepherdes* make minimal demands on a purchaser's literacy.

The almanac is styled a *shepherds'* almanac for two reasons: In their exposed, "unaccommodated" position shepherds, more than other men, know intimately not only the natural forces that play upon men but the moral forces as well. In his clear vision and plain speaking the "maister Shepeherde" who addresses the reader at the beginning of the *Kalender* declares his direct lineage from Piers Plowman. His special double perspective on natural and moral forces gives to the *Kalender* two distinct senses of

BRUCE R. SMITH

time. The first is cyclical. As a natural creature man participates in the endless repetition of seasons, and elaborate tables in the *Kalender* make it possible to reckon the moveable feasts "in perpetuity." But as a moral creature man lives out his life in a strictly delimited linear progression from birth to death. "We shepardis saythe that the age of a man is .lxxii. yere," the Master Shepherd explains,

> & that we lekene but to one holle yere. for evermore we take vi. yere for every moneth. as Jenyuere. or Feveryere. & so forthe for as the yere chaungeth by the twelve monethes. Into twelve sondry maners so dothe a man chaunge him selfe twelve. tyme in his lyfe by twelve ages and every age lasteth syxe. yere. if so be that he lyve to thre score & twelve for thre tymes vi. makethe eyghttene. & six. tymes six. makethe six and therty and than is man at the best and also at the hyghest. and twelve tymes syxe. makethe thre. score. and twelve. and that is the age of a man. (P. 10)

Not only in months but in seasons a man's life can be read as "one holle yere." A man's seventy-two years may be divided into four quarters of eighteen years each, and if we begin our reckoning with spring we discover not only a striking parallel but a sobering distinction. Beginning with eighteen years of "youthe" in spring, a man matures into eighteen years of "strength" in summer. Like the sun in the summer solstice, he reaches then his apex. Through eighteen years of "wysdome" in autumn a man then declines toward eighteen years of "age" in winter and the certain end of death (pp. 11–12). The cycle of months and seasons may begin again, but the "one holle yere" of a man's life completes its linear rise and fall. It is this double sense of time in *The Kalender of Shepherdes*—man's linear life traced out against the cycle of nature—that explains why "the peynes of hell" and "the tre of vertues" figure so prominently in the book's design.

The universe that the Master Shepherd describes is not finally, however, the relentlessly deterministic place his extended metaphor of the seasons at first implies. The stars may influence what happens to man, but still he has his free will. "Of lyvynge or dyenge," the Master Shepherd says,

> the hevenly bodyes may stere a man bothe to gode and evyll. without doute of assuerte. But yet may man withstande it by his own fre will to do what he wyll himselfe gode or badde evermore.
>
> Above the whiche inclynacyon is the might & will of god that lengeth the lyfe of man by his goodnes or to make hit short by his Justise. (P. 12)

The universe of *The Kalender of Shepherdes* is ruled over by a God who rewards good and punishes evil, but within those inescapable limits man's will to choose is more powerful than any of the outside forces that fill the *Kalender*'s treatise on astrological physiognomy. Endowed with free will but set down in a world where choices have eternal consequences, the "hero" of *The Kalender of Shepherdes* is the Mankind of medieval morality plays.

The stance the audience must take before this drama of Mankind played out against the backdrop of nature's cycle is unmistakably clear in the notice prefaced to the first *Kalender* printed in England: The printer, Richard Pynson, "and suche as longethe to hym hath made it into playne englysshe to the entente that every man may understonde it that thys boke is very profytable bothe for clerkes and laye people to cause them to have greate understondyng and in espessyall in that we be bounde to lerne and knowe on peyne of averlastinge deth" (p. 7). The connection of *Kalender* and *pastores* takes on yet another significance. The reader is to attend to the Master Shepherd's "prologue" and to the lessons of the book as a congregation listens to a preacher, as a "flock" follows its "pastor." The purchaser who takes in hand *The Kalender of Shepherdes* is to read its simple lessons, so starkly bare of any blandishments of fiction, with sober detachment from passion. Here indeed is the simplicity of the reader's role in Sannazaro's *Arcadia,* but completely turned about. There a reader succumbs to the voluptuous delights of metaphor, passion, and fantasy; here the reader must be braced for solemn lessons in straight talking, self-control, and the fact of death.

Compared with the reader's role in pastoral romance or almanac, the task set by classical eclogues is complicated indeed. No narrator, no insistently immediate "I" or priestly Master Shepherd, steps forward amid the dramatic monologues and dialogues of Vergil's *Bucolica* to give the reader a fixed perspective on the personages that come and go in such numbers and so confusingly often; no easily recognizable boundaries ground the poems in fictional space and narrative time. Nor were literary precedents much help to the poems' first readers. That Vergil should model his verses on such an out-of-the-way poet as Theocritus, whose *eidyllia* were already two centuries old and were written in an obscure literary language something like rustic Doric Greek, seems to justify William Berg's suggestion that Vergil prided himself on making his first major collection of poems as difficult as possible. *Neoteri,* "the new crowd," Cicero scornfully branded Vergil and his literary generation.[4]

Vergil's text, perplexing enough in its own right, was not all that Renaissance readers encountered when they took in hand one of the great folio editions of the poet's collected works. Four centuries after Vergil's death the grammarian Servius wrote the learned commentary on Vergil's major works that became an integral part of the received text in the Middle Ages and Renaissance. What the text of the eclogues strategically leaves out, Servius' commentary in effect provides: an omniscient, omnipresent narrator to give the reader a fixed point of view. Servius' interests in the text become perforce the reader's interests in the text. With Servius to guide them, medieval and Renaissance readers of the *Bucolica* found themselves pursuing etymologies and the literal meanings of proper names, noting the sources that Vergil had used, and speculating about the historical personages and historical events alluded to in the text. The adjustment of perspective that seemed necessary in the fourth century A.D. was even more radical nine hundred years later. To the simple frame of Servius' commentary Renaissance editors of Vergil added so many modern frames of commentary that often a folio page would contain less than a dozen lines of the original text. The edition of Vergil's principal works printed by Lucantonio Giunta (Venice, 1533 et seq.), for instance, includes not only Servius' *commentarius* but two running *explanatii,* one by Antonio Mancinelli (1452–1504) and another by Josse Badius (1462–1535), in addition to *castigiones* of the text by Giovanni Piero Valeriano Bolzani (1477–1558).

Of all the parts of Vergil's text that cry out for explanation, the second eclogue is surely the most insistent. No sooner has Tityrus, newly settled down in the pastoral fields, offered overnight shelter to the dispossessed shepherd Meliboeus at the end of the first eclogue than we find ourselves confronted in the second eclogue with a single spokesman, Corydon, who for sixty fervid lines vents the frustrations of what is quite clearly sexual passion. The object of his affections is no maiden but another shepherd, Alexis. An objective narrator first sets the stage:

> A herdsman Corydon burned for fair Alexis once,
> Alexis, master's love; nor any hope had he.
> Yet to the beech grove's shadowy height he came
> whenever able. There, alone, these artless words
> he used to fling in empty earnest at the woods and hills:
>
> ["]Cruel Alexis, are my songs of no account to you?
> Have you no pity? You will force me, in the end, to die.["]
>
> (1–7)

With its unmistakable echoes of the Cyclops' lament for Galatea in Theocritus' idyll 11, this eclogue seems almost a parody of the love-languor that characterizes Theocritus' personae. In the context Vergil gives it, Corydon's lament poses an implicit criticism of Tityrus' vision of pastoral peace in eclogue 1.[5] Such thematic subtleties, however, are four hundred years beyond Servius' vision. His interest in the eclogue is primarily historical, and he offers five possible interpretations. All of them assume that Corydon speaks for Vergil himself. Alexis, then, may be Alexandrus, one of Asinius Pollio's serving-boys who struck Vergil's fancy one day at lunch and came home with him as a gift from his master. Vergil is known to have had a love for boys, Servius notes, though not in a morally foul sense (*nec . . . turpiter*). Or Alexis may be Caesar, "beautiful in his deeds and his glory." Or he may be the son of Caesar, whom Vergil praises to gratify the father. Then again, he may be Corydona, the son of Asinius Pollio. Or, finally, he may be a boy that Pollio himself took a liking to. At the time Pollio was garrisoning a part of Italy beyond the Po and was presiding over the division of lands alluded to in the first eclogue.[6]

Renaissance interest in Vergil's text was less single-minded. In an often reprinted preface to Vergil's works, Cristoforo Landino (1424–1504), luminary in Lorenzo de' Medici's circle of Neoplatonist intellectuals and author of an allegorical commentary on the *Divine Comedy,* first praises Vergil's depiction of rustic manners. Not even the actor Roscius could better him in that. But beneath these realistic trappings Vergil covers up (*contegit*) greater matters: "even though he never lays aside the shepherd's mask, he nevertheless hides away [*abscondit*] another sense, far loftier than that ordinary one, so that his work is graced with a twofold argument [*duplici argumento*]: he can serve the one that is manifest while he carries through the one that lies hidden." It is a sign of Vergil's divine powers that he concerns himself with "humble characters out of the First Age."[7] These propositions Landino reiterates in connection with eclogue 2 in particular and goes on to offer two readings, one historical and one philosophical. Corydon is Vergil and Alexis is Caesar. Landino's main interest, however, is in what the eclogue has to say about beauty. *Formosum,* the first word in the poem, leads Landino to the distinction between *forma* and *materia* and to a lecture on the true source of beauty in form, not substance.[8] Such niceties may at first seem presbyopic as only a Neoplatonist critic can be, but in effect Landino's view restores to Vergil's text something of the metaphorical force it had lost with Servius. Humanist educators were even more overtly moral in their reading of the text. Erasmus singles out the second eclogue for special attention in his *De ratione studii* (1511 et seq.) and recommends that schoolmasters teach the eclogue as an illustration of failed friendship. Corydon the countryman and Alexis the courtier lack the likenesses that have bound together history's great

friends. Melanchthon takes another pedantic tack. Next to Corydon's last
words—"What rules apply to love?"—Melanchthon places a marginal tag
that turns the narrator's closing of the scene into an *argumentum ab utili*:

> Ah, Corydon, Corydon, what senselessness possessed you?
> A vine, half-pruned, awaits you on the leafy elm—
> rather, why not find at least a thing to mend
> with wicker (crying to be used) and pliant rush?
> You'll find, if this one spurns you, a new Alexis.⁹

When Renaissance readers set out to read Vergil's *Bucolica,* they encountered, then, not only a difficult and allusive text but several ready-
made ways of looking at it. The several lines of approach mapped out in a
folio edition of the text were not necessarily exclusive of each other, but
neither were they necessarily compatible, particularly in the matter of allusions to actual persons. Unlike their prototype Servius, Renaissance commentators on Vergil's eclogues were synthetic in their interpretations.
Mancinelli and Badius rehearse Servius' identifications of Alexis with
Alexandrus or Caesar (Mancinelli makes Alexandrus a grammarian), and
Giovanni Ludovico Vives suggests an identification with Cornelius Gallus, the amorous soldier of eclogue 10, but Landino, Erasmus, and Melanchthon testify to less literal interests in Vergil's text.¹⁰ In sum, the
ancient and modern commentators whose glosses were printed alongside
Vergil's text would invite Renaissance readers to consider that text in five
different ways. In the speeches of Vergil's shepherds they would find (1) a
depiction of rustic manners to be marveled at, (2) allusions to real persons
and real events to be deciphered, (3) parallels with earlier authors to be
noted and admired, (4) philosophical argument to be thought about, and
(5) a moral message to be acted upon. All five perspectives, we should
note, are addressed in E. K.'s scholion on *The Shepheardes Calender.*
    There is something very uncomfortable to post-Romantic readers about
a book of poems that comes equipped with a prosaic commentary. Poetry,
we feel, is too ineffable for that. Even the most difficult poems we are ac-
customed to approach directly, perhaps via a short introduction or fore-
word. Footnotes of more than minimal length seem intrusions that
threaten imaginative illusion. Nor are footnotes the same thing as a commentary. Footnotes are like handrails beside stairs, there to be used if
needed. Commentaries of the sort Servius, Badius, and Landino provide
figure as essential parts of the architecture: They demand to be taken in at
the same time as the text itself. The kind of reading implied by text-with-
commentary is utterly alien to the Romantic notion of the reader as a self-

effacing collaborator with the author, cooperating with his imagination to make the fiction complete. Here is no willing suspension of disbelief to fill out an illusion but active engagement of irony to distance the illusion. The result is to make reading a poetic text inescapably a self-conscious, indeed self-critical, act. Reading Vergil as Renaissance readers read him entailed an extraordinary ability to hold in balance multiple perspectives on a single passage at the same time.

II

The three genres Spenser brings together in *The Shepheardes Calender* each demands, then, something radically different from the reader. Pastoral romance disarms criticism and lulls the reader into uncomplicated delight in language and feeling. *The Kalender of Shepherdes* talks straight truth and demands a listener with self-reflective detachment. Vergil's *Bucolica,* at least as Renaissance readers encountered it, forces the reader to find his own way among multiple interpretations: Never losing sight of the beauties of language and image, the reader must constantly watch for historical allusions, parallels with earlier authors, philosophical argument, moral lessons. The reader of classical eclogues, unlike the reader of pastoral romance or sermonizing almanac, can take nothing for granted but must perforce become an active participant to find order and coherence in the verses.

How, then, does Spenser reconcile such radical differences when he combines romance, almanac, and eclogue in *The Shepheardes Calender*? The history of criticism of his book would indicate that he perhaps has not. In the four centuries since the *Calender* was published readers have tended to assume one of three perspectives: They have settled into the comfortable role of reader of romance and lost themselves in Colin's splendidly articulate passion, or they have stood back with the Master Shepherd and clucked their tongues in moral superiority, or they have followed the scholiasts so far into the book's thematic and structural complexities that Colin's passion seems remote and incidental. There is good reason for such divergent responses. Spenser's uneasy combination of pastoral romance and moral almanac involves an essential ambiguity that not even E. K. can explain away. "Now as touching the generall dryft and purpose of his Aeglogues," E. K. declares in his epistle to Harvey,

> I mind not to say much, him selfe labouring to conceale it. Onely this appeareth, that his unstayed yougth had long wandred in the common Labyrinth of Love, in which time to mitigate and allay the

heate of his passion, or else to warne (as he sayth) the young shepheards .s. his equalls and companions of his unfortunate folly, he
compiled these xii. Aeglogues, which for that they be proportioned
to the state of the xii. monethes, he termeth the SHEPHEARDS
CALENDAR, applying an olde name to a new worke.[11]

In E. K.'s remark we can hear the voice of the Master Shepherd: "this
boke was made for them that be no clarkes to brynge them to greate un-
derstondynge." Sixteenth-century readers apparently took Spenser—or at
least E. K.—at his word: Very many of the earliest recorded remarks on
The Shepheardes Calender commend the book's high morality and implicitly reject Colin as a hero.[12] But didactic fervor is only one of two alternatives that sort rather oddly. Spenser may have written the *Calender* to warn
others of his unfortunate folly, but before that possibility E. K. mentions
another: "to mitigate and allay the heate of his passion." On the surface of
it, there might not seem to be a contradiction here. After all, we might listen to Colin's plaintive outpourings with the disapproving detachment
that Spenser's didactic purpose would seem to demand. But evidence of
how many sixteenth-century readers read the book, no less than our own
first instincts, runs contrary. If they were not praising the *Calender*'s morality in warning young lovers against the perils of passion, the earliest
readers of the volume were paying passionate Colin Clout the compliment
of imitation, heedless of the very ironies that other readers were prizing.
Virtue or virtuosity—the *Calender*'s first readers seem to have been divided
in which to admire.

Readers since the advent of New Criticism have been much more alert,
of course, to all the thematic issues touched by Colin's career, but they
have still tended to either a "romantic" reading of Colin or a "moral"
reading. On the one hand such critics as A. C. Hamilton, enchanted like
certain sixteenth-century readers with the brilliant verses Colin speaks in
his own person and with his remarkably polished poems that other shepherds rehearse in April, August, and November, have praised Colin as the
compleat poet.[13] Isabel MacCaffrey and Patrick Cullen, on the other hand,
attentive like the scholiasts of Vergil to complexities of theme and structure
in the *Calender*'s design, have assumed the Master Shepherd's view and
pronounced Colin an antihero, a failed poet who never uses his powers to
rise above nature's destructive cycle of time.[14] To understand how Spenser
guides the reader among such divergent alternatives we must forget the
scholarly introductions that give us an unfair advantage by telling us in advance what to look for and what to feel and instead imagine what it would
be like to take *The Shepheardes Calender* in hand as its first readers did.

What kind of book is this? a purchaser might well have asked, picking up *The Shepheardes Calender* from among the ballads, Puritan theological tracts, and polemical pamphlets in Hugh Singleton's shop at the sign of the golden tun. The appearance of the fifty-page quarto would have offered no ready answer. Hugh Singleton was not a "literary" printer at all, and in the same year he printed *The Shepheardes Calender* he barely escaped having his right hand chopped off as a reprimand from Her Majesty's Government for publishing John Stubbs' *The Discoverie of a Gaping Gulf Whereinto England Is Like to be Swallowed by An Other French Mariage.* A purchaser might, then, have expected something topical and controversial. *The Shepheardes Calender* would not have been disappointing, especially in the "moral" eclogues for May, July, and September, when E. K. positively requires the reader to see political and ecclesiastical figures behind Spenser's rather obvious pseudonyms.[15] The physical design of *The Shepheardes Calender* would have suggested something more pretentious, however, than a propaganda pamphlet. The visual clues must in fact have been rather contradictory: Pastoral dialogues with a running commentary would have suggested the highbrow reading of expensive scholarly editions of Vergil's eclogues; the calendar format, with woodcuts for each of the months, would have suggested the lowbrow reading of cheap almanacs aimed at a popular market.

We may be sure that the physical design of *The Shepheardes Calender* was carefully planned. Though the work passed through the hands of at least four different printers in the course of its five editions in the sixteenth century, though it was completely reset each time, the format of the book changed not at all until it was reprinted in the folio edition of Spenser's complete works in 1611, twelve years after Spenser's death. Each of the five quarto editions preserves the same arrangement of the same woodcuts, with black-letter type for the eclogues themselves and small roman type for E. K.'s commentary. Scorned though it is by many modern editors, who pick out only those notes that seem pertinent, E. K.'s commentary must have been seen as an integral part of the book, since it was faithfully reprinted—misinformation, miscitations, and all—in every edition down to the eighth reprinting in 1653.[16]

By 1579 woodcut illustrations were common to all three of the genres brought together in *The Shepheardes Calender*. Several editions of Sannazaro's *Arcadia* display woodcut frontispieces, but none of them is tied closely to the text. The same poses appear interchangeably in other books with pastoral settings. The view of one shepherd declaiming to five auditors (Venice: Georgio Rusconi, 1515) may, for example, depict the key episode in which Sincero tells his sorrowful story to the inhabitants of Arcadia, but the illustration seems more decorative than narrative—a visual complement to the languorous atmosphere evoked in Sannazaro's prose.[17]

In editions of Vergil two distinct traditions of illustration had emerged in the course of the sixteenth century. Only two illustrated manuscripts of Vergil are known to have survived from antiquity, and Vergil's scholarly rather than popular appeal during the Middle Ages inspired very few illustrated manuscripts then. The Italian tradition of illustrating Vergil in the sixteenth century adapts the conventions and the mood of the late classical manuscripts; the German tradition continues the conventions and the mood of the medieval manuscripts. The Vergilius Romanus manuscript (Codex Vaticanus Latinus 3867), for example, offers illustrations for the eclogues that simply place the speakers, two or three as the case may be, in a landscape. Narratively these miniatures tell us little about the verses they belong with: The illustration for the first eclogue (see fig. 1) shows us Tityrus piping under a tree while Meliboeus speaks his complaint with

FIGURE 1. Illustration for Vergil's first eclogue, from Codex Vaticanus Latinus 3867 (prov. Italy or Gaul, second half of the fifth century). Reproduced by permission from Erwin Rosenthal, *The Illuminations of the Vergilius Romanus* (Zurich: Urs Graf, 1972).

arm outstretched.[18] The two speakers could be talking about anything. Many Renaissance Italian editions of Vergil's works include only one illustration for all the *Bucolica,* and directly or indirectly that one illustration recalls the Vergilius Romanus manuscript not only in the poses of the figures but in the essentially decorative rather than narrative connection between illustration and text. The single woodcut for the eclogues in Bernardino Stagnino's edition of Vergil's works (Venice, 1507), shown in figure 2, was copied in other Venetian editions of Vergil (Bartholomeo Zanni, 1508 et seq., and Alexandro Paganini, 1510 et seq.), as well as in at least one edition of Sannazaro's *Arcadia* (Milan: Augustino da Vimercha, 1518), before it inspired much finer adaptations in editions of Vergil's works printed by Hieronymo Scoto (Venice, 1555 et seq.) and Giovanni Maria Bonelli (Venice, 1558 et seq.), the latter shown in figure 3. Reproduction of this design not only with eclogues other than the first in Bonelli's editions but with Sannazaro's *Arcadia* in da Vimercha's edition shows how readers of the text looked to the illustrations mainly for atmosphere.[19]

The Renaissance German tradition of illustrating Vergil, on the other

FIGURE 2. Illustration for Vergil's first eclogue, from *Bucolica, Georgica, Aeneis* (Venice: Stagnino, 1507).

FIGURE 3. Illustration for Vergil's first eclogue, from *Universum Poema* (Venice: Bonelli, 1558).

hand, replaces the simple Italian landscapes with large, vigorous woodcuts that dress the protagonists unselfconsciously in modern costume, just as medieval illuminations had done, and crowd them into a tapestrylike space that can accommodate sequential events simultaneously, even when the same character has to appear more than once in the same picture. Banners inscribed with the characters' names make it inescapably clear that the pictures are linked to a narrative text (see fig. 4).[20]

Woodcuts in *The Kalender of Shepherdes,* finally, are less decorative or narrative than emblematic: They take the moral theme of the book, particularly its vision of Everyman seen against the cycle of time, and give that theme a graphic immediacy that even an unlettered purchaser would not forget (see fig. 5).

As befits a work that brings together elements of prose romance, classical eclogue, and moral almanac, Spenser and his illustrator have deftly fused visual traditions from all three genres in designing woodcuts for *The Shepheardes Calender.* Like the illustrations in editions of Sannazaro's *Arcadia* and in Italian editions of Vergil, the woodcuts of *The Shepheardes Calender* provide atmosphere. They give us a visual sense of the speakers and place them in landscapes that reflect the moods of the changing seasons. In the

FIGURE 4. Illustration for Vergil's first eclogue, from *Opera,* ed. Sebastian
Brant (Strasburg: Grüninger, 1502).

woodcut before "Maye," shown in figure 6, we see in the upper left the
two speakers of the poem, Piers and Palinode, posed in a springtime landscape. But we also see what Piers and Palinode talk *about*. Moving clockwise
—that direction may be intentional—we see first Piers and Palinode as
they appear in the dramatic frame of the poem (1–16), then in the center
the "shole of shepeheardes" whom Palinode has seen that morning going
a-maying with their queen, Lady Flora (19–36), then on the right the

FIGURE 5. Illustration from *The Kalender of Shepherdes*
(London: Richard Pynson, 1506).

mother goat warning her son in Piers's tale (174–226), and finally, sweeping back to the left, the same foolish kid caught in the fox's wicket (282–93). Continuing this clockwise motion, the viewer has only to glance up and to the right to return his eyes to Piers and Palinode still disputing, which is where indeed the poem ends (306–17). Spenser and his illustrator have cleverly adapted to *The Shepheardes Calender* the narrative technique of German illustrations of Vergil, in which sequential events can be presented simultaneously within the same picture space. One element remains in the "Maye" woodcut which appears neither in illustrations of pastoral romance nor in illustrations of Vergil. Rather ominously hanging over the whole scene is the appropriate sign of the zodiac as it would figure in illustrations to *The Kalender of Shepherdes*. As these signs change from month to month we are never allowed to forget the great cycles of time against which the protagonists, and Colin in particular, play out the linear narrative of their lives.

The visual clues that *The Shepheardes Calender* offers a reader are, then,

FIGURE 6. Illustration for "Maye," from *The Shepheardes Calender* (London: Hugh Singleton, 1579).

challenging and conflicting clues: In physical design the volume declares affinities with almanacs, eclogues, and pastoral romances, and each of these would ask the reader to begin the volume with different assumptions, different skills, different expectations. Amid such bewildering visual clues E. K. in his prefatory matter would have been attended to as a voice of authority. To begin with, the patronage invoked for such a physically small volume is formidable. The title page dedicates *The Shepheardes Calender* "To the Noble and Vertuous Gentleman most worthy of all titles both of learning and chevalrie M. Philip Sidney," and E. K.'s introductory epistle openly solicits patronage for "the new Poete" from the F. R. Leavis of sixteenth-century English academia, Gabriel Harvey. Here is a book that takes itself seriously. For the experience of reading such a self-consciously significant text, E. K.'s prefatory matter sets up six expectations, in this order: (1) in breadth of vision and in craft of language the anonymous poet aspires to the role of "the new Chaucer"; (2) the language of the work is controversial; (3) the author has used homely trappings "to unfold great matter of argument covertly . . . following the example of the best and most auncient Poetes"; (4) as an aid for understanding "old wordes and harder phrases," for remarking "many excellent and proper devises both in wordes and matter," and for demonstrating how "in this kind" the work in hand is "equal to the learned of other nations" E. K. has provided "a certain Glosse or scholion"; (5) the eclogues —or, more properly, "Aeglogues," "conversations of shepherds"—may be divided into "three formes or ranckes," "Plaintive," "recreative," and "Moral"; and (6) time is a crucial thematic concern, since as E. K. explains at some length, the author has consulted all the best authorities in deciding whether to begin the *Calender* with spring in March or with "the incarnation of our mighty Saviour and eternall redeemer the L. Christ" in January during the twelve days of Christmas. In effect, a reader is directed to give very close scrutiny to language, theme, and structure.

Turning to the poems themselves, a first-time reader is at once confronted with a problem of perspective. Not one voice speaks in "Januarye" but three, and they speak at cross purposes. The first voice, presumably that of E. K. in his role as commentator, sets out the "Argument" of the January eclogue: "Colin cloute *a shepheardes boy complaineth him of his unfortunate love, being but newly (as semeth) enamoured of a countrie lasse called* Rosalinde." Readers will not have to use much ingenuity in inferring the narrative situation. They will, however, have to listen closely to catch the tone of the next speaker. Following the example of Vergil in his second eclogue, an anonymous narrator sets the stage for Colin's monologue:

> A Shepeheards boye (no better doe him call)
> When Winters wastful spight was almost spent,
> All in a sunneshine day, as did befall,
> Led forth his flock, that had bene long ypent.
> So faynt they woxe, and feeble in the folde,
> That now unnethes their feete could them uphold.
>
> All as the Sheepe, such was the shepeheards looke,
> For pale and wanne he was, (alas the while,)
> May seeme he lovd, or els some care he tooke:
> Well couth he tune his pipe, and frame his stile.
> Tho to a hill his faynting flocke he ledde,
> And thus him playnd, the while his shepe there fedde.
>
> ("Januarye" 1–12)

What sort of attitude has this narrator to poor love-struck Colin? Certainly not the studied objectivity we have already observed in Vergil's beginning. The two asides the narrator allows himself—"A Shepeheards boye (no better doe him call)," "pale and wanne he was, (alas the while,)"—as well as his comparison of the shepherd's countenance to the downcast look of his sheep all betray a gentle irony that sounds something like Spenser's model poet Chaucer. The narrator's sly comic touch is apparent, too, in the way he has passion-choked Colin break off his monologue at the end of the eclogue, with one line still to go to complete the rhyme. This the narrator, less carried away himself, obligingly supplies. His songs may please country shepherds, Colin laments, but they fail to move Rosalind in "the neighbour towne":

> ["]Wherefore my pype, albee rude *Pan* thou please,
> Yet for thou pleasest not, where most I would:
> And thou unlucky Muse, that wontst to ease
> My musing mynd, yet canst not, when thou should:
> Both pype and Muse, shall sore the while abye.["]
> So broke his oaten pype, and downe dyd lye.
>
> ("Januarye" 67–72)

Irony like the narrator's is one thing Colin lacks completely.

E. K., on the other hand, has only too much irony. After Colin has thrown himself to the ground in despair, after the narrator has quietly summoned the gathering night, up steps E. K. in his academic gown:

> COLIN Cloute) is a name not greatly used, and yet have I sene a Poesie of M. Skeltons under that title. But indeede the word Colin is Frenche, and used of the French Poete Marot (if he be worthy of the name of a Poete) in a certein Aeglogue. Under which name this Poete secretly shadoweth himself, as sometime did Virgil under the name of Tityrus, thinking it much fitter, then such Latine names, for the great unlikelyhoode of the language. (Gloss to "Januarye")

How are we to take such a learned dissertation on a name that suggests rags, hobnailed boots, and dishes of clotted cream? Twentieth-century critics have been unanimous in taking E. K. at face value. Particularly if we identify him with Gabriel Harvey and recall the career of that doyen of dons, we find it hard to take E. K.'s gloss as anything but a scholarly puff to make Spenser's poem seem erudite and serious. Spenser himself, however, may have taken a different view. In the postscript to one of his published letters to Harvey, Spenser announces plans to publish his *Dreames* (now lost) by themselves, since they are "growen by meanes of the Glosse, (running continually in maner of a Paraphrase) full as great as my *Calendar*. Therin be some things excellently, and many things wittily discoursed of *E. K.*"[21] "Wittily"? By *wit* Spenser may, of course, mean "ingenuity," not "humor," but when we are confronted with *such* ingenuity the distinction between the two may not be so sharp. The whole passage seems rather arch—Spenser goes on to say that the pictures are "so singularly set forth, and purtrayed, as if *Michael Angelo* were there, he could (I think) nor amende the best, nor reprehende the worst"—and Spenser could be implying that in its context E. K.'s gloss is not to be read with a straight face.

Having sampled what Servius, Mancinelli, Badius, Landino, Vives, and Melanchthon have to say about the suspect passion of Vergil's Corydon for Alexis, we are in a position to appreciate the element of overkill in E. K.'s gloss on Hobbinol. Colin introduces Hobbinol into his complaint as the voice of conscience, a good angel who constantly tries to pull Colin out of the amorous mire and set him on the road to poetic glory. The suggestion of Hobbinol as a rival love is quite clearly metaphorical:

> It is not *Hobbinol,* wherefore I plaine,
> Albee my love he seeke with dayly suit:
> His clownish gifts and curtsies I disdaine,
> His kiddes, his cracknelles, and his early fruit.
> Ah foolish *Hobbinol,* thy gyfts bene vayne:
> *Colin* them gives to *Rosalind* againe. ("Januarye" 55–60)

E. K.'s note on this passage sounds like Hollofernes at his best:

> Hobbinol) is a fained country name, whereby, it being so commune and usuall, seemeth to be hidden the person of some of his very speciall and most familiar freend, whom he entirely and extraordinarily beloved, as peradventure shall be more largely declared hereafter. In thys place seemeth to be some savour of disorderly love, which the learned call paederastice: but it is gathered beside his meaning. For who that hath red Plato his dialogue called Alcybiades, Xenophon and Maximus Tyrius of Socrates opinions, may easily perceive, that such love is muche to be alowed and liked of, specially so meant, as Socrates used it: who sayth, that in deede he loved Alcybiades extremely, yet not Alcybiades person, but hys soule, which is Alcybiades owne selfe. And so is paederastice much to be preferred before gynerastice, that is the love whiche enflameth men with lust toward woman kind. But yet let no man thinke, that herein I stand with Lucian or hys develish disciple Unico Aretino, in defence of execrable and horrible sinnes of forbidden and unlawful fleshlinesse. Whose abominable errour is fully confuted of Perionius, and others.
>
> (Gloss to "Januarye")

So much in excess of the occasion is such hollow-frenetic rhetoric that we can hardly take E. K. as our solitary guide through the landscape of

The Shepheardes Calender. Coupled with what Spenser has to say about E. K.'s wit, prolix prolusions like this one make us suspect that E. K.'s commentary may be a kind of academic in-joke. E. K. represents one way of confronting a literary text: detached, analytical, aware of precedents, full of schemes, but curiously aloof from the emotional force of the poetry. His commentary figures as a parody of a certain kind of overly zealous reader, a sixteenth-century example of *The Pooh Perplex* or *The Overwrought Urn*. What E. K. lacks Colin has in only too much abundance: passion. To read *The Shepheardes Calender* "romantically," to revel only in language and feeling, is clearly to pass from one extreme to the other. The way between these extremes lies with the curiously reticent narrator. His condescension toward Colin bespeaks an awareness of a larger world, of larger thematic issues, beyond Colin's ken; the Chaucerian gentleness of his irony bespeaks a sympathetic understanding of Colin's passion.

III

In "Januarye" a reader of *The Shepheardes Calender* is presented, then, with three ways of reading the text: with Colin's passionate abandon, with E. K.'s analytical detachment, with the narrator's balanced irony. Careful readers should have no trouble getting their bearings. Colin's passion is ever so gently but ever so certainly mocked in the narrator's introduction and conclusion; E. K.'s commentary, with its pedantic digressions and dogmatic misinformation, needs no ironist, at least for readers who know Servius, Badius, Landino, and Melanchthon. But "Januarye" may cause some confusion. The narrator disappears after the first eclogue and does not return alone until "December." In the meantime, readers must make their own way among the *Calender*'s crowded cast of spokesmen, must make their own decisions about how much of E. K.'s lectures to take seriously, and must make up their own minds about Colin's position as later eclogues offer new points of thematic reference.

Spenser has good thematic reasons for forcing his reader to find a workable strategy unaided. *The Shepheardes Calender* belongs to a tradition of works in Western literature that could all take the name of the most recent major exercise in the tradition: *A Portrait of the Artist as a Young Man*. Vergil's *Bucolica*, Dante's *La vita nuova*, Spenser's *Calender*, Wordsworth's *Prelude*, Joyce's *Portrait*—each of these works is the manifesto of an acutely self-conscious young artist; each is a gathering in of the artist's accumulated experience, each is a preparation for the "epic" work that the artist has set for himself ahead. Behind the manifesto as a product there is a process through which the young artist has arrived at a sense of himself and his task, a process through which he has placed himself in relation to his craft, to received tradition, to his readers, to society at large, and to the self of which the artist is but one aspect. The selves on which Vergil, Dante, Spenser, Wordsworth, and Joyce turn the artist's objective eye seem curiously alike despite the centuries that separate them. Vergil's Tityrus, Daphnis, and Gallus, the passionate persona of Dante's lyrics, Spenser's Colin, Wordsworth's youthful "I," and Joyce's Dedalus are all sensitive, passionate figures who lack the larger perspective, the experience of life and the practice of craft, possessed by the artist who presents them to the reader. They are self-contained but not yet self-possessed. Suddenly or gradually, with pain or with ease, the mature artist has transcended this private self whose portrait he now can draw by standing back and looking on with irony of tenderness or ridicule or a combination of both.

The Shepheardes Calender, like other works in the "portrait" tradition, is both a testament to the young author's discovery of his identity as an artist and a record of how he made that discovery. There is a particularly telling similarity in how Joyce's *Portrait* and Spenser's *Calender* end. Just as Stephen Dedalus emerges from a third-person hero into a first-person diarist who is preparing to leave Ireland and begin his career as a writer, so the dying Colin of "December" is left behind by the self-confident "I" who steps back from *The Shepheardes Calender* in the envoy and looks at his finished work almost as if it were a piece of sculpture. He takes his leave in a perfect square of twelve lines of twelve syllables each:

> *Loe I have made a Calender for every yeare,*
> *That steele in strength, and time in durance shall outweare:*
> *And if I marked well the starres revolution,*
>   *It shall continewe till the worlds dissolution.*
> *To teach the ruder shepheard how to feede his sheepe,*
> *And from the falsers fraud his folded flocke to keepe.*
>   *Goe lyttle Calender, thou hast a free passeporte,*
> *Goe but a lowly gate emongste the meaner sorte.*
> *Dare not to match thy pype with Tityrus hys style,*
>   *Nor with the Pilgrim that the Ploughman playde a whyle:*
> *But followe them farre off, and their high steppes adore,*
> *The better please, the worse despise, I aske nomore.*

If a reader has charted his way through the *Calender* watchfully enough, this sudden shift in perspective should come as no surprise. For Spenser has so arranged the interplay of genres in *The Shepheardes Calender* that a reader himself must recapitulate the process through which Spenser has arrived at his final position of delicately poised irony. Reading the *Calender* as a pastoral romance with Colin as hero, a reader would miss the ecclesiastical and political controversies, the philosophical issues, the moral considerations that transform Colin the pastoral lyric lover into Spenser the epic narrative poet. Reading the *Calender* as an almanac in the tradition of *The Kalender of Shepherdes,* the reader would see only one difference between lover and artist: a recognition of human mortality. Reading the *Calender* as a collection of classical eclogues with a learned commentary, the reader would miss the poignancy of Colin's plight. What is needed, of course, is a reading strategy that combines all three: the imaginative sympathy of pastoral romance, the moral rigor of *The Kalender of Shepherdes,* the perspicacity of classical eclogues. The reader who has discovered that has discovered Spenser's own perspective as an artist and has mastered the special kind of reading demanded by *The Faerie Queene.*

Georgetown University

NOTES

1. On the geometrical symmetry of the *Calender*'s design see A. C. Hamilton, "The Argument of Spenser's *Shepheardes Calender,*" in *Spenser: A Collection of Critical Essays,* ed. Harry Berger, Jr. (Englewood Cliffs, N. J.: Prentice-Hall, 1968), pp. 30–39. On the *Calender*'s cyclical design see S. K. Heninger, Jr., "The Implications of Form in *The Shepheardes Calender,*" *SRen* 9 (1962), 309–21; and Maren-Sofie Røstvig, "*The Shepheardes Calender*—A Structural Analysis," *RMS* 13 (1969), 49–75.

2. Jacopo Sannazaro, *Arcadia,* trans. Ralph Nash (Detroit: Wayne State University Press, 1966), p. 153. Hereafter cited in the text.

3. *Le Compost et Kalendrier des bergiers,* 1st ed. (Paris, 1493), was first translated into Scots dialect and printed at Paris in 1503. Richard Pynson printed the first English translation at London, 1506. My quotations come from the transcript of Pynson's text printed in H. Oskar Sommer, ed., *The Kalender of Shepherdes* (London: Kegan Paul, Trench, Trübner, 1892). Citations in the text are to vol. 3. Figure 5 is reproduced from vol. 3, sig. A-2^r.

4. William Berg, *Early Virgil* (London: Athlone Press, 1974), pp. 15–22. Citations in the text are to this edition.

5. Ibid., pp. 113–14; Eleanor Winsor Leach, *Vergil's "Eclogues": Landscapes of Experience* (Ithaca: Cornell University Press, 1974), pp. 146–58.

6. Servius, *In Vergilii Bucolica et Georgica commentarii,* ed. G. Thilo (1887; rpt. Hildesheim: Olms, 1961), vol. 3, p. 18.

7. Rpt. in Vergil, *Opera* (Venice: Giunta, 1533), fol. 6. Landino's critical bent is fully exemplified in D. C. Allen, *Mysteriously Meant: The Rediscovery of Pagan Symbolism and Allegorical Interpretation in the Renaissance* (Baltimore: The Johns Hopkins Press, 1970), pp. 142–54.

8. Rpt. in Vergil, *Opera* (Nuremberg: Koberger, 1492), fols. 3v–4.

BRUCE R. SMITH

9. Philip Melanchthon, *Opera,* ed. C. G. Bretschneider, vol. 19 (Brunswick: Schwetschke, 1853), cols. 299–300. Melanchthon also accepts the identification of Alexis with Augustus Caesar. On Erasmus' interpretation see T. W. Baldwin, *William Shakspere's Small Latine & Lesse Greeke* (Urbana: University of Illinois Press, 1944), vol. 1, p. 91.

10. Mancinelli's and Ascensius' commentaries are printed in Vergil, *Opera* (Venice, 1533); Vives's commentary, in Vergil, *Universum poema* (Venice: Bonelli, 1558). The annotated edition of Vergil's works printed by Henry Bynneman (London, 1570) notes simply, "Pro Corydone Virgilium, pro Alexi Augustum intellige." Peter Ramus is virtually alone among Renaissance commentators in preferring to take the second eclogue simply as an expression of passion: "mihi magis placet communem locum, et communem affectum fictis nominibus a poeta cantari, ut sine tropo res simpliciter intelligatur, praesertim cum Theocriti imitatio constet" [to me it is more pleasing to assume that a commonplace and a common feeling are being sung by the poet using fictional names, so that the matter is understood simply, without a trope, especially since it is put together in imitation of Theocritus] (Vergil, *Bucolica,* ed. P. Ramus [Paris: Wechelus, 1558]).

11. *The Works of Edmund Spenser: A Variorum Edition*, ed. Edwin Greenlaw, et al., 11 vols. (Baltimore: The Johns Hopkins Press, 1932–57), vol. 7, p. 10. All quotations are from this edition.

12. William Wells, ed., "Spenser Allusions in the Sixteenth and Seventeenth Centuries, Part 1, 1580–1625," *SP* 68 (1971), 3–172.

13. Hamilton, "The Argument."

14. Isabel G. MacCaffrey, "Allegory and Pastoral in *The Shepheardes Calender*," in *Critical Essays on Spenser from ELH* (Baltimore: The Johns Hopkins Press, 1970), pp. 116–37; and Patrick Cullen, *Spenser, Marvell, and Renaissance Pastoral* (Cambridge, Mass.: Harvard University Press, 1970), pp. 120–48. A more balanced view of Colin emerges in Richard Helgerson's essay "The New Poet Presents Himself: Spenser and the Idea of a Literary Career," *PMLA* 93 (1978), 893–911. Helgerson places Colin amid the conflict between two contradictory Renaissance ideas of the poet: as a youthful scribbler of private amorous trifles and as the *vates* of classical antiquity, the "seer" who addresses himself to cosmic issues and inspires public action.

15. H. J. Byron, "Edmund Spenser's First Printer, Hugh Singleton," *The Library,* 4th ser. 14 (1933), 121–56. On topical allusions in the moral eclogues see Paul E. McLane, *Spenser's "Shepheardes Calender"* (Notre Dame: Notre Dame University Press, 1961), pp. 140–57, 158–74, 175–87, 188–202, 203–15.

16. For a thorough discussion of the publishing history of *The Shepheardes Calender* see Francis R. Johnson, *A Critical Bibliography of the Works of Edmund Spenser Printed Before 1700* (Baltimore: The Johns Hopkins Press, 1933), pp. 2–10. By 1579 there is evidence that printers and readers were beginning to see differences in subject-matter associations between black-letter type that imitated common "secretary hand" and roman type that imitated humanist handwriting and books from Italian presses. Henry Bynneman's edition of Vergil's works (1570), Lord North's English translation of Plutarch's *Lives* (1579), and Thomas Watson's Latin translation of Sophocles's *Antigone* all appeared as carefully designed, carefully printed imitations of the best Italian editions of the classics. But there are plenty of exceptions to this trend: Abraham Fleming's English translation of Vergil's eclogues (1575), Thomas Newton's anthology *Seneca His Tenne Tragedies* in English translations (1581), and Arthur Hall's English translation of books 1 to 9 of the *Iliad* (1581) are all printed at least partly in black letter. Perhaps the "low" style of pastoral prompted that choice in the case of Fleming's Vergil. Of the eleven publications assigned to Hugh Singleton by the *STC* between 1577 and 1581 I have been able to examine five. Stubbs' *Discoverie*

is neatly printed in roman type, three small theological tracts are printed in black letter, and *The Shepheardes Calender* combines both.

17. Illustrations for Sannazaro are catalogued in Max Sander, *Le livre à figures italien depuis 1467 jusqu'à 1530*, vol. 3 (Milan: Hoepli, 1942–43), 1164–66.

18. There is a thorough discussion of the origins and conventions of these illustrations in Erwin Rosenthal, *The Illuminations of the Vergilius Romanus* (Zurich: Urs Graf, 1972), from which volume I have reproduced figure 1. Medieval scholars generally assign the Vergilius Romanus to Italy or Gaul in the second half of the fifth century A.D. The manuscript was brought to Aachen by Charlemagne and afterward resided in the Abbey of St. Denis before being returned to Italy in the fifteenth century, when it appears in an inventory of manuscripts owned by Pope Sextus IV (1471–1484). The other late classical manuscript with illuminations, Codex Vaticanus Latinus 3225 (the "Vergilius Vaticanus"), dates from the early fifth century and provides only one illustration for all the *Bucolica.* Though much more sophisticated in execution and distinctly Byzantine in feeling, this illustration places Tityrus and Meliboeus in poses remarkably similar to those in the Vergilius Romanus. See J. de Wit, *Die Miniaturen des Vergilius Vaticanus* (Amsterdam: Swets & Zeitlinger, 1959), pl. 6.

19. Italian illustrations of Vergil are catalogued in Sander, *Le livre à figures italien*, 3. 1313–18; and in Carlo Enrico Rava, *Supplement à Max Sander: Le Livre à figures italiens de la Renaissance* (Milan: Hoepli, 1969), p. 161. Designs for the woodcuts printed by Sagnino are attributed to Zoan Andrea Vavassore, after an illustrated MS in the monastic library of Bobbio. See Giuliano Mambelli *Gli annali delle edizione virgiliane* (Florence: Olschki, 1954), p. 49. The adaptation of Vavassore's design for Bonelli's edition of Vergil (fig. 3) is printed with eclogues 1, 5, 6, and 9, all four in the same edition.

20. Theodore K. Rabb, "Sebastian Brant and the First Illustrated Edition of Vergil," *Princeton Library Chronicle* 21 (1960), 187–99. On French illustrations of Vergil see Robert Brun, *Le livre français illustré de la Renaissance* (Paris: Picard, 1969), pp. 312 ff. The edition of Vergil's works in French translation printed by Christophe Langelier (Paris, 1540) belongs in spirit and technique to the Strasburg tradition. Two other editions (*Les bucoliques* [Paris: Jehan de la Garde, 1516] and *Les oeuvres* [Paris: Galiot du Pre, 1529]) make use of twelve separate blocks depicting single figures and pieces of scenery that can be combined and recombined to fit the different narrative circumstances of each eclogue.

21. *Three Proper, and wittie, familiar Letters* (1580), rpt. in *Var.* 10.18.

JUDITH M. KENNEDY

The Final Emblem of
The Shepheardes Calender

THE FINAL emblem of *The Shepheardes Calender*, "Merce non mercede,"
is to be found at the very end of the volume immediately following the
epilogue or envoy.[1] It is not introduced as an emblem, nor is it assigned to
a character, but it is clearly of the same nature as the emblems appended to
the eclogues, being particularly close in type to Willye's emblem for August, "Vinto non vitto." The first question that naturally arises about
"Merce non mercede" is, What does it mean? The other emblems, even
the missing "Colins Embleme" for December, are all sufficiently glossed
by E. K. to leave readers with the impression that they have at least some
understanding of their meaning, but E. K.'s comments on the envoy or
epilogue are confined to an introductory remark of justification of claims
the poet makes in this final apostrophe to his book. The *Variorum* offers no
comment at all on "Merce non mercede," but editors occasionally have
provided at least a translation. Gilfillan gives "For recompense, but not for
hire"; his translation is adopted by D. Laing Purves. Child gives "Done
for itself and not for profit." MacLean annotates "For reward [in the sense
of substantial and intelligent response] not for hire [or salary]."[2] These
three translations are substantially the same, but Gilbert, in the course of
arguing that "Merce non mercede" is in fact Colin's emblem for December, misplaced through the printer's error, states that *merce* means "wares,
goodes, merchandise," and that *mercede* refers to the "reward" of the
poet, or fame. His implied translation is then "Riches of the world perish,
but not the poet's reward."[3] In a letter in answer to Gilbert, Syford apparently accepts the assigning of the emblem to Colin and agrees that *mercede*
is used in the sense of "'misericordia' or 'pity' or 'mercy'." The translation to be derived from this sense is not entirely clear; I quote the final sentences of Syford's letter: "The Calendar is to the better please, the worse
despise. In other words, Spenser wants others to like it, at least the better
ones. As for the worse, let them be scorned, or perhaps, he would have
added, let them scorn. He asks no more,—only their generosity, pity,
mercy—'merce non mercede'."[4]
Because these comments show that there is little agreement on the

meaning of "Merce non mercede," it is at first sight surprising that such scant scholarly attention has been devoted to the phrase, but the neglect becomes more understandable in the light of what seems to be a general lack of interest in the emblems of *The Shepheardes Calender*. With the exception of the debate about the missing emblem for December, commentary in the *Variorum* is chiefly limited to discussion of possible sources. Critics frequently omit any mention of the emblems from their interpretations of the eclogues, and even Patrick Cullen, whose full discussions often embrace a consideration of the emblems and who suggests in a footnote that "Merce non mercede" may have been "intended to speak for the *Calender* as a whole,"[5] does not consistently include the emblems as an integral part of the eclogues nor devote much time to considering their meaning. It is my belief that the final emblem does indeed speak for several of the main themes of the *Calender* as a whole, and that it belongs to Immerito, whose name is punningly explained by it. .

The emblems of *The Shepheardes Calender* belong to that particular family of devices known as the *mot,* a group akin to the *impresa,* in relation to which Paolo Giovio "enjoys a primacy analogous to that of Alciati for the emblem."[6] In his prefatory letter to Samuel Daniel's translation of Paolo Giovio, N. W. distinguishes between *imprese* and emblems thus:

> *Impreses* manifest the special purpose of Gentlemen in warlike combats or chamber tornaments. *Emblems* are generall conceiptes rather of moral matters then perticulare deliberations: rather to give credit to the wit, then to reveale the secretes of the minde.[7]

In "To the Frendly Reader," Daniel enlarges upon the manner in which such "Devises" declare "inward pretended purposes and enterprises" and "discover our secret intentions"; he divides them into four kinds, one of which is the mot. Of mots, "which truly are of great excellencie if they bee gallantly composed," he gives the following main characteristics: (1) "this word *mot* signifieth as much as *Gnome,* a short sentence or posie"; (2) "the mots which are chiefly used, are either amorous or grave, and they beare a great grace if they be perfectly composed with their circumstances and properties"; (3) they should be short, preferably not exceeding a verse in any tongue, and using only part of a Latin or Greek hexameter; (4) "better are they esteemed being taken out of some famous author"; (5) "above all, if it be possible, let them leave some scruple whereon to meditate, to him who either readeth or heares them"; (6) "it is lawfull to use them without figures, although that *Paulus Jovius* vainly termeth them so used, soules without bodies."[8] In the body of the dialogue Giovio constantly emphasizes the wit and originality of *imprese*. Altogether, "the framing of an *Impresa* is the adventure of a readie and phantasticall braine."[9] Puttenham, too, shows enthusiasm for the form and indicates that it deserves to be held in high esteem:

> This may suffice for devices, a terme which includes in his generality all those other, viz. liveries, cognizances, emblemes, enseigns and impreses. For though the termes be divers, the use and intent is but one whether they rest in colour or figure or both, or in word or in muet shew, and that is to insinuat some secret, wittie, morall and brave purpose presented to the beholder, either to recreate his eye, or please his phantasie, or examine his judgement, or occupie his braine or to manage his will either by hope or by dread, every of which respectes be of no little moment to the interest and ornament of the civill life: and therefore give them no little commendation.[10]

By the specially marked attention E. K. gives each emblem in his gloss, he shows that he fully appreciates that in these enigmatic sentences Spenser is displaying his "readie and phantasticall braine" and is intending "to insinuat some secret, wittie, morall and brave purpose" to the reader. Individual glosses frequently show E. K.'s enjoyment of the punning, riddling nature of the emblems, and particularly of the Italian ones. For example in the gloss to Colin's emblem for January, E. K. picks up the pun on *anchóra* ("yet," "withall") and *ancora* ("an anchor") when he says that "yet leaning on hope" Colin "is somewhat recomforted."[11] In the gloss to Colin's emblem for June he awakes the reader's suspicion of further hidden meaning by his bland conclusion: "which is all the meaning of thys Embleme," and his gloss to the "very ambiguous" August emblems is in itself wittily enigmatic. E. K.'s glosses remind us that a good mot should tease the mind, or "leave some scruple whereon to meditate," and may bear more than one meaning. Puttenham is particularly enthusiastic about the richness of interpretation possible for Heliogabalus' device both in its original form and even more in its adaptation to Queen Elizabeth, praising particularly its "subtilitie and multiplicitie of sense," and zestfully spelling out its meanings.[12]

It is very much to be regretted that Puttenham did not exercise his ingenuity in exploring the "subtilitie and multiplicitie of sense" of the final emblem of the "Gentleman who wrate the late shepheardes Callender,"[13] for the two words Spenser balances across his negative are richly multiple and ambiguous. Modern Italian distinguishes between *merce* and *mercé*. *Merce* is derived from the Latin, *merx, mercis,* and its primary meaning is "ogni bene economico trasportabile," or goods or wares. Although it is used predominantly of worldly goods, the *Dizionario Enciclopedico Italiano* (1957) cites poetic usages by Dante and Petrarch referring to merit accumulated for the eternal life and to the riches of virtue adorning a lady. *Mercé* (or *merzé*) is a truncated form of *mercede* or *merzede,* which is from the Latin *merces, -edis,* derived from *merx, mercis.* The primary meaning of *mercede* is payment for work (the laborer is worthy of his hire), but it can also mean recompense or reward, both spiritual and temporal; meritorious works; pity or grace. *Mercé* shares with *mercede* the sense of recompense or reward and is more common than *mercede* in the sense of pity or grace (whether these aids are sought from the lady or from God). It can also be used in the sense of thanks. Florio does not distinguish between *merce* and *mercé.*[14] His relevant entries are as follows:

> Merce, *as* Mercatantia, *as* Mercede. Also *mercies, thankes, gramercies, commiseration, pittie, ruthe, compassion. Also wages or hire, the rewarde of science.*
> Mercede, *a rewarde, a meede, a hire.*
> Mercatantia, *as* Mercadantia.
> Mercadantia, *merchandise or ware.*

Spenser's final emblem wittily exploits the multiple senses of these two closely related words, finding in diversity a unity appropriate to an admirer of Tasso and Ariosto. This mot is both amorous and grave, and it is perfectly composed with the circumstances and properties both of the poem and of its author. It partly discovers the secret intentions of the amorous, poetic, and religious debates of the *Calender,* and it further declares the inward pretended purposes and enterprises of Immerito. The ensuing few pages will explore what "Merce non mercede" means in amorous, poetic, and religious terms, both within and beyond *The Shepheardes Calender.*

The amorous theme of *The Shepheardes Calender* is sounded dominantly in the story of Colin and Rosalind. Colin painfully loves the town-bred Rosalind, who scorns his rural music. Despite her scorn, Colin is hopeful of winning her love. He himself scorns Hobbinol, who seeks his love with gifts: "Ah foolish *Hobbinol,* thy gyfts bene vayne: / *Colin* them gives to *Rosalind* againe" ("January" 59–60).

In "April," Hobbinol laments the loss of Colin's love and describes the pitiable condition to which Colin's unrequited love for Rosalind has reduced him. Thenot marvels that Colin should have the skill of a poet, yet lack the discipline "to brydle love." Thenot sees Colin as blinded by love, and "lewdly bent." Hobbinol sardonically views him as "a greater fon, /

That loves the thing he cannot purchase." Hobbinol's cynicism seems justified by the events lamented in "June," when Colin tells Hobbinol of Rosalind's faithlessness, causing Hobbinol to exclaim that she is "voide of grace" (115).

After this central low point, the story of Colin's love for Rosalind develops unexpectedly. There is no reconciliation, or clearing up of misunderstanding, nor does Colin in disillusionment reject love. Instead, "August" offers a sestina of lament that is not without hope (contrary to "Già speme spenta," the emblem for June), but is dedicated to woe only "till safe and sound / She home returne, whose voyces silver sound / To cheerefull songs can chaunge my cherelesse cryes." In "October," Piers forcefully corrects Cuddie's pessimistic view of the effects of Colin's love:

> Ah fon, for love does teach him climbe so hie,
> And lyftes him up out of the loathsome myre:
> Such immortall mirrhor, as he doth admire,
> Would rayse ones mynd above the starry skie.
> And cause a caytive corage to aspire,
> For lofty love doth loath a lowly eye.   (91–96)

In "November," Thenot speaks of Colin's muse "Lulled a sleepe through loves misgovernaunce," but since he invites Colin to sing a song to "advaunce" his "loved lasse," the misgovernance would seem to be on Colin's part, rather than on love's. Colin himself seems now capable of bridling love and puts aside amorous lays as inappropriate to the winter season, accepting instead Thenot's suggestion that he elegiacally celebrate Dido. In "December," Colin regrets that the passing of his poetic powers robs Rosalind of her due garland and finally bids adieu to the "deare, whose love I bought so deare." As E. K. says, this stanza "is a conclusion of all. where in sixe verses he comprehendeth briefly all that was touched in this booke." But E. K. is misleading in his summary of the last two verses, which emphasize not Hobbinol, but a last "à Dieu" to Rosalind.

Before considering how "Merce non mercede" relates to Colin's love for Rosalind, some other shepherd lovers should be noted. In "February," Cuddie is complacently content that he has won Phyllis with "a gyrdle of gelt" and scorns Thenot's warning, "Thou art a fon, of thy love to boste, / All that is lent to love, wyll be lost." Given this materialistic approach to love, Cuddie's pejorative attitude to Colin's love in "October" is understandable and revealing. Two other shepherds taken unwarily in the snare of love are Thomalin in "March" and Perigot in "August." The pains of both these shepherds are commented upon with wry sympathy by Willye; they reveal the honey and gall of the common experience of love.

These common lovers will die if they meet "gracelesse griefe" ("August," 113); the materialistic lover, Cuddie, can see "lordly love" only as "a Tyranne fell," reminiscent of "Cupide, oure lord" in ·The Parlement of Foules, and looking forward to Busirane. Such lovers are like Chaucer's lower order of birds, unable to understand the courtly forbearance of the eagles, and certainly incapable of the restless spiritual and intellectual seeking of Chaucer's dreamer in the Parlement. Colin is the heir to both characteristics, and "Merce non mercede" speaks to his amorous experience within the Calender, and to Immerito's later statements on love under the same poetic pseudonym. For the Colin of the first half of the Calender, the emblem quite conventionally in terms of courtly love seeks the mercy or pity or favor of the beloved rather than material reward. However, Colin's attitude toward Hobbinol's gifts, and Hobbinol's condemnation of Colin for loving what he cannot purchase, show an incomplete understanding of the nonmaterial nature of true love. Furthermore, the favor being sought, like the mercy and grace sought even by the royal tercel, is sublunary, no more than the natural satisfaction of the call of kind. After Colin loses the hope of this kind of satisfaction, his attitude to love changes. The grace that he now seeks as guerdon from his apotheosized love is indicated in the latter part of The Shepheardes Calender, explicated at the end of Colin Clouts Come Home Againe, and celebrated in the vision of the Graces in The Faerie Queene. In the latter part of the Calender Rosalind is to Colin an "immortall mirrhor" of "Beauty, which is an excellent object of poeticall spirites" ("October" 93, and gloss). Rosalind has become to Colin much more a Belphoebe than an Amoret, and as such she is viewed and addressed in a manner akin to that suitable for Elisa/Cynthia/Gloriana. She is "of divine regard and heavenly hew, / Excelling all that ever ye did see" (CCCHA 933–34), and all that Colin asks of her is

> that I may her honour paravant,
> And praise her worth, though far my wit above.
> Such grace shall be some guerdon for the griefe,
> And long affliction which I have endured.
>
> (CCCHA 941–44)

Rosalind, the poetic symbol of inspiring love and beauty, is one step up the stair of heavenly aspiration. The majesty and princely power of Elisa draw the aspiring poet further up the stair. Immerito's emblem declares that he desires from these potent poetic symbols of the beloved the bountiful grace of favorable countenance, rather than any carnal or financial meed.

The theme of the nature and function of the true poet is also carried mainly through the story of Colin. His role as lover is inextricable from his role as poet, but in his poetic role he has further important functions as eulogist and elegist, and as exemplar and leader. In "June," although he disclaims Hobbinol's view of him as able to draw the Muses after him and purports himself to be indifferent to praise, blame, or renown, yet in exalting Tityrus/Chaucer as his mentor and model he emphasizes the growing fame of Tityrus' skill. Similarly, all Colin's modest disclaimers about his "rugged and unkempt" rhymes are contradicted by the respect and reputation he has won among his fellow shepherds, by his association with Chaucer, Vergil, the Muses, Orpheus, and Pan, and by his own virtuoso performances: the dazzlingly brilliant forms in "April," "August," and "November," the formal stanza of complaint in "January" and "December," and the eight-line, two-rhyme stanza of "June" handled as a dialogue so that the tightness of the form is transcended by conversational ease in a manner worthy of the master he is here imitating (c.f., for example, Chaucer's "Fortune"). Some aspects of the theme of the poet's duties and rewards are crystallized in the debate between Cuddie and Piers in "October." Cuddie is discouraged by the lack of material support available to him, and rejects all Piers' arguments that the rewards of poetry are to be found in encouraging and celebrating virtue in this world, and ultimately, through "aspyring wit," returning to its true home, heaven. If "Merce non mercede" had been the emblem of the October eclogue, it might have been possible to apply it to the poetic theme in diametrically opposite senses, derived from the crossed meanings of the words: for Piers "Thanks, not hire," and for Cuddie "Wages, not [spiritual] reward." But the final emblem is placed after the envoy which claims immortality for the *Calender* and an enduring, though modest, fame. This fame draws life from the poem's didactic function and is therefore associated with the poetic ideal expressed by Piers. In the overarching sense of the emblem, *merce* must mean here at its most material "the rewarde of science" as opposed to *mercede* as financial meed, or wages. The reward of science is in this world the grace, favor, thanks and approval of "the better"; in heaven it is a higher grace, but not a grace earned as wages. Spenser's position on the kind of reward that a poet should expect in this world is stated fairly frequently in later poems. The bounty of Cynthia, so highly praised in *Colin Clouts Come Home Againe,* is certainly more a matter of gracious countenance than money or other tangible goods. The poet's relation to his prince or patron is similar to the right courtier's, who serves

> Not so much for to gaine, or for to raise
> Himselfe to high degree, as for his grace,
> And in his liking to winne worthie place.
> (*Mother Hubberds Tale* 774–76)

It behooves "mightie Peeres" in support of the Muses "with their noble countenaunce to grace / The learned forheads, without gifts or gaine" (*The Teares of the Muses* 81–82). This bountiful circle of grace, independent of material gain, is wonderingly commented on by Florio in his praise of the relationship between Spenser and Leicester: "Curteous Lord, Curteous Spenser, I knowe not which hath purchast more fame, either he in deserving so well of so famous a scholler, or so famous a scholler in being so thankful without hope of requitall to so famous a Lord." (*Var.* 7.642).[15]

The third major subject of *The Shepheardes Calender* is religion. The Calender will live "To teach the ruder shepheard how to feede his sheepe / And from the falsers fraud his folded flocke to keepe" (Envoy). The true shepherd achieves "timely death" ("December" 150), which joyfully releases him into "The fieldes ay fresh, the grasse ay greene" ("November" 189) of heaven. The debates of May, July, and September show that it is not easy to find "the grene path way to life" ("November," gloss to emblem) of death in Christ. Even a well-intentioned shepherd such as Diggon may be "bewitcht / With vayne desyre, and hope to be enricht," and find himself among those whose "ill haviour garres men missay / Both of their doctrine, and of their faye" ("September" 74–75, 106–07). The final emblem of *The Shepheardes Calender* is an affirmation of true faith, the anchor in all troublous seas of doubt. It affirms the faithful dependence on God's grace and rejects wages for any works or deservings. This "most wholesome Doctrine and very full of comfort" (as Justification by Faith is called in Article 11) is the cornerstone of Spenser's religious profession. The emblem calls to mind the beginning of the fourth chapter of *Romans,* where the importance of reward received by grace, and not earned as wages, is set out. In Erasmus' Latin:

> Quid enim scriptura dicit? Credidit autem Abraham Deo, et imputatum est ei ad iustitiam. Ei vero qui operatur, merces non imputatur secundum gratiam, sed secundum debitum. Porro ei qui non operatur, sed credit in eum qui iustificat impium, imputatur fides sua ad iustitiam.　　　　　　　　　　　　　　　　(*Rom.* 4.3–5)[16]

These verses are translated in the Geneva Bible thus:

> 3. For what saith the Scripture? Abraham beleved God, and it was counted to him for righteousness.
> 4. Now to him that worketh, the wages is not counted by favour, but by dette, (Bishops' Bible—not receved of grace, but of duetie.)
> 5. But to him that worketh not, but beleveth in him that justifieth the ungodlie, his faith is counted for righteousness.

The Final Emblem of *The Shepheardes Calender*

In verse 4, "worketh" is marginally glossed "Meriteth by his workes," and in verse 5, "worketh not" is marginally glossed "That dependeth not on his workes, nether thinketh to merit by them."

In terms of the religious debates of the eclogues, the final emblem indicates that the doubts and difficulties of this world can only be resolved by faith in the grace of God and asserts the truth of the doctrine of justification by faith, a doctrine crucially important in the division between the Roman and Protestant churches, as is clearly shown in, for example, Hooker's *A Learned Discourse of Justification* or Van Der Noot's *Theatre for Worldlings*. The true believer looks to the bountiful grace of God for reward and totally rejects the crassly mercenary view of God's gifts expressed by Palinode: "Good is no good, but if it be spend: / God giveth good for none other end." As the emblems for May, and E. K.'s gloss on them, make clear, Palinode is being seduced from the right way of true religion by the "falsers" of faith. Morrell and Diggon also in varying degree are weakened in their faith by their mercenary views (cf. "July" 211–12 and "September" 74–75).

In relation to the poet, the maker, the emblem places in perspective all the desires and aspirations and achievements, however noble and enduring, of this world: Immerito seeks to be justified by faith, reposing his trust in the "merce" or grace of God, rather than seeking the reward or wages ("merces") of his own works. The "modesty topos" of the *Calender* takes on deeper meaning and new vitality when seen from this perspective. Poetic convention is transcended by religious conviction, and Spenser could say with Hooker "we acknowledge a dutiful necessity of doing well, but the meritorious dignity of well doing we utterly renounce."[17]

It is not always easy imaginatively to recapture the vitality and fervor of religious conviction and debate in Spenser's time. Few today know St. Paul's Epistle to the Romans "by rote and without the book," and exercise themselves "therin evermore continually, as with the daily bread of the soul,"[18] or learn to recite the eloquent answers of the young scholar in Nowell's *Catechisme*. The answer to the question about rewards and wages may serve as a reminder of how close Spenser's poetic vocabulary in describing his beloved and his prince comes to the language of religion:

Ma. But God doth allure us to good doing wyth certaine rewardes, both in this life and in the life to come, and doth covenaunt wyth us as it were for certayne wages.

Sch. That reward, as I have sayd, is not geven to workes for their worthinesse, and rendred to them as recompense for deservinges, but by the bountifulnesse of God, is freely bestowed upon us without deserving. And justification God doth geve us as a gift of

hys owne deare love toward us and of hys liberalitie through
Christ. When I speake of Gods gift and liberalitie, I meane it free
and bountifull wythout any our desert or merite: that it be Gods
mere and syncere liberalitie, which he applyeth to our salvation
onely whom he loveth and which trust in hym, not hyêred, or
procured for wages, as it were a marchandise of hys commodities
and benefites used by hym for some profite to hym selfe, requiring againe of us some recompense or price: which once to thinke,
were to abate both the liberalitie and majestie of God.[19]

Spenser was a consciously ambitious poet. If he had not been so successful, his claims to be the heir of Vergil and Chaucer, his hope to overgo
Ariosto, and his lavish praise of his poetic persona Colin would seem ludi-
crously egotistical. But his high aspirations and great achievements are
held in the steady perspective of divine perfection, knowing that "God re-
wardeth abundantly every one which worketh, yet not for any meritorious dignity which is, or can be, in the work, but through his mere mercy,
by whose commandment he worketh."[20] "Immerito" is not just the conventionally modest pseudonym of the fledgling epic poet, trying his wings
in appropriately humble pastoral flight, but a statement of faith by the
Christian poet. From his earliest work to his last, England's prince of pastoral, amorous, and epic poets subordinated all his ambitions to attaining
"That Sabaoth's sight" through his faith in "th' exceeding grace / Of
highest God that loves his creatures so, / And all his workes with mercy
doth embrace."
     It is unlikely that this essay has fully searched out the "inward pretended
purposes and enterprises" and "secret intentions" discovered gnomically
in the exquisite wit of the final emblem of *The Shepheardes Calender,* but it
may persuade that "Merce non mercede" should be considered as Immerito's emblem, which in this capacity provides Spenser's readers something
"whereon to meditate."

St. Thomas University

Notes

1. *The Works of Edmund Spenser: A Variorum Edition*, ed. Edwin Greenlaw et al., 11
vols. (Baltimore: The Johns Hopkins Press, 1932–57), vol. 7, p. 120. All quotations from
Spenser are from this edition, with modernization of i, u, and v.

2. Edmund Spenser, *Poetical Works*, ed. George Gilfillan (Edinburgh: James Nichols, 1859), vol. 4, p. 298; *The Canterbury Tales and Faerie Queene,* ed. D. Laing Purves (Edinburgh: Nimmo, 1870), p. 582; Spenser, *Poetical Works,* ed. Francis J. Child (Boston: Little, Brown, 1860), vol. 4, p. 374; Hugh MacLean, ed., *Edmund Spenser's Poetry,* A Norton Critical Edition (New York: Norton, 1968), p. 424n.

3. Allan H. Gilbert, "The Embleme for December in the *Shepheardes Calender*," *MLN* 63 (1948), 181–82.

4. Constance M. Syford, "Merce non Mercede," *MLN* 63 (1948), 435–36.

5. *Spenser, Marvell, and Renaissance Pastoral* (Cambridge, Mass.: Harvard University Press, 1970), p. 97n.

6. *Enciclopedia Italiana*, 1949 ed. (Rome: Istituto Poligrafico dello Stato, 1951), vol. 18, p. 938.

7. *The Complete Works in Verse and Prose of Samuel Daniel,* ed. A. B. Grosart (1885–96; rpt. New York: Russell and Russell, 1963), vol. 4, pp. 11–12.

8. Ibid., pp. 16–17, 22–23.

9. *The Worthy tract of Paulus Jovius, contayning a discourse of rare inventions, both Militarie and Amorous called Imprese. Whereunto is added a Preface . . . By Samuell Daniell* (London, 1585), sig. Eiiv. Available in "English Books 1475–1640" (Ann Arbor: University Microfilms), R. 296.

10. *The Arte of English Poesie,* ed. Gladys Willcock and Alice Walker (Cambridge: Cambridge University Press, 1936), pp. 107–08.

11. E. K. perhaps also has in mind Thomas Vautrollier's device "Anchora Spei" which passed to Richard Field when he married Vautrollier's widow and which has become very familiar to Spenser's readers through Field's use of it for the 1596 *Faerie Queene.* See R. B. McKerrow, *Printers' and Publishers' Devices in England and Scotland 1485–1640* (1913; rpt. London: The Bibliographical Society, 1949), p. 183, and Device 222.

12. Ibid., p. 103.

13. Ibid., p. 63.

14. John Florio, *A Worlde of Wordes, Or Most copious, and exact Dictionarie in Italian and English* (London, 1598). Available in "English Books 1475–1640" (Ann Arbor: University Microfilms), R. 540.

15. See Eleanor Rosenberg, *Leicester, Patron of Letters,* (New York: Columbia University Press, 1955), p. 353. I thank Professor A. C. Hamilton for drawing this quotation to my attention and for other helpful suggestions during the preparation of this paper.

16. *The new Testament in Englishe after the greeke translation annexed wyth the translation of Erasmus in Latin* (1550). *STC* 2821. Available in "English Books 1475–1640" (Ann Arbor: University Microfilms), R. 110. Verse 4, in the Vulgate (Ei autem qui operatur, merces non imputatur secundum gratiam, sed secundum debitum), is cited in Langius, *Novissima Polyanthea* (Frankfurt: 1613), p. 808, under "Merces, Sententiae Biblicae."

17. *A Learned Discourse of Justification,* in *Of the Laws of Ecclesiastical Polity,* ed. Christopher Morris (London: Everyman, 1963), p. 24.

18. Tyndale's rendering of Luther's preface to the Epistle to the Romans, in *William Tyndale,* ed. G. E. Duffield, (Philadelphia: Fortress Press, 1965), p. 120.

19. A. Nowell, *A Catechisme, or first Instruction and Learning of Christian Religion* (1571), sig. Oiiii[r-v]. *STC* 18709. Available in "English Books 1475–1640" (Ann Arbor: University Microfilms), R. 327; where see also *STC* 18701, *Catechismus, etc.* (1570), sig. Oiv[r-v].

M. At praemiis tamen tum in hac vita, tum in futura nos ad bene agendum invitat
Deus, et quasi mercede quadam nobiscum paciscitur.

JUDITH M. KENNEDY

A. Merces illa non pro dignitate, ut dixi, operibus tribuitur, et illis quasi gratia pro meritis refertur, sed Dei benignitate gratis praeter meritum, in nos confertur. Iustitiam verò Deus nobis pro sua in nos charitate, et liberalitate per Christum dono dat. Dei donum liberalitatemque quum dico gratuitam, et sine mercede, aut merito nostro benignam intelligo: ut sit mera synceraque Dei liberalitas, quàm ad nostram modo, quos diligit, quique illi fidimus, salutem referat, non conducta, aut mercenaria, quasi quaedam commodorum utilitatumque suarum mercatura, quàm ad fructum aliquem suum exerceat, aliquod vicissim premium, aut pretium à nobis repetens: qua sola vel cogitatione Dei benignitas, simul et maiestas minueretur.

20. Hooker, *A Learned Discourse*, p. 67.

ALEXANDER DUNLOP

The Drama of *Amoretti*

A LITTLE MORE than ten years ago I noted a pattern of calendar symbolism in *Amoretti* based on the correspondence of sonnets 22, 62, and 68 to the dates of Ash Wednesday, the Feast of the Annunciation, and Easter in the year 1594. This pattern has been accepted by most commentators on *Amoretti*, but with reservations that reflect, I think, a conflict still present in Spenser criticism generally. Some have found Spenser's precisely calculated pattern an unlikely and inappropriate expression of amorous sentiment; others have found the simple pattern an inadequate expression of the allegorical mentality.

Criticism of *Amoretti* seems to be caught in an impasse between numerologists and traditionalists. At one extreme the late Josephine Waters Bennett, rejecting entirely the notion of calendar symbolism in *Amoretti*, saw the sequence in a historical, representational context.[1] At the other extreme, A. Kent Hieatt and Alastair Fowler, exploring various possibilities of symbolic structuring, both have focused mainly on abstract, symbolic aspects of the sequence.[2] In the present supplement to my earlier work on *Amoretti* I want to suggest that we may break the impasse by approaching the sequence from a different standpoint.

Professors Bennett, Hieatt, and Fowler have studied two different aspects of *Amoretti:* the narrative-historical aspect, which is the author's *donnée,* and the symbolic aspect, which embodies the author's evaluation of the conventional and historical materials with which he works. Through the symbolic framework of *Amoretti* Spenser places the narrative-historical details in a universal context. But the lover is a character who makes his own evaluation of the situation. I suggest that in the study of the lover's viewpoint we may find an essential link between traditionalists and numerologists.

The basis for this approach to *Amoretti* is the recognition that Spenser is speaking to us not directly but indirectly through the persona of the poet-lover. The poet-lover is a semifictional dramatic character interposed between the author and the reader. His directly demonstrated reactions to the circumstances of courtship form the dramatic element of *Amoretti,* an element that commentators have almost entirely neglected.[3]

That the poet-lover is specifically identified as Edmund Spenser, author of *The Faerie Queene,* makes him no less fictional than the Dante of the

Commedia. The personal details—the references to his work on *The Faerie Queene,* to his friend Lodowick Bryskett, and to his three Elizabeths, the calendar symbolism linking the work to 1594, and the connection to the *Epithalamion* celebrating his own marriage—are a means of relating the particular to the general and the universal.[4] The personal element is subsumed in the didactic purpose of the sequence, which is to dramatize how one progresses toward a truer understanding and enjoyment of love.

Once we abandon the notion that Spenser the author is speaking to us directly we gain a critical detachment from the sonnets that permits us to see the imperfection of the poet-lover. "Vntrainde in louers trade" (51) and limited by his human nature, during most of the sequence he is troubled by his passion, confused, caught in the emotional flux of the moment. Finally, like Dante, he is led to a fuller understanding and a more meaningful love. Each individual sonnet, then, represents not the completeness of vision of Spenser the author, but the emotional state of the lover at one stage of his development.

The lover's imperfection introduces an important element of irony. Through the symbolic framework of the sequence Spenser makes the lover's amorous experience a part of the larger pattern of the religious experience of Lent, Holy Week, and Easter. The religious framework is expressed numerologically, in a different mode and on a different level than the discourse of the lover, who is wrapped in the cloud of his own desires. The lover's failure to relate his personal experience to the larger pattern of spiritual truth is the source of his imperfection and the basis of the irony of *Amoretti.* The lover is an ironic figure because he fails to see what Spenser expected his readers to know: that the little loves—*amoretti*—of this world are imitations of God's great and universal love.

The symbolic pattern that is not apparent to the lover becomes apparent to the reader only relatively late in the sequence. Hunter has found it difficult to accept the idea that Spenser expected the reader to understand all the sonnets in terms of a concept that is not fully expressed until late in the sequence.[5] Spenser was less concerned with the psychology of reader response than with figuring forth truth as perfectly as possible—a truth that he believed to exist apart from its perception. He was concerned with reader response to the extent that he manipulated the veil of allegory in order to require the reader to engage in retrospective analysis, certainly not to relieve him of that responsibility. For finally the process of reading *Amoretti* becomes analogous to the perception of truth in a life that Spenser saw imbued at every point with elusive but often demonstrable signs of spiritual truth.

Amoretti is a comedy in the Dantesque sense. Its outcome is felicitous on every level. The lover wins his lady and also a deeper understanding of love at the same time that Christ by his passion and resurrection does "triumph ouer death and sin" that man "may liue for euer in felicity" (68). Yet from the limited perspective of the poet-lover the drama is intermittently comic and tragic:

> Sometimes I ioy when glad occasion fits,
>   and mask in myrth lyke to a Comedy:
> soone after when my ioy to sorrow flits,
>   I waile and make my woes a Tragedy.   (54)

Until the sonnets of Holy Week (62–68) the lover is condemned, largely by his own shortsightedness and failure to understand, to "wast and weare away in terms unsure, / twixt feare and hope depending doubtfully" (25). He does not see that the period of trial is beneficial and necessary.

The Lover's education proceeds in three steps. The first is the period of trial and privation. This period provides an opportunity for the lover to demonstrate steadfastness and loyalty in the face of adversity. It serves perhaps to heighten the desire of the lover, or at the least provides an opportunity to demonstrate how greatly he loves the lady. It both tests and develops the faith that he needs to persevere. Perhaps most important of all, privation at one level serves to redirect the poet's love to a higher level.

Though the lover is limited in his understanding of love and of himself, he is in no way malicious. He must have enough faith or knowledge to recognize, at least at times, that the period of trial and denial is salutary. This recognition is expressed in the sonnets in which he praises the lady's pride or welcomes his suffering, such as 24 or 25. But he must also be weak and ignorant enough to need the period of trial and denial. His weakness is the weakness of common humanity. With a measure of faith and steadfastness on his part, and a measure of grace on the part of his lady and his Lord, he can go a long way toward overcoming this inherent human weakness.

The lover's guide in the preparatory part of his education is the lady:

> For with mild pleasance, which doth pride displace,
>   she to her loue doth lookers eyes allure:
> and with sterne countenance back again doth chace
>   their looser lookes that stir vp lustes impure.
> With such strange termes her eyes she doth inure,
>   that with one looke she doth my life dismay:
> and with another doth it streight recure,

> her smile me drawes, her frowne me driues away.
> Thus doth she traine and teach me with her lookes.   (21)

The most important aspect of the lady's character is her constant obduracy. Except for a smile of encouragement in sonnets 39 and 40, there is no sign that the lady is in any way moved by the lover's histrionics until sonnet 60. In her outward behavior she is as unmoved as, in the lover's words, "a senceless stone" (54). His efforts to move her are "fruitless work" (23): "So doe I weepe, and wayle, and pleade in vaine" (18).

We know nothing of her inner emotional state, because we see her only through the lover's eyes, and he, "lyke Narcissus vaine" (35), is concerned only with his own. The lover presents us a lady with two distinct aspects —that of the cruel "fayre proud" and that of the "donna angelicata"—but these are clearly projections of the lover's volatile, emotional reactions to the lady's unchanging obduracy. Until her submission in 67 the lady never takes any action more drastic than a look or a smile. It is the lover who imputes to her "smyling lookes" either guileful cruelty or gracious mercy as his varying moods incline him to proud protest or to humble plea. The only exception to Elizabeth's restraint is her burning of his letter mentioned in 48, and even here, the lover interprets it as inaction rather than action; it did not mean that she actively rejected him, but that she "would not heare" him. When she finally does submit, it is not because of his arguments, but rather "of her owne goodwill" (67).

Just as the lover is not all wrong in his approach to the lady, the lady is not absolute in her rejection of him. She is properly unyielding, but she continues to receive his suit. She "lyke the Spectator ydly sits / beholding me that all the pageants play"; but she does not leave the performance. Rather "she bids me play my part" (18), and she watches "with constant eye" (54). This constancy, this willingness to continue, shared by the lover and the lady, is the foundation of love. The lady must be intriguing enough to attract the lover, but restrained enough to maintain his intense desire without providing any satisfaction on the initial level of his desire. She is a figure of constancy and stability, with a perhaps instinctive wisdom related to those qualities, in contrast to the fitfulness, instability, and shortsightedness of the lover. It is interesting to note that the characteristics of Spenser's Elizabeth are precisely those of another Renaissance lady of the same name, the Mona Lisa, whose restraint and whose enigmatic smile have power to evoke widely varying reactions.[6]

Just as Vergil can lead Dante only so far, the scope of the lady's guidance is limited. Elizabeth's role, like Vergil's, is limited to the human level, to that which man can achieve on his own power.[7] But her wisdom is great, for she understands her own limitations and his, as he indicates in sonnet 58: "Weake is th'assurance that weake flesh reposeth / in her owne power." Like Vergil's, her guidance is preparatory; it accords with and leads up to divine guidance. Her function has both a positive and a negative aspect. There is something divine in her that leads him on and something forbidding in her that rejects the amorous expression of his lower soul, gradually preparing him for the recognition that he must direct his energies into a higher channel.

We know that the lady is modestly encouraging yet unyielding. All the rest of what we are told about her in the first sixty sonnets—that she is cruel, deceitful, proud, and insensitive—really tells us nothing about the lady, but a great deal about the lover, and it is this factor that is of primary importance. It is the change in the distraught, emotional lover as he gradually achieves new insights into the nature of love that is the primary dramatic element in *Amoretti*. On the surface the lover's state seems to worsen during the course of the sequence. Though there are periods of elation in sonnets 39 and 40 and in the sonnets around 68, we find him tortured and rejected at the beginning of the sequence and we leave him pining and alone at the end. But the drama of *Amoretti* is not on the surface, it is within the lover. It is not the drama of a hero conquering a lady, but that of a more of less average man standing the trials of love, that of a man conquering himself. His notions of warfare put forth in sonnets 1 through 21 are all wrong. He cannot conquer the lady. Conceivably he could conquer the lady's body, but he could not "conquer" the lady into any relationship of true love, for conquest implies unwilling submission, and true love, Spenser tells us, is a matter of "mutuall good will" (65). The notion of conquest is foreign to Spenser's concept of love. Rather the lover must by his constancy prove himself worthy to accept the gift of her love. Unbeknown to the lover this is what has been happening in sonnets 22 through 60.

During the first stage of his education, the poet's love is in an intermediary stage between sense and spirit and is centered in the heart, which according to Thomas Wright is the "corporal organ and instrument" of the passions: "the very seate of the Passions, is the heart, both of men and beasts."[8] The activities of the lover are like those of the ladies in the parlor of Alma's castle (*FQ* II.ix.34–35). Not concupiscible, the poet's love is nevertheless attached to the mortal Elizabeth. Yet, as Pietro Bembo tells us, "souls being immortal, can never be contented with a mortal thing."[9] The passion for earthly beauty must be elevated to a passion for the spiritual source of beauty:

That with the glorie of so goodly sight,
The hearts of men, which fondly here admyre
Faire seeming shewes, and feed on vaine delight,
Transported with celestiall desyre
Of those faire formes, may lift themselues vp hyer,
And learne to loue with zealous humble dewty
Th'eternall fountaine of that heauenly beauty.

(*HHB* 15–21)

In the medical sonnet (50), observing that the heart is "of all the bodie chiefe," the lover mistakenly insists that the lady should "seeke first to appease / the inward langour of my wounded hart." Bright and Burton prescribe instead scriptural readings or physical exercise as cures of love melancholy.[10] The lover must learn to control rather than appease his heart and so raise love above the level of the sensitive soul. This was indicated as early as 22, when the lover recognized that "her temple fayre is built within my mind," and he vowed that he would build her there an altar, "and on the same my hart will sacrifise." As Lever perceptively commented in *The Elizabethan Love Sonnet,* "the heart is to be led like a sacrificial victim, into the temple of the mind, and burned there."[11] The lover is led to this sacrifice of the lower soul by the lady's example of chaste and steadfast love; by Christ's example of perfect love, which he only gradually learns to relate to his own love; and, in the final group of sonnets, by temporary physical separation from his beloved.

He suffers in this first stage of his courtship largely because he has not yet learned to love on the spiritual plane. He is concerned chiefly with himself, with "th'importune suit of my desire" (23). This becomes more important to him than his civic and poetic responsibilities: "Great wrong I doe, I can it not deny, / to that most sacred Empress my dear dred, / not finishing her Queene of Faery" (33). His "importune suit" even distorts his spiritual values: "Whom then shall I or heauen or her obay? / . . . my lower heauen, so it perforce must bee" (46). His love is a Pandora's box (24) of stormy passions (e.g., 56), complaints (32), pleas (55), bribes (27), disguises (54), and threats (36), rather than a "sacred bowre" of "simple truth and mutuall good will" where "pride dare not approach" (65).

Sonnets 58 and 59, two of the most beautiful of *Amoretti,* distinguish between the lover's pride and the lady's self-assurance. The curious line "By her that is most assured to her selfe," placed above sonnet 58, was explained some years ago by the suggestion that "by" here means "concerning" in accord with one sixteenth-century usage.[12] In the context of the dramatized education of the lover this explanation is unnecessary. "By her" means just what we would normally take it to mean: that these are the words of the lady. They explain how he has erred and what he should have learned in this preparatory period. His efforts to conquer the lady by his wiles and pleadings and rebukes have been acts of pride. "Ne none so rich or wise, so strong or fayre, / but fayleth trusting on his owne assurance," she tells him in 58. This is the lesson which the lady has taught him, the insight which he has had to gain from his period of trial in order to be ready to receive "the lesson which the Lord vs taught" (68). The lover's response in the next sonnet, 59, conveys the recognition that her self-assurance, in contrast, has not been "stubborn pride," as he had insisted all along, but the wisdom of one who "Keepes her course aright," and ultimately the source of his own happiness. The second and most important step in the education of the lover is the revelation of perfect, selfless love through the celebration in Holy Week of Christ's passion. A considerable period of preparation was necessary before the lover was ready for this revelation. It is here that the religious framework of the sequence begins to become apparent and that we look back and see that this period was Lent. The lover had to demonstrate loyalty, steadfastness, desire to be united with the lady, faith that he could attain his goal, and, above all, a love untainted by selfishness or pride. These are of course also the qualities required of the Christian in the quest for spiritual union with God.

The guide in the second part of the lover's education is Christ, who provides the preeminent example of love, as Spenser declares in his resurrection hymn, sonnet 68:

> And that thy loue we weighing worthily,
>   may likewise loue thee for the same againe:
>   and for thy sake that all lyke deare didst buy,
>   with loue may one another entertayne.

In the final couplet, addressed to the lady, the lover draws the moral conclusion:

> So let vs loue, deare loue, lyke as we ought,
>   loue is the lesson which the Lord vs taught.

True love is not a matter of wooing and winning, of courtship and conquest; it is ultimately a gift of grace, sonnets 67 and 68 suggest. The bond of love, as Spenser conceives it, depends on three things: the proven worth of the lover, the freely-willed submission of the lady, and the grace of God. The lover is granted the latter two at the culmination of his period of trial in the Holy Week sonnets 62 through 68.

The irony of the first part of the sequence resulted from the lover's failure to recognize that he must change before the lady could relent. The turning point, as A. Kent Hieatt has suggested, is sonnet 62.[13] Here the lover begins to show awareness of his own shortcomings. He has felt himself more sinned against than sinning in his furious warnings to the lady not to spill his "guiltlesse blood" in 38. In 24 he had declared "that she to wicked men a scourge should bee, / for all their faults with which *they* did offend" (italics mine). Here he includes himself among the offenders as he resolves to "fly the faults with which *we* did offend" (italics mine). He now resolves to "change eeke our mynds and former liues amend, / the old yeares sinnes forepast let vs eschew." Indeed, the third quatrain of sonnet 62 suggests that the new year's joy promised in the sonnet is contingent upon the act of penitence that he describes in the second quatrain.

In sonnet 62 for the first time in *Amoretti* he uses "we" to refer to himself and the lady. "Fayre proud" is in process of becoming "fayre loue." Heretofore he has carefully guarded his ego, his separate identity: "Fondnesse it were for any being free, / to couet fetters, though they golden bee," he had declared in sonnet 37. By sonnet 65 he has learned to value a new liberty within captivity, as he urges the lady to "make him bond that bondage earst did fly." The theme is carried one step further in the Easter sonnet to Christ, who did "bring away / captiuity thence captiue vs to win."

The third step in the education of the lover is separation from the beloved. On the symbolic level the Christian is separated from the physical presence of Jesus after the ascension and is left awaiting reunion with God. On the narrative-historical level we may assume that there was a temporary separation prior to the marriage celebrated in *Epithalamion*. On both levels the effect of this separation is a raising of the lover's interest and desire to a spiritual level. This provides him with the right focus as he awaits reunion with his God and provides the basis for a higher bond of love between the lover and his bride here on earth.

During the third part of his education, which occurs in the last twenty-one sonnets, he is deprived of the physical presence of his guides. He must now make the final transfer of his affections to the spiritual level in preparation for reunion with his God and with his lady. In the context of Spenser's modified Neoplatonism, this concentration on the spiritual is the closest man can come in this life to God and to true love.

In relation to the dramatic structure of the sequence this third section is something of an appendix, starting a new drama, beginning a new problem. On the symbolic level the progression from revelation to anticipation of fulfillment is a logical one; it defines the limits of human experience according to Spenser's religious values. Dramatically, however, the problem of the first sixty sonnets is resolved in the Holy Week sonnets. The irony that pervades the first sixty sonnets is dispelled as the lover begins to sense the deeper truth that is then finally revealed to him in 68. In the final group of sonnets he becomes an ironic figure again, as he faces new problems without really understanding them, though of course he is much advanced over his previous state.

The stages of development in the last twenty-one sonnets are distinct. The first seven sonnets form a group, of which the first three celebrate the new stage of their relationship and the next four show that the lover has not yet fully assimilated the lesson of the Holy Week sonnets. In all of these first seven sonnets the poet-lover is concerned with the enjoyment of love "here on earth" (72). His education is clearly not yet complete. In 69, though he praises her "honor, loue and chastity" he celebrates his "conquest," and refers to her as his "glorious spoile." The second spring sonnet, 70, is a simple *carpe diem* poem concerned with earthly time and earthly pleasures. In 71, adapting the spider image of 23, he gloats that she has fallen captive in his "cunning snare." Sonnet 72 provides the key to this series of six sonnets:

> Oft when my spirit doth spred her bolder winges,
>   In mind to mount vp to the purest sky:
>   it down is weighed with thoght of earthly things
>   and clogd with burden of mortality.
> Where when that souerayne beauty it doth spy,
>   resembling heauens glory in her light:
>   drawne with sweet pleasures bayt, it back doth fly,
>   and vnto heauen forgets her former flight.

Perhaps understandably, in light of recent events of the courtship, the lover is preoccupied with earthly things. The concreteness of these "here on earth" sonnets culminates in the introduction in 74 of his three Elizabeths: mother, queen, and future wife. In the following sonnet that magical name is washed away in the sand, demonstrating the vanity of the things of this earth, our names and our bodies and the little loves attached to them. Poetry, as the lover protests at the end of the sonnet, can provide permanence and fame that can escape death. But even this is a fame of body and name, a fame among things here on earth:

Vayne man, sayd she, that doest in vaine assay,
a mortall thing so to immortalize,
for I myselfe shall lyke to this decay,
and eek my name bee wyped out lykewize.

This event seems to signal a shift in the lover's relationship to the lady. Hereafter there is a change in the lover's attitude, characterized by a clear distinction between himself and his thoughts, and between the lady and her image or idea. Sonnets 76 and 77 are perhaps the most sensuous of *Amoretti,* but it is only his thoughts which enjoy the sensuous delights:

And twixt her paps like early fruit in May,
whose haruest seemd to hasten now apace:
they loosely did their wanton winges display,
and there to rest themselues did boldly place.
Sweet thoughts I enuy your so happy rest,
which oft I wisht, yet neuer was so blest.

The couplet makes clear the distinction between himself and his thoughts. Sonnet 77 exploits the same principle, concluding: "Her brest that table was so richly spredd, / my *thoughts* the guests, which would thereon have fedd" (italics mine).

The sense of presence, confidence, and concrete materiality that pervades the sonnets immediately following the Easter victory has given way to a sense of separation and the lover's almost pathetic awareness of being on his own: "Lackyng my loue I go from place to place, / lyke a young fawne that late hath lost the hynd" (88). The lover becomes like a child left in the house alone. First he indulges his fantasies, as we have seen in 76 and 77. Later, he will fall prey to his fears (84 through 86). At the end these emotions will have been concentrated in the earnest desire for the return of those who love him, and we leave him anxiously waiting (87 through 89).

The process is an extension of his education in love. He notes that her "ymage yet I carry fresh in mynd" (78), and in her absence he learns to direct his thoughts not to her physical being but to this image, to the spiritual being of the lady: "Cease then myne eyes, to seeke her selfe to see, and let my thoughts behold her selfe in mee" (77). He shows a still clearer awareness of the idea in 79 as he distinguishes from her physical beauty the lady's "gentle wit, / and vertuous mind":

Only that is permanent and free
from frayle corruption, that doth flesh ensew.

> That is true beautye: that doth argue you
> to be diuine and borne of heauenly seed:
> deriu'd from that fayre Spirit, from whom al true
> and perfect beauty did at first proceed.

This is true beauty, and love of this is true love, in contrast to our earthly *amoretti,* because it partakes of God's love. Ultimately it is love of God, of "that Fayre Spirit, from whom al true / and perfect beauty did at first proceed."

If we compare sonnet 80 with 33, the two sonnets in which the poet mentions his work on *The Faerie Queene,* we find that his new love has wrought significant change in him and in his attitude toward his work. In 33 he renounces the "tedious toyle" because of "a proud loue, that doth my spirite spoyle." In 80 he declares that he "stoutly will that second worke assoyle," refreshed, not spoiled, by his praise of the lady," the contemplation of whose heauenly hew, / my spirit to an higher pitch will rayse."

Sonnets 80 through 82 are the culmination of the theme of self-expression. The poet has felt unable all along to express the strong feeling in his heart. In sonnet 3, considering the beauty of the lady, he was tongue-tied: "So when my toung would speak her praises dew, / it stopped is with *thoughts* astonishment" (italics mine). Thought was stunned and stopped because the heart had gained control. In 81, praising "her gentle spright," he concludes: "The rest be works of nature's wonderment, / but this the worke of *harts* astonishment" (italics mine). His mind has regained control, his love has been raised above the level of the sensitive soul, and he can speak again: In 82 he declares that the "lofty argument" of his poems in her praise "vplifting me, / shall lift you vp vnto an high degree."

The repetition of sonnet 35 as 83 is not a mistake, as many have supposed, but a highly expressive device reflecting Spenser's emphasis on the spiritual essence behind the physical presence.[14] It is a function of the dramatic irony of the sequence that the same words may be wrong in one place and right in another depending on the spirit in which they are spoken, the meaning that the lover attaches to them. That meaning is revealed in the dramatic context. At 35 the poet declared his preoccupation with the lady to the exclusion of all other aspects of earthly creation. This reflected the imbalance of his soul, his spoiled spirit, and in fact it occurs just two sonnets after his renunciation of his responsibilities in 33. At 83 the poet declares his preoccupation with spiritual rather than physical beauty; this reflects the elevation of his love and the restoration of balance to his soul. It occurs three sonnets after his rededication to his work, after the physical departure of the lady, and after a series of sonnets in which he has refocused his vision on the spiritual rather than the physical presence of the lady.

A final trial awaits the lover still. Jealousy, envy, and spite now enter to plague him in sonnets 84, 85, and 86. An understanding of the dramatic nature of *Amoretti* is particularly important for an appreciation of these three sonnets, because here perhaps more than anywhere else in the sequence it is not so much what the lover says but how he says it that conveys the primary meaning. These sonnets may be addressed to another man or other men whose intrusion into the relationship he fears, but they may also be addressed to his own heart, from which he fears a renewed outbreak of passion that might intrude in the spiritual peace that he has attained.

Sonnet 84 depicts the lover's reaction to the idea of an intrusion into his relationship with the lady. His reaction shows reverential love: He will permit only "pure affections" and "modest thoughts" to approach her, and he does not want her disturbed with word of his "sad plights," though earlier he had been very eager to tell her about them. The most important aspect of his reaction is fear of intrusion. Left on his own he is particularly vulnerable to fear, which visits us most when we are alone.

In 85 he seems to think the world criticizes his praise of the lady. His reaction here, as in 84, shows a certain emotional agitation. He is on the defensive, but this is not a reasoned defense. He begins, for example, by name-calling: the world "cannot deeme of worthy things"; it is like the "Cuckow" that chatters witlessly in order to obscure the sweeter notes of the Mavis (thrush). We will recall that it was he himself who invoked the Cuckow to call his lady to love in the first spring sonnet, 19. What this sonnet shows is not any evidence of real intrusion or envy, but his fear of these things.

In 86 the poet, who earlier had himself bitterly and forcefully rebuked the lady, reacts to the insult of some "venemous toung." His reaction ("Let all the plagues and horrid paines of hell / vpon thee fall") is itself venomous to say the least. The emotional agitation suggested vaguely in 84 and more clearly in 85 has reached a high pitch in 86. It is as though the lover is being pursued by the furies whom he mentions at the beginning of 86.

The emotionalism of these sonnets gives way in the final sonnets to a mood of pensive anticipation. All his interest and energy has now effectively been transferred to a spiritual love, of which the object has temporarily been removed beyond the realm of his present experience. The result is the death of this life, which can no longer satisfy him: "Ne ioy of ought that vnder heauen doth houe, / can comfort me." Only reunion with his love can bring life to his living death: "Dark is my day, whyles her fayre light I mis, / and dead my life that wants such liuely blis."

I have tried to analyze *Amoretti* as a sequence of sonnets dramatizing the poet's experience in love. The plot of the drama is the personal development of the lover as reflected in the poems. The irony of the drama results from his inability to relate his personal experience to the larger context of religious values embodied in the symbolic framework that the reader can see, but that the lover, of course, cannot.

This approach to *Amoretti* is, I believe, a middle way, synthesizing the insights of those who see the sequence in a representational, historical context and those who sometimes convey the impression that it exists in a wholly abstract context of religious and calendrical symbolism. *Amoretti* is both a simple love story expressing common human experience and an abstract composition delineating Spenser's Christian concept of universal love. Between the lines of the lover's outcries we read the simple story, and through the symbolic framework we learn what it means, but the central drama is within the lover himself. It is not that of winning the lady, nor yet that of Christ's passion and resurrection, but that of the lover's progress toward a higher love. The human and the divine are the basic and essential levels of meaning, but it is the progress that man can make toward the divine that forms a bridge between the two and ties them together in a bond that has practical moral meaning for the reader. The drama of the lover's experience in gaining insight into the meaning of love is the aesthetic center of the work, uniting commonplace story and cosmic symbolism.

Auburn University

Notes

1. Josephine Waters Bennett, "Spenser's *Amoretti* LXII and the Date of the New Year," *Ren Q* 26 (1973), 433–36. Cf. my "The Unity of Spenser's *Amoretti*," in *Silent Poetry,* ed. Alastair Fowler (London: Routledge & Kegan Paul, 1970), pp. 153–69.

2. A. Kent Hieatt, "A Numerical Key for Spenser's *Amoretti* and Guyon in the House of Mammon," *YES* 3 (1973), 14–27; Alastair Fowler, *Triumphal Forms: Structural Patterns in Elizabethan Poetry* (Cambridge: Cambridge University Press, 1970), pp. 180–82.

3. Others who have referred to dramatic elements in *Amoretti* in recent years include Louis L. Martz, "The *Amoretti*: 'Most Goodly Temperature'," in *Form and Convention in the Poetry of Edmund Spenser,* ed. William Nelson (New York: Columbia University Press, 1961), pp. 146–68; also, Waldo F. McNeir, "An Apology for Spenser's *Amoretti*," *Die Neueren Sprachen* 14 (1965), 1–9.

4. See Rudolf Gottfried, "Autobiography and Art: An Elizabethan Borderland," in *Literary Criticism and Historical Understanding,* ed. Phillip Damon (New York: Columbia University Press, 1967), pp. 109–34.

5. G. K. Hunter, " 'Unity' and Numbers in Spenser's *Amoretti,*" *YES* 5 (1975), 39–45.

6. Professor McNeir has noted this similarity in "An Apology," p. 9.

7. Robert G. Benson draws a slightly different comparison in his excellent "Elizabeth as Beatrice: A Reading of Spenser's *Amoretti,*" *South Central Bulletin* 32 (1972), 184–88.

8. *The Passions of the Minde in Generall* (1604; rpt. Urbana; University of Illinois Press, 1971), p. 33.

9. *Gli Asolani* (1505), trans. Rudolf B. Gottfried (Bloomington: Indiana University Press, 1954), p. 183.

10. Timothy Bright, *A Treatise of Melancholie* (1586; rpt. Amsterdam: Theatrum Orbis Terrarum, 1969), p. 255; Robert Burton, *The Anatomy of Melancholy* (1621; rpt. Amsterdam: Theatrum Orbis Terrarum, 1971), p. 626–62.

11. J. W. Lever, *The Elizabethan Love Sonnet* (1956; rpt. London: Methuen, 1966), p. 107.

12. Martz, "The *Amoretti,*" p. 163. Martz attributes the suggestion to William Nelson and Leicester Bradner.

13. Hieatt, "A Numerical Key," p. 19. It is interesting to note that if we count sonnets 62 through 89 plus the nine separately spaced anacreontic stanzas plus the twenty-four stanzas of *Epithalamion,* we find that 62 marks precisely the beginning of the second half of the *Amoretti-Epithalamion* volume. Alastair Fowler, *Triumphal Forms,* p. 181, suggests another possible array, noting that the identical sonnets, 35 and 83, are centrally placed in the *Amoretti-Epithalamion* volume if we count each of the four capitalized anacreontic stanzas as one unit. Perhaps it is a case of multiple ordering.

14. See Fowler, *Triumphal Forms,* p. 181. Also, James Nohrnberg, *The Analogy of the Faerie Queene* (Princeton: Princeton University Press, 1976), pp. 68–71. Nohrnberg notes several pairs of related sonnets whose placement he feels may be significant: the New Year's sonnets 4 and 62; the angel sonnets 17 and 61; the spring sonnets 19 and 70; the Lent-Easter sonnets 22 and 68; the spider sonnets 23 and 71; the *Faerie Queene* sonnets 23 and 80; the repeated sonnet 35 and 83; and the idea sonnets 45 and 88. To this list of related sonnets might be added the two smile sonnets 39 and 40 and the two sonnets of dereliction 33 and 46, all symmetrically placed between 22 and 57; the two floral blazons 26 and 64, symmetrically placed between 22 and 68; and the five "thou" sonnets, 5, 22, 39, 68, and 86.

MARGRETA DE GRAZIA

Babbling Will in
Shake-speares Sonnets 127 to 154

*T*HE OXFORD ENGLISH DICTIONARY suggests that *babble* is
onomatopoetic in origin, an imitation of baby talk, of the early labials infants make. *Ba-Ba* became *babble* in order to denote more sophisticated
nonsense syllables. For Elizabethans, however, the word stemmed from a
more grown-up endeavor—the attempt to build a proud tower reaching
unto heaven, a presumption God penalized by confusing tongues.[1] *Babble*
evolved from *Babel,* a cognate of *Babylon* which patristic tradition traced to
the Hebrew *balal,* "to confound."[2] If the word applied with particular apt-
ness to the prattle of infants, it would have been because babbling was, after Babel, the native tongue of all speakers.

This history of *babble,* like most Elizabethan etymologies, tells more
about the beliefs of those who accepted it than about linguistic origins.
Babble was linguistically related to the tower of that name because it was
related causally. Babble was the result of the presumptuous building of
Babel. Because of this proud act, men had difficulty communicating not
only when speaking different languages but even when sharing the same
tongue.

What the etymology does not reveal is that, for Elizabethans, language
began to deteriorate some two millennia before Babel. Adam, according to
them, did share the language of God, traditionally held to be Hebrew. He
demonstrated his mastery of this language when he assigned names to the
animals exactly corresponding to their natures—an accomplishment Genesis records. But that was in the beginning. Adam and Eve, once they lis-
tened to a voice other than God's and modified their own accordingly, lost
access to this divine tongue. Fallen Adam and his descendants still possessed its outward form, but no longer understood the truths inhering in
its vocabulary and syntax. The Fall, therefore, was not only moral and intellectual; it was linguistic. Adam's sin of pride set off a process of linguistic deterioration to which succeeding generations, the likes of Cain, no
doubt contributed. Babel brought this process to a climax. Because of the
builders' pride, their desire to make a name for themselves by reaching unto
heaven, language lost its superficial as well as its essential relation to the

divine original. From this point on, outwardly and inwardly, a man's words clashed not only with the Creator's Word and the truth of Creation, but with the words of other men.[3]

Like so many Old Testament events, Babel could recur in the life of every Christian. Pride, assertions of will, could break down language just as it did for Adam and Eve, Nimrod and the builders. The explanation implicit in the *Babel-babble* etymology was not restricted to history, to what had once happened on a plain in the land of Shinar. "What may a man then say of the most part of mens discourses, and deuices, who liue in these dayes?" asks one of Shakespeare's contemporaries. "Truely, that it is but babble, that is Babel."[4] Built in the word was a perpetual reminder that the desire in any man's heart to build proud Babels—architectural, intellectual, or any other—generates linguistic confusion.

If, for Elizabethans, pride confused the language of biblical and contemporary speakers, would it not have affected fictional speakers in the same way? In Elizabethan literature, Babel's cause of pride may entail its effect of broken communication. In Elizabethan sonnet sequences, the cause looms large. The sonnet form itself and its conventional motive stress the relation of sonnets to pride or willfulness, to inordinate self-esteem.

A sonnet or *sonetto* is a diminuitive sound, *sono* or *suono*. *Sono* is also the first person of the verb *essere,* to be. Petrarch reminds readers of the origin of *sonetto* by rhyming its two roots in the first quatrain of the first sonnet of his *Canzoniere*. The derivation suggests that the typical sonnet sound might be self-assertion, variations on the theme "I am." Sonnets are addressed to and frequently named after the beloved, but the beloved is typically made in the image of the lover. The author's name can figure as significantly as, if less prominently than, the beloved's. Petrarch mythologized around the rock and arc embedded in his name; Sidney converted himself (if in name only) from Philip, "horse-lover," to Astrophil, "star-lover"; Greville decoded his name, "Greiv-ill," to communicate his despair; and even as minor a sonneteer as Alexander Craig plays on his name's craggy designation and assigns it to his mistress Lithocardia (fortunately not recognizing his most nominal kinship with Petrarch). Furthermore, a sonneteer composes sonnets to persuade his mistress to comply with his will or desire. This is true whether his sonnets take the form of flattery, insult, prayer, or anecdote. A sonneteer designs sonnets to advance his designs, to evoke from his beloved a positive response in word and deed.

Shakespeare's sonnets fall readily into this context of proud verse. Both the sonnets to the fair youth and those to the dark mistress originate in pride—artistic pride in the one, sexual in the other. And the pride in both cases manifests itself in forms recalling Babel's tower.[5] In the fair youth sonnets, the poet considers his sonnets poetic edifices constructed to out-last architectural monuments, towers, and pyramids built of marble, gold, and brass. By such structures, he would make an eternal name for himself or his surrogate beloved. In the dark mistress sonnets, the poet's ambi-tions are less grandiose although perhaps no less Babylonic in Elizabethan eyes. Fulke Greville identifies his lover's rising urge with the builders' pre-sumption in sonnet 39 of *Caelica.* His brazen attempt to "embabylon" himself in the venereal skies of his mistress Caelica incurs the confusion of language. Greville's convoluted and opaque profane sonnets could be seen as the outcome of such high hopes. Shakespeare's sonnets, issuing from the poet's overweening desire to extend himself in time and space, could be plagued by the same linguistic confusion. Francis Davison's lover in *A Poetical Rhapsody* is the victim of such a fate: "That like th'accursed Rabble / That built the Towre of Babble, / My wit mistaketh, / And unto nothing a right name doth giue."[6]

The title of Shakespeare's sonnets as it appears on the frontispiece of the 1609 Quarto—*Shake-speares Sonnets*—makes it possible to extend the com-parison between Babel-builders and sonnet-makers. The compound sur-name touches on both aspects of the self-elevating enterprise.[7] The sonnets concern the proud shaking of two spears, two sharp instruments. The shaking of one—a stylus's point—forms script. The shaking of the other—a phallic blade—makes love. The to-and-fro movement of the liter-ary spear is the subject of the sonnets to the fair man. The up-and-down motion of the sexual spear, the "inflaming" brand of 153 and 154, is the subject of those to the dark woman. That everyone knows that the son-nets are also William's sonnets (Will-I-am's I-ams) should further heighten expectations of hearing Babylonic overtones, especially in son-nets that begin when someone by the name of Will renominates black "fair."

I

Will begins his sonnets to or about his dark mistress by declaring that a general linguistic revolution has set off a personal romantic one. Because in the current idiom "black" has usurped and banished "fair," Will over-throws romantic convention and takes on a suitably dark mistress: "But now is blacke beauties successiue heire"; "Therefore my Mistersse eyes are Rauen blacke."[8] According to his manifesto, Will's loving of black is merely a concession to the times. Radical innovations in language have dictated his amorous uprising.

Subsequent sonnets cast doubt on this propagandist justification. Is the ideal of black as universal as he claims, "euery toung saies beauty should looke so"? Others contest his claim in 131 and flatly deny it in 148. And is it, as he argues, current phraseology that determines his amatory bent? Sonnets 132 and 140 indicate that it is the other way around. If his mistress would satisfy his passion in 132, he will "sweare beauty her selfe is blacke." Were she, on the other hand, to betray him in 140, he would retaliate by speaking "ill." Sonnet 138 illustrates the true causal relation between Will's desire and language. Because he wants to lie with his mistress, Will tells and credits lies. His purpose in calling black "fair" is to promote and ratify his illicit desire.

The desire prompting Will to speak has one object—to evoke his mistress's sexual pity, her "deep kindnesse." Her black eyes are compelling from start to finish because their funereal hue (127, 132) betokens a readiness to mourn, to be sexually compassionate. He urges her other parts to emulate their "pretty ruth" ("sute thy pitty like in euery part" [132]), specifically the part to which his looks are "ouer-partiall" (137). He covets her glances because they intimate her "cunning" (139);[9] dark glances promise acts of darkness ("In nothing art thou blacke saue in thy deeds" [131]); occular black circles project the circle of her genital "naught" or "nothing" that is nothing like the bright, wholesome circle of the sun.[10] It is on this circular hole, "the baye where all men ride" (137), that his eyes, like hers, are "anchord." This visual fixation accounts for his various disorders of vision (137, 148, 149), for according to sixteenth-century physiology, prolonged focus on "things" venereal dims the eyesight.[11] Will's final reference in the singular to the long-standing object of his desire ("my mistres eye" [153]) makes it clearer still that it is the single black hole or "naught" that has always been the target of his digital "one" (136) as well as his sole objective in speaking.[12]

By calling black "fair," Will flatters his black mistress, thereby warming her to him. In 152, he admits that he has misused language to "inlighten" her. He hopes to brighten her with his neologisms, "to put faire truth vpon so foule a face" (137) just as the glamorizing hands of 127 were "Fairing the foule" with cosmetics. He performs this enlightening process when he transforms her drab traits to "rare" in 130, her blackness to beauty in 132, "the very refuse" of her deeds to "strength and warrantise of skill" in 150. Such transformations work to "inlighten" her in another sense. They would make her sexually light or lighter, though she is already the commodious "baye where all men ride" (137).[13]

By calling black "fair," he would flatter himself also, by idealizing his devotion to her. His forward reassignment of names enables him to ennoble his adulterous passion with "deepe othes of thy deepe kindnesse / Othes of thy loue, thy truth, thy constancie" (152). He has pressed into self-serving service not the word *fair* alone, but its synonyms—beautiful, good, and true. One inversion upheaves the aesthetic, moral, and epistemological foundation of language. On any of these displaced levels, Will can justify his desire: judge her black the "fairest" (131), classify her "common place" his "seuerall plot" (137), honor her as "made of truth" (138), dismiss facts of her promiscuity as slander (131, 140), and write off his depravity as "no want of conscience" (151).

Ironically, Will's specialized vocabulary does not promote communication, at least not the kind he values. Only in 138 where flattering lies lead to horizontal lying could his speech be considered effective. Typically, language sets Will and his mistress apart: They speak to quarrel, accuse, and insult (134, 139, 140, 142, 149). His words, as he admits, have been "vainely exprest" (147) in three senses. Stimulated by sexual pride or vanity, he has addressed himself to her *vanus* or "naught" and to no purpose, in vain. Will, failing to "inlighten" will and its object, darkens or obscures language. His speech takes on the denigrating properties of will. "Worship of [her] defect" (149) makes his language defective.

Will's use of his own name illustrates the decline. He expands and confuses its reference both as a proper and a common noun so that it comes to mean nothing, the "nothing" he solicits in 136. As a proper name, *Will* names Will anonymous rather than singling him out from other individuals. His own name becomes a blanket designation for the innumerable applicants for admission to her "treasure" "full with wils" (136). As a common noun, *will* no longer refers to the power of choice that distinguishes man from beast. Instead it designates the involuntary appetite that he shares with them. He thus casts off the name marking his place both in society and creation in order to assume one that will introduce him "untold" to his mistress's "common place" (137). He goes further still when he asks to be called not by name but by "nothing" (136). For by that synecdochic cancellation, he obliterates such distinctions as subject-object, male-female, name-being, one-none. Names preserve distinctions that expressions of indiscriminate or blind desire could better do without.

Rhetoric and syntax no less than vocabulary betray Will's yearning for "naught" or "naughtiness."[14] Privative tropes and negative constructions modify his destructive desire. Lack of freedom (slavery, imprisonment), dearth of funds (bankruptcy, indebtedness, poverty), physical defects (blindness, wounds, pain, sickness, death) best denote his depraved experience in which only will exists in abundance ("Will too boote, and Will in ouer-plus" [135]) and that commodity is always reducible to "nothing," as in 136. Negative descriptions are paralleled by a syntax of negation. Affirmations are made through denial, from the opening "blacke was not counted faire" to the concluding "water cooles not loue." He compares his mistress to what she does not resemble ("My Mistres eyes are nothing like the Sunne" [130]) and describes his love for her with a catalogue of senses and faculties that do not love her ("I doe not loue thee with mine eyes" [141]). He and his mistress address one another with negative constructions. She says "I hate . . . not you" (145) and accuses him of saying "I loue thee not" (149). He puts requests to her negatively: "O Call not me to iustifie the wrong" (139), "Let no vnkinde, no faire beseechers kill" (135), "vrge not my amisse" (151). Descriptions of his own state take the negative form: "am I not free" (134), eyes with "no correspondence with true sight" (148), "No want of conscience" (151). The threefold pun of "periurde eye" (152) contains lust's cancellation of Will's power to see, to affirm, and to exist. Because forsworn, his "aye" approximates denial, his "eye" denotes blindness, and his "I" suggests nonbeing.

Will's desire so thoroughly infiltrates language that acts of speech conflate with acts of love. "Lying" denotes both the satisfaction of Will's appetite and the kind of speech that would attain it: "I lye with her, and shee with me" (138).[15] Verbal license or "misuse" is prerequisite to sexual liberties or "misuse" (152). Tongues and pens are simultaneously instruments of verbal and sexual expression. Another organ besides that of speech is aroused by his mistress' blackness ("euery toung saies beauty should looke so" [127]), just as another inscribing tool besides a pen writes *en gros* (133) in Will's place ("He learnd but suretie-like to write for me" [134]). Lips at once make and break, seal and profane both verbal contracts (with oaths) and sexual contact (with kisses)—"those lips of thine, / That haue prophan'd their scarlet ornaments, / And seald false bonds of loue" (142). The same gesture would quiet both types of activity. Would she kindly "turne back" in true venereal fashion, she would "still" both the noise of his "loude crying" and the motion of the "discontented" part (143).[16]

Language, once appropriated by desire, loses its proper association with reason.[17] Desire's observations contradict reason's assessment, giving rise to paradox. In 138, Will says of his mistress, "I do beleeue her though I know she lyes," taxing his affirmation with the conflicting claims of desire ("I do beleeue her") and of reason ("I know she lyes"). The same conflict recurs when he records that his eyes "know what beautie is" yet take it "the worst to be" (137) and when he notes "the very refuse of thy deeds" yet esteems it as "strength and warrantise of skill" (150). When reason, "angry that his prescriptions are not kept" (147), retires from the fray, language disintegrates altogether: "My thoughts and my discourse as mad mens are, / At randon from the truth vainely exprest." His mad formulations verge on nonsense, the verbal counterpart to his moral "naughtiness."

With reason or *logos* gone or on the wane, Will's language cannot be logical. Contradictions crop up within single sonnets. In 139, for example, he begins with the plea, "O Call not me to iustifie the wrong" and continues with, "Let me excuse thee." From sonnet to sonnet, too, he contradicts himself. He announces, "My Mistres eyes are nothing like the Sunne" in 130 but compares them to it in 132. He bids his mistress, "Tell me thou lou'st else-where" in 139 and in the next sonnet forbids her to mention her infidelities. The law of noncontradiction, the basis of Aristotelean logic, clearly is not operating in Will's dialectic.

Will commits one logical fallacy, *repetitio principii,* with particular frequency. Throughout the sonnets, he begs the quesion, presenting proofs as questionable as what he intends to prove by them. Thomas Wilson, in his widely read *Rule of Reason,* calls this fallacy the "Cuckowes song" because "the same is repeated that was spoken before."[18] He finds it exceptionally common among "self-willed folke that followe lust" and gives an example: "beyng asked why thei will dooe this and that thei aunswere streight, Marie because I will dooe it." The generalization applies squarely to Will's reasoning: The proof of his conclusions typically lies in his own will.[19] His reasoning matches that of Wilson's exemplary lover even down to his expletive, for Will swears aplenty as if to back his assertions with more than his impotent say-so.

The syllogistically structured 127 introduces us to Will's habitual form of sophistry. There he attempts to demonstrate that the reason for his will lies in language and circumstance. As we have seen, however, the explanation lies in his will alone. Other sonnets follow the same captious circularity. In 131, he groans a thousand times to prove his contention that his mistress has "the power to make loue grone." In 138, as if to play on his personalized fallacy, he explains that he and his mistress lie to one another in order to lie together. In the more complex example of 151, Will sets out to prove his mistress the source of his conscience (his firsthand knowledge of sin), warning that he will "guilty of my faults thy sweet selfe proue." He begins with the universal premise that "conscience is borne of loue," proceeds to identify her as "loue," and then concludes that conscience is born of her, that is, she is guilty of his faults. He proves her "loue," however, by showing that conscience is born of her (she provokes his incriminatory risings and fallings). In other words, she is "loue" because she gives birth to conscience, yet she gives birth to conscience because she is "loue." His conclusion merely repeats one of his premises, and the argument goes nowhere.

Again and again Will's logic tautologically turns on itself. His attempts to find reasons or arguments in defense of his faults rebound, invariably pointing back to his own will as cause. Like flesh that requires "No farther reason" than that it "may, / Triumph in loue" (151), Will tries to make appetite a reason unto itself. But there are no valid reasons to rationalize his risings.[20] There are no probable proofs to support his sexual proving, the "blisse in proofe" (129) he longs to demonstrate in "things of great receit" (139)

In sonnets 127 to 154, language is will's mouthpiece. Like "neglected child" pursuing distracted mother in 143, Will cries out for what he wants. The sonnets verbalize groans like the thousand he gives forth in evidence of his love's power in 131. Love of black colors or discolors each outburst in form as well as subject. Will's rhetoric, grammar, and logic all take on the negative predicates of his shady passion.

II

It is as if a new and different Will were speaking in 146. This sonnet does, it is true, describe the soul's pathetic condition by privative states— the poverty, starvation, and death to which fleshly urges have reduced it. But the sestet impels the soul through penance to convert these to the positive terms of affluence, aggrandizement, the death of death that promises life. Similarly, negation functions to affirm: "death once dead, ther's no more dying then." "No" denies the negative substantive "death" in order to affirm its opposite. Distinguishing this sonnet still more is its irrefutable logic: What is sinful or ephemeral should be spurned; the demands of the flesh are sinful and ephemeral; therefore, these demands should be spurned (and spiritual ones embraced instead). No voice opposes the reasonable exhortation and sets up paradox. Echoes of the Pauline mystery support it: "So shalt thou feed on death, that feeds on men, / And death once dead, ther's no more dying then."

Sonnet 146 gives voice to a new will or desire, one whose object is God rather than a black mistress. It expresses the need for spiritual reconciliation rather than carnal union. It is this new concern for divine not profane mercy, for charity not lust, that straightens out Will's diction.[21] Thomas Wilson recommends the same remedy to those afflicted by Will's habitual logical fallacy. If speakers would consign their wills to God, the fallacy would correct itself: "God graunt all our willes, to stande euer with his will, and then I doubte not but this harme shall with ease be auoided."[22]

The substitution of God's charity for will's lust is also the traditional antidote to Babel. Writers from the Middle Ages to the sixteenth century saw Pentecost, the event that secured the tansmission of God's Word in all tongues, as God's explicit revocation of Babel. After this miracle, linguistic confusion need no longer prèvail. Conflicting tongues, whether of nations or of individuals, could be united if based on God's Word of charity.[23] Such a universal foundation would obviate superficial variety and thereby overcome Babel's barriers to communication.

Will, however, does not apply the standard remedy to his linguistic (and moral) confusion. Sonnet 147 may explicitly refer to his rejection of the spiritual alternative held out in 146: "My reason the Phisition to my loue, / Angry that his prescriptions are not kept / Hath left me." Without reason to direct him to the desire that makes it possible to "feed on death," Will's "Desire is death." Without the hope of forgiveness offered by reason's love, he is literally "desperate," hopeless. He cannot convert willful terms to "terms diuine" so that his discourse (insofar as there can be discourse without reason) is "as mad mens," "At randon from the truth vainely exprest."

Will does make a few motions to rephrase himself but, as usual, ends up only repeating himself. Confession leads to a rededication to, rather than a repudiation of, error. In 147, after describing his "disease," he diagnoses its cause: "For I haue sworne thee faire, and thought thee bright, / Who art as black as hell, as darke as night." He does not, however, apply the remedy prescribed by his "Phisition." He admits again to his distorted vision in 148, but imputes it to her sexual "cunning" rather than his own pride, just as he holds her guilty of his faults in 151. Finally in 152, he gives a full reckoning of his perjured statements: "For I haue sworne deepe othes of thy deepe kindnesse: / Othes of thy loue, thy truth, thy constancie." The tense of his final admission, however, indicates that he has not renounced them: "more periurde eye, / To swere against the truth so foule a lie." The final two sonnets epigrammatize Will's inability to change despite his awareness of his moral disease. Knowing himself "sick withall," Will "the helpe of bath desired . . . But found no cure." Incorrigible, he reverts to what he knew in 147 was "that which longer nurseth the disease" —"His mistres eye," the cause of his infection from the beginning.

The prescription of 146, Wilson's corrective measure, and Babel's antidote can have no effect on Will's chronic ailment. His illicit passion involves more than the tumescent puffing-up he takes pride in in 151. His offense pertains more to spirit than body. Will draws the distinction himself in explaining that it is the impulse of "one foolish heart" rather than the allurement of "sensuall feast" that drives him on (141). A gloss from an Elizabethan homily on idolatry indicates both the nature and extent of Will's offense. It identifies lust for a harlot with idolatry and refers us to "the word of GOD, out of the which the similitude is taken" for an explanation:

> Doeth not the worde of GOD call Idolatrie spirituall fornication? Doeth it not call a gylte or painted Idole or Image, a Strumpet with a painted face? Bee not the spirituall wickednesses of an Idols inticing, like the flatteries of a wanton harlot? Bee not men and women as prone to spirituall fornication (I meane Idolatrie) as to carnall forni-cation?[24]

In worshipping his mistress's black "nothing," Will has "made flesh a deity."[25] The flesh he deifies is his own as well as his mistress's, for idola-tors are indistinguishable from their idols. "Thei that make them are like unto them," warn Psalms 115 and 135, two psalms suggested by the wording and subject of 137.[26] Augustine's definition of pride as the per-verse imitation of God applies exactly to Will's doing.[27] In creating his idol, Will inverts God's incarnation by making flesh the word. That his idolatry also strains to make something out of nothing, a prerogative that is God's alone, but succeeds only in unmaking or nullifying fair, bright-ness, and truth adds another twist to his perversity.[28]

Will's parody of God's incarnate Word is extensive. His love of his mis-tress's defects or "refuse" is modeled on Christ's love regardless of merit; Will, however, loves the lack of merit itself while Christ loves in spite of it. Will seeks grace and pity but in the form of sexual favors; his mistress, however, has an infinite capacity not for giving but for receiving, in her thing "of great receit" (136) that like "The sea all water, yet receiues raine still" (135). He constrains the administration of her usurious grace with an eye-for-eye golden rule ("Roote pittie in thy heart that when it growes, / Thy pitty may deserue to pittied bee" [142]) and concludes more with a curse than blessing ("If thou doost seeke to haue what thou doost hide, / By selfe example mai'st thou be denide"). Love of his mis-tress leads to recriminations (lust is "full of blame" [129]) rather than for-giveness, self-righteousness rather than contrition. In violation of the two-fold principle of charity, Will loves his mistress as he hates himself and his neighbors (149). His relation to his mistress and his friend is a trinity (she, like the Holy Ghost, is the mutual love of both), all three being identical in substance (will) but distinct in relation (one person of their trinity vari-ously cohabits another).

Central to Will's parody of Christian love is his rebaptism. In order to be admitted to his mistress's body rather than the body of Christ's church, to become "one" with her "common place" and its transient occupants rather than with Christ's community, Will changes his Christian name from one denoting a spiritual relation to one promoting physical union: "Make but my name thy loue, and loue that still, / And then thou louest me for my name is *Will*" (136). He prefers to incorporate himself in his mistress's black that he has sworn "fair" rather than be incorporated into the church, Christ's black but fair bride according to the traditional interpretation of the Song of Solomon. His self-administered baptism would effect an anatomical union with his mistress rather than a spiritual one with God through which he would participate not in Christ's resurrection but in the risings she monitors in 151, the nimble leaping of "blessed wood" she activates in 128, thus subjecting himself to the sexual doom and salvation she dispenses in 145. Because baptized in her name (and he calls her "loue" in 151) rather than Christ's, the salubrious waters of 153 and 154 prove inefficacious. He resigns himself to reimmersion in her contaminating, raging hole or well that is sponsored by her black eyes: "the bath for my helpe lies, / Where *Cupid* got new fire; my mistres eye."

These distorted reverberations of God's Word reveal how deeply Will's desire has penetrated language. It has corrupted not only its formal elements of rhetoric, grammar, and logic, but its very foundation in charity, in the principle capable of resolving Babel's confusion. Such linguistic apostasy has its origin in Will's initial barring of "fair" from his vocabulary. The "black" or "nothing" he establishes in its place excludes divinity. Will chooses to love what God is not: the primordial state of nothing from which creation was made and would revert if not sustained by Him. In Sidney's and Golding's translation of De Mornay's *A Woorke Concerning the Trewnesse of the Christian Religion* (1587), this state is termed "not-being" or evil and is defined as a "bereving or diminishing of the good qualities which things ought naturally to have." Creatures retain "a certeyne inclination . . . whereby they tend naturally to nothing" that increases when they turn away from God's sustaining Being or Goodness. The treatise's Platonic and Christian terms both pertain to Will's attraction to "nothing": "In the very Soule of man, the evil that is there is a kind of darknesse, for want of looking up to ye light of the sovereyne mynde which should inlighten it."[29]

Given their full weight, Will's nullifying words work to undo creation and obstruct God's light. By loving the antithesis of "Being" and "Light," Will goes about "Slandring Creation" in a much more profound and irreversible way than the simulators of fair he censures in 127. They imitate God's creation while he denies it. The truth he has consciously and repeatedly sworn against (151) is God's truth. By swearing, he calls upon God who is Truth to make his lies good, thereby asking him to bear witness against himself.[30] Will's willing or, more accurately, nilling amounts to a prodigious denial and one—the only one—that cannot be revoked.

The final two sonnets, both variations on a Greek epigram describing an attempt to quench Cupid's flame, are often considered anticlimactic. After all, the closing sonnet repeats what the previous one has just said, itself a repetition of an ancient refrain that has been translated many times before.[31] Still this rutted and pointless recital must be seen as a fitting conclusion to Will's babbling. It is the final step in the downgrading of language we have witnessed throughout his sonnets importuning the dark mistress. Will's language, ineffectual, negative, illogical, and irreversible, concludes in dead-end stammer. A change of heart might have unbabelized and revitalized his speech, but the ungodly denial involved in counting black "fair" allows for no such conversion.

Georgetown University

NOTES

A brief version of this paper was delivered at the convention of the Modern Language Association, Chicago, 30 December 1977.

1. "No direct connexion with *Babel* can be traced, though association with that may have affected the senses." *OED.*

2. Gen. 11.9 suggests such a derivation, and Augustine builds on it in *City of God* 14.4. The *OED,* however, states that no such Semitic root can be found and gives the Assyrian *bāb-ilu,* gate of God, as the possible origin.

3. For a documented account of the history of Adam's language and its confusion at Babel in the sixteenth century, see my "Shakespeare's View of Language: An Historical Perspective," *SQ* 30 (1978), 374–88.

4. Simon Goulart, *A Learned Summarie Upon the Famous Poeme of William of Saluste,* trans. Thomas Lodge (London, 1621), "Babylon," p. 173.

5. The numerological structure of the *Sonnets* may itself suggest a proud monument. See Alastair Fowler, *Triumphal Forms: Structural patterns in Elizabethan Poetry* (Cambridge: Cambridge University Press, 1970), pp 183–97.

6. "Allusion to the Confusion of Babell," in Francis Davison's *A Poetical Rhapsody* (1602–1621), ed. Hyder Edward Rollins, 2 vols. (Cambridge, Mass.: Harvard University Press, 1931), vol. 1, p. 78. I wish to thank Thomas P. Roche, Jr., for this reference.

7. Examples of Shakespeare's dissection of names in the plays are abundant, such as Fal-staff, Tear-sheet, Mal-volio, Pro-spero. See Harry Levin's "Shakespeare's Nomenclature," in *Essays on Shakespeare,* ed. Gerald Chapman (Princeton: Princeton University Press, 1965), pp. 59–90.

8. All quotations from Shakespeare's sonnets are from the facsimile of the 1609 quarto edition in Stephen Booth's *Shakespeare's Sonnets* (New Haven: Yale University Press, 1977).

9. Booth, ibid., notes a pun on "cunn" in "conscience" in sonnet 151.1, 2, 13, p. 526, that should also be applied to "cunning" in 139.

10. For eye as vulva, see ibid., notes to 136.2 (p. 470), 148.7–9 (p. 521), and 153.9 (p. 535). On sexual "nothing," see note to 20.12 (pp. 164–65).

11. On lust's effect on the eyes, see ibid., 129.1 (p. 442).

12. For the sexual reference of hole, bath, well, and valley in 153 and 154, see ibid., general note to 153 (pp. 533–34).

13. For *light* as sexually compliant, see Eric Partridge, *Shakespeare's Bawdy* (1947; rev. ed. London: Routlege and Kegan Paul, 1968), p. 137.

14. Shakespeare's use of "nothing" shares with *nequam-nequitiam* and naught-naughtiness a triple reference—quantitative, moral, and anatomical.

15. In the version of this sonnet that appeared in *The Passionate Pilgrim*, reprinted in Booth, *Sonnets,* pp. 476–77, Will describes the crucial romantic function of a habitual "soothing tongue." In Will's idiom, the phrase refers both to truthful mouthpiece and placating codpiece.

16. Compare Venus' compromising position in "Venus and Adonis," line 594. Note 9, above, also applies to "discontent" in 153.

17. On the near synonymity of language and reason, see Pierre de La Primaudaye's discussion in *The French Academie: Fully Discoursed in Foure Books,* trans. Thomas Bowes, Richard Dolman, W.P. (London, 1618), p. 378.

18. *The Rule of Reason Conteinying The Arte of Logique* (1553), ed. Richard S. Sprague, Renaissance Studies Series 6 (Northridge: California State University, 1972), p. 198.

19. Will's assertion in 121, "I am that I am," is an example of begging the question: Cause and effect, premise and conclusion are identical. The logic is appropriate to proclaim God's self-subsistence but presumes too much in the likes of Will.

20. On "the phonetically and ideationally related" *reason* and *rising,* see Booth, *Sonnets,* note to 151.8 (p. 527).

21. Similar clarifications of style accompany the conversion from profane to divine love in Fulke Greville's *Caelica* and in Barnabe Barnes's *Parthenophil and Parthenophe* and *A Divine Century of Spiritual Sonnets.* Richard Waswo notes the shift in the former in *The Fatal Mirror: Themes and Techniques in the Poetry of Fulke Greville* (Charlottesville: University Press of Virginia, 1972), pp. 106–08.

22. Wilson, *Rule of Reason,* p. 198.

23. My article, "Shakespeare's View of Language," pp. 378–79, describes the tradition that saw Pentecost as the resolution of Babel's confusion.

24. "The III part of the Sermon against Perill of Idolatry," *Certaine Sermons or Homilies Appointed to be Read in the Time of Queen Elizabeth I* (1623), ed. Mary Ellen Rickey and Thomas B. Stroup (Gainesville, Fla.: Scholars' Facsimiles & Reprints, 1968), p. 61.

25. Variants of this phrase refer to similar perverse incarnations in Sidney's *Astrophil and Stella* (4), Greville's *Caelica* (103), and Shakespeare's *Love's Labors Lost* (4.3.74).

26. Quoted by Booth, *Sonnets,* 137.2 (p. 474).

27. *Confessions* 2.6.

28. The futility and presumption of such an attempt are apparent in Sir John Davies' "Nosce Teipsum": "Of nought no creature ever formed ought, / For that is proper to th'*Almighties* hand." *The Poems of Sir John Davies* ed. Robert Krueger (Oxford: The Clarendon Press, 1975), lines 63–64.

MARGRETA DE GRAZIA

29. *The Complete Works of Sir Philip Sidney,* ed. Albert Feuillerat (Cambridge: Cambridge University Press, 1923), vol. 3, pp. 289, 290, 291.

30. The following sixteenth-century gloss on Proverbs 6.19 draws out the implications of Will's swearing against the truth: "when by their false othe they cal God vnto witnesse of their lies, they would spoile him of this trueth, and consequently, that he should be no GOD: for seeing he is the trueth, he cannot stand without it." Michael Cope, *A Godly and Learned Exposition upon the Prouerbes of Solomon,* trans. M. O. (London, 1580), p. 92^v.

31. For the Greek original and its numerous sixteenth-century variants, see James Hutton, "Analogues of Shakespeare's Sonnets 153–54: Contributions to the History of a Theme," *MP* 38 (1941), 385–403.

HUGH MacLACHLAN

The "carelesse heauens":
A Study of Revenge and Atonement
in *The Faerie Queene*

*And almost all things are by the Law purged with blood, and without
sheading of blood is no remission.*—Hebrews 9.22

AS GUYON and his Palmer journey in search of Acrasia's Bower, they
come upon the mortally wounded Amavia, whose first words raise a question of fundamental importance for a theological reading of the Book of
Temperance and also for an increased understanding of the battle between
Arthur, Cymochles, and Pyrochles over the exhausted Guyon in canto
viii:

> But if that carelesse heauens (quoth she) despise
>   The doome of iust reuenge, and take delight
>   To see sad pageants of mens miseries
>   As bound by them to liue in liues despight,
>   Yet can they not warne death from wretched wight.
> (*FQ* II.i.36)[1]

This distraught lament points us toward one of the primary thematic con-
flicts that unite the first eight cantos of Book II.

Amavia laments what seems to her to be a universe which lacks divine
justice, a universe either apathetic or wantonly malicious, which does not
offer vengeance on the acts of sinful men (and women). Instead, it leaves
man destitute of heavenly protection, scorning his misery and permitting
him only the opportunity of suicidal despair. If, as Amavia believes, man
exists in a world of "carelesse heauens" in which there is no system of divine retribution, he is forced to bear responsibility for justice himself. And
those who are "capable" of extracting justice must do so both for themselves and for others who are the victims of evil but too weak to retaliate
themselves. This is the situation which Spenser explores in the series of ad-

135

ventures in which Guyon finds himself prior to his collapse after the temptations of Mammon's Cave.

The theme of revenge is, of course, to be found everywhere in the Elizabethan and Jacobean theater. Hamlet, Hieronymo, Bussy, and countless other stage characters plotted, schemed, pondered, strangled, poisoned, stabbed, butchered, and generally destroyed both others and themselves, physically and spiritually—all in the name of private revenge. Senecan tragedy, popular throughout the period, had pointed the way, and neo-Senecan plays kept the blood hot. From Italy came the *novelle,* filled with Mediterranean passions, extravagant tortures, and dire revenge, all of which served to confirm the average Elizabethan's belief that the Latins were not only papists and therefore theologically damned but also, in many unfortunate cases, maniacs and therefore morally reprehensible as well. These Italian monsters entered England in their original tongue and in French translations, and after the mid-1560s could be relished in William Painter's *Palace of Pleasure* and other lurid English equivalents. Moreover, that complementary and related Italian craze, duelling, reached England during this period, and the code of honor espoused by it enjoined revenge on all its practitioners. All this contemporary background has been well surveyed by critics.[2] The purpose of this paper is not to examine their work and their disagreements concerning the acceptability of personal revenge in the Elizabethan and Jacobean theater (for they tend to agree that the moralists and theologians universally condemned it) but to apply their insights to *The Faerie Queene,* a moral and theological work, where the first eight cantos of Book II can be read as a study of the nature and necessity of blood vengeance, first from a pagan or classical perspective, and then from the perspective of Christian reconciliation—a movement from personal revenge to divine vengeance and ultimately to divine forgiveness in the figure of Prince Arthur.[3]

There were essentially three ways in which writers in the sixteenth century could discuss the validity of personal revenge: first, as a theological problem created by divine injunction ("Dearly beloued, auenge not your selues, but giue place vnto wrath: for it is written, vengeance is mine: I will repaye, saith the Lord" [Rom. 12.19]);[4] second, as an ethical problem, since in the moral handbooks of the period vengeance was viewed as a sin stirred into existence by such passions as wrath, envy, jealousy, and ambition; and, finally, as a political and social problem, since the private revenger took punishment into his own hands when it had been left in certain situations (again by divine injunction) to the king and state. (The ruler, St. Paul tells us, "is the minister of God to take vengeance on him that doeth euil" [Rom. 13.4].) Private revenge as a legal problem is predictably explored in Book V, the Book of Justice, and as an issue is too complex to be given treatment in the present paper.[5] Here I am concerned with the Book of Temperance, in which we are presented with an anatomy of vengeance as an ethical and theological problem for man. As Spenser portrays him, Guyon is revealed to be ostensibly Christian, though in practice he conceives of the world in a classical and, therefore, essentially pagan manner. As a consequence, he is forced to confront the spiritual and psychological problems inherent in a system of personal justice (and injustice), ultimately accepting both his own sinfulness and in Arthur a divine mediator upon whom God's wrathful vengeance against all mankind (including Guyon) can justly be imposed.

The motif of blood vengeance and the stain of blood guilt runs deep through much of the first two books of *The Faerie Queene* as well as late Elizabethan and all of Jacobean drama. The world of departed spirits wandering the underworld crying for revenge was repeatedly evoked on the London stage. The apparent ghost of Hamlet's father demands restitution for his poisoning; Macbeth, staring at an apparition of the murdered Banquo cries: "It will have blood, they say; blood will have blood." Richard III is haunted on the eve of Bosworth by the specters of those he had destroyed, rubbing their hands in anticipation of his blood to be spilt the next day. So also in Book I of *The Faerie Queene* Sans Joy arrives at the House of Pride, his brother slain by Redcrosse, seeming to "nourish bloudy vengeaunce in his bitter mind" (I.iv.38); and when he is confronted by Duessa, she appeals to him in good pagan fashion: "Let not his loue, let not his restlesse spright / Be vnreueng'd, that calles to you aboue / From wandring *Stygian* shores, where it doth endlesse moue." He replies:

> Ded is *Sans-foy*, his vitall paines are past,
> Though greeued ghost for vengeance deepe do grone:
> He liues, that shall him pay his dewties last,
> And guiltie Elfin bloud shall sacrifice in hast.   (I.iv.48–49)

When he catches sight of his dead brother's shield during the battle with Redcrosse, he cries to Sans Foy's ghost:

> Ah wretched sonne of wofull syre,
> Doest thou sit wayling by black *Stygian* lake,
> Whilest here thy shield is hangd for victors hyre,
> And sluggish german doest thy forces slake,
> To after-send his foe, that him may ouertake?

Goe caytiue Elfe, him quickly ouertake,
  And soone redeeme from his long wandring woe;
Goe guiltie ghost, to him my message make,
  That I his shield haue quit from dying foe.   (I.v.10–11)

Even Arthur, for a moment at a loss how to explain the vitality of the apparently immortal, ghostly figure of Maleger,

                    doubted, least it were some magicall
  Illusion, that did beguile his sense,
  Or wandring ghost, that wanted funerall,
  Or aerie spirit vnder false pretence,
Or hellish feend raysd vp through diuelish science.

                                                    (II.xi.39)

These primitive worlds of sin, communal pollution, and personal or tribal atonement with other men or with the gods are associated predictably with the powers of evil in *The Faerie Queene*. The concepts control Sans Joy in his desire to avenge his brother by sending Redcrosse to "redeeme" his wandering ghost. And when Duessa confronts Night and demands revenge for the death of one of her children, the goddess promises an unrestricted vendetta against "The sonnes of Day" (I.v.25) and the imposition of the *lex talionis:*

Yet shall they not escape so freely all;
  For some shall pay the price of others guilt:
  And he the man that made *Sansfoy* to fall,
  Shall with his owne bloud price that he hath spilt.

                                                    (I.v.26)

When Redcrosse comes to "auenge" the knight who had committed suicide at Despaire's urging, he himself invokes this view of justice: "What iustice can but iudge against thee right, / With thine owne bloud to price his bloud, here shed in sight?" (I.ix.37). And Despaire turns the *lex talionis* against him by pointing out that

All those great battels, which thou boasts to win,
  Through strife, and bloud-shed, and auengement,
  Now praysd, hereafter deare thou shalt repent:
  For life must life, and bloud must bloud repay.   (I.ix.43)

Despaire, of course, throughout his debate with Redcrosse argues from the point of view of unmitigated Old Testament justice in which God is falsely portrayed solely as a god of wrath and vengeance. This view of the Old Testament god is balanced only at the last moment by Una's reminder that the same god does not demand vengeance on sinful man, for "Where iustice growes, there grows eke greater grace" (I.ix.53).

The belief in a world of primitive retributive justice which both Despaire and Redcrosse espouse is not, however, fully rebutted in Book I because Spenser's attention there is on man's spiritual relationship with his God.[6] Redcrosse's primary lesson is that all men are sinful and so none, including himself, can justly be accounted righteous. Legally and theologically Despaire is right (though only half right): God is just, man is sinful, and justice demands punishment for sin—in this case death. Redcrosse, however, is taught in the House of Holiness that God is also merciful to man. Thus, although he can do nothing to make himself righteous, man can gain absolution and salvation through divine grace. But Despaire's argument that Redcrosse's "great battels" of "bloud-shed, and auengement" will ultimately demand talion is not answered in Book I if we consider the *lex talionis* as also defining a *human* relationship. This second relationship is not explored until Book II.

The very first episode in Book II anticipates the issue of careless heavens raised by Amavia's lament. Archimago, meditating "auenging woe" (II.i.2) against Redcrosse, comes upon Guyon and deceives him into believing that Duessa (in disguise once more) has been ravished and that her attacker remains unpunished. In concluding his description of the lady's predicament, the magus invokes the gods: "Witnesse ye heauens, whom she in vaine to helpe did call" (II.i.10). God has not responded to the apparently distressed lady's plea for protection; and Guyon, moved to outrage, rhetorically replies: "And liues he yet . . . that wrought this act, / And doen the heauens afford him vitall food?" (II.i.12). Immediately his "fierce ire" is ignited, and he sets off in "zealous hast" without his Palmer to find this recreant knight. Promising the distraught lady "reuenge," he reaches Redcrosse (who he has been told is the ravisher) "inflam'd with wrathfulnesse" and is only stopped in his heat at the last moment by the sight of the red cross on the knight's shield, the "sacred badge of [his] Redeemers death" (II.i.27). Though they are brothers of the same Order of Maydenhead, only this final warning saves Guyon and Redcrosse from conflict. In spite of Guyon's acknowledgment of Redcrosse's reputation for goodness (II.i.19), he is more than ready in his impulsive anger to cast that and their brotherhood aside in his desire to offer justice to an unknown lady whose plight the heavens have apparently ignored—and on only hearsay evidence.

This early conflict introduces the reader to the question of whether there is divine retribution to structure justice in this world and offers us (and Guyon if only he would truly accept it) a complex positive answer—a divine redeemer (symbolized by Redcrosse's shield). Guyon, however, like other heroes in the poem, has the experience but misses the meaning. Although he has *acknowledged* the idea of personal divine care, he has already *acted* (and later will continue to act) as though the heavens are, in fact, careless. Thus in the following cantos he must be confronted with a detailed theological and psychological analysis of the human condition and both the necessity and the reality of divine care and retribution in the figure of Prince Arthur.

The story of Amavia is for Guyon (as it is for Spenser) a paradigm of the human predicament, but one which the knight interprets in wholly classical and pagan terms. Harry Berger has, I think, correctly stressed the extent to which the Knight of Temperance is a model of the Aristotelian ideal and as such is self-reliant within his moral universe. As the book progresses there is, he notes, a change in the "perceived" metaphysics of Guyon's world from classical to Christian: In the first seven cantos the cosmos is thought by the characters to be controlled by fortune or chance, but in the last five cantos there is revealed behind this force a system of divine concern.[7] The argument is well founded, and the movement from a self-reliant aristocrat to an Everyman figure which he sees in Guyon finds its parallel, I believe, in a movement from the knight's assumption that man must seek personal revenge (or act as an agent of justice for those too weak to seek their own) to an acceptance of the reality of divine retribution. And this second movement is controlled likewise by Guyon's final rejection of careless heavens—the world of fortune—and his acknowledgment of divine intervention in human affairs.

When Guyon comes upon Amavia, the first words he hears remind us of his earlier mistake with Redcrosse, for like Archimago she complains that the "carelesse heauens" refuse to give man "iust reuenge" for wrong done to him. She then continues:

> But thou, sweet Babe, whom frowning froward fate
>   Hath made sad witnesse of thy fathers fall,
>   Sith heauen thee deignes to hold in liuing state,
>   Long maist thou liue, and better thriue withall,
>   Then to thy lucklesse parents did befall:
>   Liue thou, and to thy mother dead attest,

> That cleare she dide from blemish criminall;
>   Thy little hands embrewd in bleeding breast
> Loe I for pledges leaue. So giue me leaue to rest. (II.i.37)

It has been argued that this episode is concerned with original sin (Ruddy-mane's stained hands) and Baptism (the Nymph's Well), and that in Mordant (Mort-dant) we have the figure of the fallen Adam, "death-giver" to all mankind.[8] Amavia, it would seem, is the fallen Eve. Like Guyon, however, she lives in a pagan universe: The heavens do not participate in human affairs; and mankind, she suggests, suffers because of fortune or fate and not because it is guilty of original sin (see also II.i.50). Indeed, she maintains that she dies "cleare . . . from blemish criminall," and moments later raises her hands "As heauen accusing guiltie of her death" (II.i.49). From a Christian perspective this is theologically unsound, but Guyon himself (not adept, of course, at reading allegories of which he himself is a part) is puzzled by Amavia's and Mordant's predicament. "What direfull chance, armd with reuenging fate, / Or cursed hand hath plaid this cruell part" (II.i.44), he asks, struggling with various (and wrong) possibilities as he so often does. He does not recognize that the bloody hands of their child represent the curse of original sin passed from father to son, and his moralization of this "image of mortalitie" can be read totally as a classical solution to the human situation:

> Then turning to his Palmer said, Old syre
>   Behold the image of mortalitie,
>   And feeble nature cloth'd with fleshly tyre,
>   When raging passion with fierce tyrannie
>   Robs reason of her due regalitie,
>   And makes it seruant to her basest part:
>   The strong it weakens with infirmitie,
>   And with bold furie armes the weakest hart;
> The strong through pleasure soonest falles, the weake through smart.

> But temperance (said he) with golden squire
>   Betwixt them both can measure out a meane,
>   Neither to melt in pleasures whot desire,
>   Nor fry in hartlesse griefe and dolefull teene.
>   Thrice happie man, who fares them both atweene:
>   But sith this wretched woman ouercome
>   Of anguish, rather then of crime hath beene,
>   Reserue her cause to her eternall doome,
> And in the meane vouchsafe her honorable toombe.

> Palmer (quoth he) death is an equall doome
>> To good and bad, the common Inne of rest;
>> But after death the tryall is to come,
>> When best shall be to them, that liued best:
>> But both alike, when death hath both supprest,
>> Religious reuerence doth buriall teene,
>> Which who so wants, wants so much of his rest:
>> For all so great shame after death I weene,
> As selfe to dyen bad, vnburied bad to beene.   (II.i.57–59)

As she dies, Guyon, like Amavia herself, accuses "fortune, and too cruell fate, / Which plunged had faire Ladie in so wretched state" (II.i.56). His explanation of her death is ethical, not theological, and focuses on the betrayal of reason to the tyranny of the "raging passion." His solution, also ethical, is temperance, which "can measure out a meane" between the contending passions. While a Christian reader can agree with Guyon's anatomy of the mind, it is essentially an Aristotelian psychology he espouses and therefore also pre-Christian and compatible with Guyon's essential paganism. Moreover, Guyon concurs with Amavia's belief in her innocence at death (II.i.58). The reason she has committed suicide, he argues, is not that she is guilty of sin but that she was fated (doomed) to die at this moment. Thus she deserves honorable burial. It can be argued that Guyon's next words to the Palmer are a Christian assertion of the Last Judgment, but Tantalus and Ixion in Hades and the classical heroes wandering Elysium should remind us that the words and the philosophy can be found in Virgil as well as in St. Paul and the Gospels.

Guyon reveals even more clearly his pagan perspective in his reason for burying Mordant and Amavia, for "who so wants, wants so much of his rest." Protestants of the sixteenth century believed that spirits of the dead were at rest, no matter what state their bodies were left in: They rested firmly either in heaven or hell. Roman Catholics, who believed in purgatory, thought that men might return from the dead to ask that good deeds be done in order to shorten their time there. But both Protestants and Catholics agreed that burial or lack of burial was not the issue involved in the question of wandering spirits.[9] It is, however, for Guyon, as it had been for Antigone. Moreover, his ceremony over the grave sounds more pagan than Christian.

> The dead knights sword out of his sheath he drew,
>> With which he cut a locke of all their heare,
>> Which medling with their bloud and earth, he threw

Into the graue, and gan deuoutly sweare;
Such and such euill God on *Guyon* reare,
And worse and worse young Orphane be thy paine,
If I or thou dew vengeance do forbeare,
Till guiltie bloud her guerdon do obtaine:
So shedding many teares, they closd the earth againe.

(II.i.61)

For the pagan nature of this ceremony we might compare the hair shorn at the burial of Patroclus in the *Iliad* (23.70–74, 135–53) or the lock of hair left by Orestes on his father Agamemnon's tomb in the *Choephori* (1–10).[10] By his actions and his oath Guyon initiates a blood feud, and he becomes (along with Ruddymane, for whom he acts as a kind of godfather making promises of a blood covenant on his behalf) an avenger of blood.

Guyon's inability to wash the blood from Ruddymane's hands at the beginning of canto ii makes sense when we recognize that he does not consider the stain from a Christian perspective. Guyon, in fact, is at a loss to explain satisfactorily why the hands remain bloody:

He wist not whether blot of foule offence
    Might not be purgd with water nor with bath;
    Or that high God, in lieu of innocence,
    Imprinted had that token of his wrath,
    To shew how sore bloudguiltinesse he hat'th;
    Or that the charme and venim, which they druncke,
    Their bloud with secret filth infected hath,
    Being diffused through the senselesse truncke,
That through the great contagion direfull deadly stuncke.

(II.ii.4)

Confusing though Spenser's construction is here, the semicolon at the end of line 2 and the general syntactical structure of the stanza make it seem that Guyon cannot understand why the pagan ritual of washing in water or symbolic bath will not "purge"—a theological term here as it is in the Geneva Bible version of Hebrews (e.g., ch. 9)—this offence of Ruddymane's playing in his mother's blood. This guilt attributed to the child by Guyon is for what he believes to be an "actual" sin which Ruddymane has unwittingly or "innocently" committed; and that the knight in fact considers the act to be polluting, though the child is obviously ignorant of what it has done, is suggested in the previous stanza when Guyon brings it to the water thinking "His guiltie hands from bloudie gore to cleene"

(II.ii.3). As usual, Guyon offers alternatives to explain what he does not understand. Either God has imprinted on Ruddymane's innocent hands a sign of his hatred of those who commit murder to serve as a reminder of the child's obligation to punish Acrasia (on whose "guiltie bloud" Guyon has sworn for him an avuncular oath of vengeance), or else the parents have passed the contamination of Acrasia's poison on to the child through their blood. He does not expect the blood to leave an indelible stain; given it, he is willing to offer either a divine or a human explanation, a metaphysical or a physical one.[11] But that Guyon is *not* thinking of original sin in his explanations is shown when the Palmer rejects both as false: "And of your ignorance great maruell make, / Whiles cause not well conceiued ye mistake" (II.ii.5).

Alastair Fowler has suggested that Guyon's washing of the babe's hands is successful, that he performs the sacrament of Baptism, and that Ruddymane's hands remain bloody because in Protestant theology Baptism absolves man of the guilt but not of the effects of original sin. The burial of Mordant and Amavia becomes the shedding of St. Paul's *vetus homo*. To complete this interpretation Fowler suggests that the phoenix, a traditional image of rebirth and one associated by Guyon with Ruddymane ("And in dead parents balefull ashes bred"),[12] indicates the creation or putting on of the *novus homo*. But Guyon acts in an essentially pagan manner in this episode and because of this does not, I think, perform the sacrament of Baptism. The phoenix metaphor itself arises in a predictably pagan statement on Guyon's part: "Ah lucklesse babe, borne vnder cruell starre, / And in dead parents balefull ashes bred" (II.ii.2). Guyon's theological perspective here only repeats Amavia's metaphysics. He has some concept of a universal plan, but it is essentially mechanical, containing no suggestion of human responsibility for that plan. Ruddymane is orphaned "As budding braunch rent from the natiue tree, / And throwen forth, till it be withered." This, Guyon suggests, is a metaphor for the human predicament. But it sounds more Stoic than Christian. The tree, he implies, flourishes. Ruddymane, the bud, only begins to wither when through bad fortune (the common state of men for this pessimist) he is separated from that tree, his parents. But if Guyon were talking about original sin, his metaphor should have *begun* with a withered tree because that is the state of fallen man.[13] Read this way, the phoenix image for Guyon means only that man is forced to grow up in a world of misfortune. And the poet, rather than using the metaphor optimistically as an image of renewal, is only reminding us that original sin does not die with the parents; it lives on in their children. The phoenix here is an image not of rebirth but of redeath.

The possibility of irony is not beyond Spenser, and the double perspective on this "state of men" here measures Guyon's ignorance that his own hands are as stained as Ruddymane's. The Palmer, who knows of original sin, tells the knight to "let them still be bloudy, as befell, / That they his mothers innocence may tell" (II.ii.10). But she is *not* innocent—she cannot be, simply because she is human, and fallen. And so his words are a reminder that the child bears the "moniment" of the parents' sin, just as they themselves had carried the stain of their fathers'. The stain is to remain "as a sacred Symbole . . . to minde reuengement." For Guyon this means what it did before: The bloody hands are a reminder of the necessity to prosecute vengeance on Acrasia. For the Palmer and the poet, however, it means that God revenges the Fall of Man on all mankind, including "innocent" children—a topic not resolved until Arthur's battle with Pyrochles and Cymochles in canto viii. And so Guyon walks off determined to be a personal redeemer, determined to bring justice into an unfortunate world in which the gods, if they exist, are apparently apathetic. They may abhor the spilling of blood, but they themselves refuse to help in the administration of justice.

The episode at Medina's castle presents Guyon with a pagan anatomy of the problem of wrath and its concomitant, revenge.[14] Sir Huddibras and Sans Loy, the irascible and concupiscible appetites, are constantly at strife in their desire to rule the mind.[15] For Medina, the rational mean, their continual hostility must be caused by a "cursed euill Spright, / Or fell *Erinnys*" (II.ii.29).[16] Although she does not decide the source of this enmity, Medina goes on to offer a completely rational (and secular) argument against this passionate revenge. Even if there *were* "rightfull cause of difference," it would be better to seek friendship than to bring into existence the blood feud which grows out of anger: "Then with bloud guiltinesse to heape offence, / And mortall vengeaunce ioyne to crime abhord" (II.ii.30). Nothing is more disgraceful than "fowle reuenging rage." The Erinyes provoke us to anger and vengeance, and the product is bloodguilt. The knights in reality, however, show the effects of the distemper caused by original sin, not mentioned in this episode by Guyon, the Palmer, or Medina herself. And so Guyon leaves Ruddymane to be "tempered" by Medina—to be trained to ethical perfection as a solution to wrath, as though the ethical life were in itself sufficient to annul the consequences of the Fall. Moreover, he leaves the child there to be "taught / T'auenge his Parents death" (II.iii.2), seemingly oblivious to Medina's estimation of revenge as a foul, distempering rage. It is typical of Spenser's technique in the early cantos of each book that the situations which Guyon confronts here are personally relevant, but he mistakenly thinks that they have consequences only for others; and so he proceeds in search of Acrasia's Bower to avenge Amavia ignorant of his own sin.

Guyon's experience continues as he meets Furor dragging Phedon by the hair, urged on by Occasion "To heape more vengeance on that wretched wight" (II.iv.5). In *The French Academie* (London, 1586), La Primaudaye tells us that "*Cicero* saith, that that which the Latines call Anger *[furor]*, is named of the Grecians desire of reuenge" (p. 312). This personified passion for revenge is, of course, Phedon's own and is the product of the string of vengeful acts which Phedon recounts to Guyon after his release, acts that tell a story of revenge which could have served the Elizabethan stage. It is predictable that Phedon explains his tragedy as born of bad fortune, ignoring once more the human responsibility for maleficence asserted in Christian doctrine:

> Faire Sir (quoth he) what man can shun the hap,
> That hidden lyes vnwares him to surpryse?
> Misfortune waites aduantage to entrap
> The man most warie in her whelming lap.   (II.iv.17)

Seeing what he believes to be his lady making love to a groom, Phedon returns home, "chawing vengeance all the way" (II.iv.29); but after slaying her "innocent," he hears the truth from Pryene:

> Which when I heard, with horrible affright
>   And hellish fury all enragd, I sought
>   Vpon my selfe that vengeable despight
>   To punish: yet it better first I thought,
>   To wreake my wrath on him, that first it wrought.
>   To *Philemon,* false faytour *Philemon*
>   I cast to pay, that I so dearely bought;
>   Of deadly drugs I gave him drinke anon,
> And washt away his guilt with guiltie potion.[17]

> Thus heaping crime on crime, and griefe on griefe,
>   To losse of loue adioyning losse of frend,
>   I meant to purge both with a third mischiefe,
>   And in my woes beginner it to end:
>   That was *Pryene;* she did first offend.   (II.iv.30–31)

No clearer example of what Medina warns against could be given. And yet Guyon still fails to connect this exemplum with his own desire to avenge

A Study of Revenge and Atonement in *The Faerie Queene*

the deaths of Ruddymane's parents. He should recognize here the danger of uncontrolled vengeance which destroys not only the guilty (Philemon), but also the innocent (Claribell), and the revenger himself who seeks to cancel his fury with suicide. But again Guyon offers his only solution: "all your hurts may soone through temperance be easd" (II.iv.33).[18]

Pyrochles is Furor writ large. He smokes and burns with that wrath out of which revenge springs, and Atin's description of his master's irascible nature moves the Palmer to note: "Happy, who can abstaine, when Rancour rife / Kindles Reuenge, and threats his rusty knife" (II.iv.44). Guyon has belatedly learned caution from his mistake in thinking that he could easily control Furor; though he ignores the implications for his own psyche—that he has in himself the capacity to succumb to this impulse—he now knows how to handle the irate passion for revenge in others (II.v.9). When he defeats Pyrochles, the latter appeals for mercy, blaming (predictably) only fortune for his defeat (II.v.12). And Guyon's compassion is offered in words that have an ironic overtone: "Liue and allegaunce owe, / To him that giues thee life and libertie" (II.v.13). Guyon means, of course, himself. But the fact that the situation in this episode so closely parallels Pyrochles' similar situation with Arthur in canto viii suggests that Guyon is wrong to see himself as a "life-giver." In fact, Guyon endorses Pyrochles' belief in the vagaries of fortune as the basis for victory and defeat, for they share the same metaphysics: "Was neuer man, who most conquestes atchieu'd, / But sometimes had the worse, and lost by warre" (II.v.15). Guyon now falls into that second great trap in the code of personal revenge and atonement: He had been exposed to the possibility of punishing the innocent (Redcrosse, Claribell); now he grants mercy to the guilty. He releases Pyrochles and offers him both Furor and Occasion. Pyrochles, parody-redeemer of the worst in man, "Did lightly leape, where he them bound did see, / And gan to breake the bands of their captiuitee" (II.v.18). It is not long, however, before Furor has "his redeemer chalengd for his foe" (II.v.20). If revenge seems to lead to problems for Guyon, so does mercy. How can man ultimately be sure whom he should punish and whom he should spare?

If the irascible passion can be kindled to desire revenge (indeed, for Spenser it is an unquenchable fire: Pyrochles lives for revenge), so also can the concupiscible. Atin stirs Cymochles from his lethargy to seek revenge on Guyon for his dealings with his brother (proem to canto v). When he awakes, "As one affright / With hellish feends, or *Furies* mad vprore, / He then vprose, inflam'd with fell despight" (II.v.37), swearing "to been aueng'd that day" (II.v.38). Phaedria, however, once she has separated Cymochles from Atin (strife), is capable of causing him to forget his "care of vow'd reuenge" (II.vi.8), suggesting perhaps that her fallen *carpe diem* hedonism offers man his only philosophical (not theological) reason for rejecting the code of private revenge. This "immodest mirth" offers us, therefore, her own parody of peace for mankind and in her wandering bower a false harmony of nature and an illusory garden of prelapsarian pleasure and reconciliation for postlapsarian man.

In the Cave of Mammon Guyon most clearly displays the only other solution of the classical world to the danger of personal revenge: heroic magnanimity. Guyon can be shown to be not only the Knight of Temperance but also the Knight of pagan Magnanimity—that perfection of classical man later to be Christianized and celebrated as an ideal throughout the Renaissance.[19] And it is part of the definition of the magnanimous man in the *Nicomachean Ethics* and elsewhere that, though he takes up the cause of justice for others who have been wronged, he is quick to forgive and forget injuries done to himself. But the problem with the un-Christianized virtue is that it presumes that man has the capacity for independent perfection—indeed it celebrates its desirability—and thus the capacity to act as the judge of others who do not live up to the ideal of goodness and forgiveness. For Aristotle there was no such thing as original sin. Man was born with equal potential for both vice and virtue, and it was ultimately his personal decision which one he chose. Guyon is able in this confrontation with the values of the world to display his natural (pagan) power to reject all of its attractions. But his collapse is the defeat of a man who has assumed the reality of independent human worth. Patrick Cullen, I think, has made much the same point. "Guyon's deficiency," he suggests, "throughout the book has been an inability to see the full reality of evil. Guyon is a *naif;* a courteous young man, polite, well-brought-up, well-schooled, of a good family, but innocent . . . to the diabolic roots of evil and the fallen dimensions of his own nature. Guyon has acted like an unfallen Adam around whom the garden has fallen. . . . Guyon must learn what he found difficult to understand when Ruddymane's hands could not be washed clean, that baptism does not return man to Eden, that there remains even in the baptized Christian something of evil against which he contends."[20] He is "fallen" man, all of whose good deeds are worthless to his salvation because they are not based on faith. He is "dead" to the spiritual life.[21] He may worry whether Mammon's treasure is the product of "guiltlesse bloud" (II.vii.13) which is now blotted by "bloud guiltinesse" (II.vii.19), but the curse, if it exists on Mammon's gold, is pagan, not Christian.[22] He still cannot see that his hands are as red as Ruddymane's; and that is why he does not recognize Pontius Pilate, who is busy trying to wash his hands clean. Man cannot do it for himself any more than he can do it for others. And Guyon, like Pilate, has also fundamentally denied Christ: Both are capable of judging an innocent man guilty and a guilty man innocent because of the limiting systems of evaluation and responsibility to which they subscribe.[23]

It is after Guyon has collapsed in his ensuing state of exhaustion, having been exposed to all the failures of a system of human vengeance, a system created by what would appear to be an unconcerned or "carelesse heauen," that Spenser examines the ultimate solution. For seven cantos Guyon has struggled through a world in which divine grace has remained hidden, a world apparently (even for our knight) controlled by fortune. But Archimago's and Amavia's condemnation of divine apathy is rebutted at the beginning of canto viii:

> And is there care in heauen? and is there loue
> In heauenly spirits to these creatures bace,
> That may compassion of their euils moue?
> There is: else much more wretched were the cace
> Of men, then beasts. But O th'excceding grace
> Of highest God, that loues his creatures so,
> And all his workes with mercy doth embrace,
> That blessed Angels, he sends to and fro,
> To serue to wicked man, to serue his wicked foe.

Guyon is that "wicked man." And there *is* a careful heaven. And because there is, man is able to escape the cycle of personal vengeance and its passions. However, he must give up not only his desire to do evil (embodied in Pyrochles and Cymochles) but also his belief in his own unaided goodness (embodied in Guyon).

Having assured us of the presence of divine concern, the poet is forced to ask the question: "O why should heauenly God to man haue such regard?" (II.viii.2). In other words, this episode in which Prince Arthur battles Pyrochles and Cymochles for the fate of the unconscious Guyon is to be a study in the mystery of the Redemption. This raises a question which has puzzled critics of Book II: Why does Spenser introduce an apparently redundant angel who, having warned the Palmer of impending danger, leaves the scene, to be replaced by a second agent of divine grace— Prince Arthur. The answer perhaps lies in the first chapters of Hebrews. The argument to the Geneva Bible edition of this epistle tells us that its

> chief purpose is to persuade vnto the Ebrewes . . . that Christ Iesus
> was not onely the redemer, but also that at his comming all ceremo-

nies must haue an end: forasmuche as his doctrine was the conclusion of all the prophecies, and therefore not onely Moses was inferior
to him, but also the Angels: for they all were seruants, and he the
Lord, but so Lord, that he hathe also taken our flesh, and is made
our brother to assure vs of our saluation through him self: for he is
that eternal Priest . . . and, therefore at his comming . . . all sacrifices for sinne [ought] to be abolished.

There are four essential points here, all I believe at work in canto viii: first
that only Christ is man's redeemer; second, that at his coming the prac-
tices of the Old Testament are to cease as superseded, including "sacrifices
for sinne," (i.e., acts of personal atonement); third, that the angels are inferior to him; and fourth, that Christ was man as well as God.

Having summoned the Palmer, the angel leaves. There would seem to
be two explanations suggested in Hebrews. The angels, we are told, served
the ancient Hebrews as bearers of divine law and so represent the old covenant, a covenant of law and justice. (The word spoken by the angels to
man, we are told in the gloss to Hebrews 2.2, "was the Law giuen to
Moses by the hands of the Angels.") This raises the problem that "if the
worde spoken by Angels was stedfaste, and euerie transgression, and dis-
obedience receiued a iuste recompence of reward [i.e., an eye for an eye],
How shal we escape, if we neglect so great salvation, which at first began
to be preached by the Lord" (2.2–3). If we are guilty by the Mosaic law
which the angels bore to man, a law upon which our awareness of sin is
based and punishment imposed, how can we evade that just vengeance except by acknowledging Christ's gospel of Redemption? The angels trans-
mit to man the old law, Christ the new. When Spenser's angel departs in
favor of Arthur, the theological moment has arrived in Book II to create a
new covenant between God and man.[24] The second reason for the angel's
departure seems based on the argument in Hebrews that God chose to become man in order to be able to suffer death and to triumph over Satan
through his resurrection (2.14). Only by becoming man was God able to
absorb the punishment due to man for his trangressions. Man could not
save himself, nor could the immortal angels. Therefore, Christ "in no
sorte toke the [nature of] Angels, but he toke the seed of Abraham.
Wherefore in all things it became him to be made like vnto his brethren,
that he might be merciful, and . . . that he might make reconciliation for
the sinnes of the people" (2.16–17). Thus, while Spenser's angel can serve
and protect Guyon (II.viii.8), it cannot ultimately *redeem* him. That must
be done by Arthur, functioning as Christ in this episode.[25]

Pyrochles and Cymochles now appear, unregenerate men, stirred by Ar-

A Study of Revenge and Atonement in *The Faerie Queene*

chimago and Atin to avenge themselves on Guyon. Though the Palmer laments their desire to despoil the knight of his armor and to wreak their "vengeance on the ashes cold" (II.viii.13), the brothers reveal the inability of man to judge good and evil properly in their justifications (or rationalizations) for defaming Guyon. Cymochles argues that Guyon must have been bad (and therefore worthy of having revenge imposed on his corpse) because he is now dead and unburied: "The worth of all men by their end esteeme . . . ; Bad therefore I him deeme, that thus lies dead on field" (II.viii.14). For Cymochles, disrespect shown to Guyon's body must indicate his society's judgment of him.[26] If the one brother, however, offers at least some system for ethical evaluation, the other will settle for none:

> Good or bad (gan his brother fierce reply)
>   What do I recke, sith that he dyde entire?
>   Or what doth his bad death now satisfy
>   The greedy hunger of reuenging ire,
>   Sith wrathfull hand wrought not her owne desire?
>   Yet since no way is left to wreake my spight,
>   I will him reaue of armes, the victors hire,
>   And of that shield, more worthy of good knight;
> For why should a dead dog be deckt in armour bright?
> (II.viii.15)

Pyrochles is concerned only to vent his choleric need for revenge, and whether Guyon was good or evil is of no consequence. Revenge for him has nothing to do with morality—only mortality.

Into this world of personal, and at times immoral, revenge which can turn against even a good man like Guyon himself, a system of revenge in which not only Pyrochles and Cymochles but also Guyon takes part, Arthur enters. When he learns from the Palmer of the brothers' desire "to reuenge their spight" (II.viii.25), he offers two methods to bring peace:

> May be, that better reason will asswage
>   The rash reuengers heat. Words well dispost
>   Haue secret powre, t'appease inflamed rage:
> If not, leaue vnto me thy knights last patronage.
> (II.viii.26)

The appeal to reason, however, cannot work against fallen man's desire for personal revenge and satisfaction in order to regain lost honor, even

though Arthur offers the brothers the benefit of the doubt in his acknowledgment that they may be in the right to seek that revenge:

> Ye warlike payre, whose valorous great might
> It seemes, iust wrongs to vengeance do prouoke,
> To wreake your wrath on this dead seeming knight,
> Mote ought allay the storme of your despight,
> And settle patience in so furious heat?
> Not to debate the chalenge of your right,
> But for this carkasse pardon I entreat,
> Whom fortune hath alreadie laid in lowest seat.[27] (II.viii.27)

The Prince's decision to pass over the question of Guyon's moral state in
his appeal for mercy seems a reminder that Christ enters the world, not to
judge it, but to save it (John 12.47–48).

The next stanzas present the climax of Spenser's examination of the
question of personal revenge. Cymochles cannot understand this request
for pardon, for in his universe evil lives on after the death of the evildoer:

> To whom *Cymochles* said; For what art thou,
> That mak'st thy selfe his dayes-man, to prolong
> The vengeance prest? Or who shall let me now,
> On this vile bodie from to wreake my wrong,
> And make his carkasse as the outcast dong?
> Why should not that dead carrion satisfie
> The guilt, which if he liued had thus long,
> His life for due reuenge should deare abie?
> The trespasse still doth liue, albe the person die.
>
> Indeed (then said the Prince) the euill donne
> Dyes not, when breath the bodie first doth leaue,
> But from the grandsyre to the Nephewes sonne,
> And all his seed the curse doth often cleaue,
> Till vengeance vtterly the guilt bereaue:
> *So streightly God doth iudge.* But gentle knight,
> That doth against the dead his hand vpheaue,
> His honour staines with rancour and despight,
> And great disparagment makes to his former might.
>
> *Pyrochles* gan reply the second time,
> And to him said, Now felon sure I read,
> How that thou art partaker of his crime.
>
> (II.viii.28–30, italics mine)

A Study of Revenge and Atonement in *The Faerie Queene*

For Cymochles, Guyon's sin of having dishonored him on Phaedria's wandering island lives on though the knight himself is dead. The Prince's agreement with the knight, however, is only superficial, for he is echoing the second Mosaic commandment: Man shall not worship graven images, "for I am the Lord thy God, a ielouse God, visiting the iniquitie of the fathers vpon the children, vpon the third *generacion* and vpon the fourth of them that hate me" (Exod. 20.5). From grandsire to nephew's son—four generations. Arthur is talking not of personal sin which, in a careless universe, justifies seeking satisfaction through personal revenge, but of original sin in a *careful* universe in which God himself justly seeks revenge for human evil. And because original sin pollutes *all* mankind, personal revenge is impermissible, for all men have sinned and thus are subject to the blood code of Cymochles and Pyrochles—even the brothers themselves. No man can be good under the law, not even the best of them (Guyon): "bothe Iewes and Gentiles are vnder sinne. As it is written, There is none righteous, no not one" (Rom. 3.9–10). "Therefore thou art inexcusable, o man, whosoeuer thou art that iudgest: for in that that thou iudgest another, thou condemnest thy self: for thou that iudgest, doest the same things" (Rom. 2.1). The statement cuts two ways, however: The brothers should not judge Guyon's goodness because they also are subject to God's judgment (his law); but also it is not Guyon's job to judge Acrasia and to vow revenge on her. Arthur transfers judgment to God. But he is only acknowledging here a transfer which had been effected under the old covenant. He is also "the Mediatour of a better Testament, which is established vpon better promises" (Heb. 8.6)—a Covenant of Mercy.

It is with no chance word that Cymochles recognizes Arthur's desire to be Guyon's "dayes-man": a mediator, intercessor, one who volunteers to act as go-between, in this case between man and God, to atone for man's sins. The word is used in this sense in the Bishops' Bible version of Job 9.33. Job, a man who believed himself righteous and therefore unjustly punished by God, lamented the fact that there was no mediator between himself and God. Arthur provides that service missing under the old covenant for Guyon, another mistakenly self-righteous man. Pyrochles darkly recognizes that the Prince has chosen to be a "partaker" of Guyon's crime as Christ chooses to absorb the punishment imposed on fallen mankind in order to offer him new life. When Pyrochles strikes the Prince unprovoked, Arthur accuses him of breaking the law (of arms on the chivalric level of the allegory, of the old covenant of Justice on the theological level) and warns that he will "feele the law, the which thou hast defast" (II.viii.31). By the old law Pyrochles stands justly condemned to death because he is incapable of doing good independently of God's grace.

Hebrews suggests that God became man in order to act as mediator and to absorb man's guilt upon himself, and this explains why Arthur uses Guyon's sword in his battle against the brothers, for in so doing he partakes of humanity. The wound that he receives in his right side (II.viii.38), symbol of the Crucifixion, reminds us that "almost all things are by the Law purged with blood, and without sheading of blood is no remission" (Heb. 9.22). "How much more shal the blood of Christ . . . purge your conscience from dead workes, to serue the liuing God?" (Heb. 9.14). Thus we move from a world of inconsequential human acts of revenge and atonement on Guyon's part to one of effective divine atonement. This act of heavenly magnanimity, however, does not make man righteous; it only offers to absolve him from just blame. When Pyrochles is defeated and "now subiect to the victours law" (II.viii.50), he discovers himself subject to the rigor of the old covenant. The new covenant which the Prince bears, however, is one of divine mercy ("I wil be merciful to their vnrighteousnes, and I wil remember their sinnes and their iniquities no more" [Heb. 8.12]). And just as Christ had come into the world to save, not to judge,

> full of Princely bounty and great mind
> [Arthur] . . . not cared him to slay,
> But casting wrongs and all reuenge behind,
> More glory thought to giue life, then decay,
> And said, Paynim, this is thy dismall day;
> Yet if thou wilt renounce thy miscreaunce,
> And my trew liegeman yield thy selfe for ay,
> Life [eternal] will I graunt thee for thy valiaunce,
> And all thy wrongs will I wipe out of my souenaunce.
>
> (II.viii.51)

Pyrochles' answer reveals that he does not understand the Christian magnanimity inherent in the new covenant which he is offered and (as he had done with Guyon previously) still considers the universe to be run by fortune and not divine plan: "Foole (said the Pagan) I thy gift defye, / But vse thy fortune, as it doth befall" (II.viii.52). Good and evil, success and defeat, are for him the result of chance and natural human strength. Thus he despises Arthur's offer of grace and freely chooses to die, confirmed in this false belief—yet another Gryll.

Regretfully Arthur beheads him because "he so wilfully refused grace." The sacrifice that the Prince has symbolically made in this battle has been rejected. We are warned in Hebrews that

if we sinne willingly after that we haue received the knowledge of
the trueth, there remaineth no more sacrifice for sinnes, But a feareful loking for of iudgement, & violent fyre, which shal deuoure the
aduersaries. He that despiceth Moses Law [the law which Pyrochles
had defaced], dyeth without mercie vnder two, or thre witnesses.
Of how muche sorer punishment suppose ye he be worthie, which
treadeth vnder fote the Sonne of God, and counteth the blood of the
Testament as an vnholie thing, wherewith he was sanctified, and
doeth despite the Spirit of grace? For we knowe him that hathe said,
Vengeance *belongeth* vnto me: I wil recompense, saith the Lord. And
againe, The Lord shal iudge his people. It is a feareful thing to fall
into the hands of the liuing God.   (10.26–31)

Man must surrender his desire for personal revenge both because it is a passion and because he cannot judge clearly on whom it is ethically proper to
impose vengeance, and he must leave justice to a careful and omniscient
God. But that same God would rather encourage Medina's vision of goodwill and charity among men and between sinful human beings and God
himself instead of justly imposing divine vengeance. However, vengeance
is the Lord's, and rejection of this covenant brings man's "fate" down
upon him.

Guyon also is subject to the victor's law; and although he has performed
"good" deeds throughout his life and can usually control the passion of revenge in himself, he still believes that personal vengeance is necessary in
the face of careless heavens. He must still stand condemned for his mis-
taken classical belief in the desire for and the necessity of self-sufficiency.
But when he hears of Arthur's struggles to protect and save him, "His
hart with great affection was embayd, / And to the Prince bow[ed] with
reuerence dew, / As to the Patrone of his life" and offers himself "to be
euer bound" (II.viii.55) to his service. This decision by Guyon—a decision
which for us may seem natural and predictable, but one which for Guyon
is monumental—suggests his renunciation of the independence sought by
Aristotle's magnanimous man (one of his greatest qualities for the Greeks)
and his recognition of man's need to accept the necessity of divine patronage. It is typical of the magnanimous man, however, that he seeks to return good for good (that last infirmity of a noble, but theologically flawed
mind), and so Guyon asks what he may do to return "so great graces"
(II.viii.55), for if this can be done, the knight will no longer be in
Arthur's debt. Theologically he is assuming that there is a value in good
deeds in the process of his salvation. The Prince (like Spenser a Protestant
in his views) offers the solution to this last flaw in his thinking:

> Faire Sir, what need
> Good turnes be counted, as a seruile bond,
> To bind their doers, to receiue their meede?
> Are not all knights by oath bound, to withstond
> Oppressours powre by armes and puissant hond?
> Suffice, that I haue done my dew in place.
> So goodly purpose they together fond,
> Of kindnesse and curteous aggrace.   (II.viii.56)

Arthur's argument is a theological one: The doing of good deeds does not enable man to merit salvation, and so Guyon has no right to expect a "meed" for his acts. In fact, because man has faith and has accepted the necessity of combatting evil, good deeds are only the natural and necessary consequence. Spenser here explains the final theological basis of good works as the *consequence* of faith—a consequence that plays no part in the process of man's justification by faith alone or in his ultimate salvation.

Vengeance as a theme and revenge as a word disappear totally from Book II at the end of canto viii. And yet it can be legitimately argued that Guyon does what he sets out to do—punish Acrasia for what she has done to Mordant and Amavia. I would suggest, however, that this punishment is no longer the product of revenge. The episodes of Book II are designed to teach us (and Guyon) that there is a careful heaven and that all men are sinful, even the best. Guyon is forced to accept the fact that Ruddymane's stained hands are his own, and in so doing he must internalize what the bloody-handed babe represents—fallen man. The punishment imposed on Acrasia is better regarded, not as vengeance imposed on an external human being, but as the rejection and containment of the source of human evil which Guyon has come to recognize *in himself*. He is no longer an avenging hero but a man who has successfully come to control the intemperance that stains all fallen men, including himself.[28]

Thus Spenser shows us in these eight cantos a world in which the heavens *are* careful, both to wicked man (Guyon)—ethically good though he may be—and to his wicked foe (Pyrochles and Cymochles). The perception of a world of fortune only reveals man's blindness to a world of grace. If God does not seem to punish wickedness, it is only beause we cannot see the operation of divine justice clearly. Though wrath and the desire for personal vengeance can be controlled (though not eradicated) by human temperance, and classical magnanimity can offer the best of men a paradigm of mercy to live by, in the end it forgets that *all* men, including the best, need forgiveness. The mystery of the Redemption which Spenser questions at the beginning of this canto is solved with an understanding of divine magnanimity: grace freely given, not as just reward for the good man's goodness (for it would go to Pyrochles too, if only he would take it), but as an act of divine mercy in the face of human evil. Even divine vengeance in the end will be abated, if man will choose to accept in its stead divine love. "O th'exceeding grace / Of highest God, that loues his creatures so, / And all his workes with mercy doth embrace."

Wilfrid Laurier University

NOTES

1. *The Works of Edmund Spenser: A Variorum Edition,* ed. Edwin Greenlaw et al., 11 vols. (Baltimore: Johns Hopkins Press, 1932–57). All Spenser quotations are from this edition.

2. See Ruth Kelso, *The Doctrine of the English Gentleman in the Sixteenth Century* (Urbana: University of Illinois Press, 1929), ch. 5; Lily B. Campbell, *Shakespeare's Tragic Heroes: Slaves of Passion* (Cambridge: Cambridge University Press, 1930), ch. 1, and "Theories of Revenge in Renaissance England," *MP* 28 (1931), 281–96; Willard Farnham, *The Medieval Heritage of Elizabethan Tragedy* (Berkeley and Los Angeles: University of California Press, 1936), ch. 9; Fredson Bowers, *Elizabethan Revenge Tragedy: 1587–1642* (Princeton: Princeton University Press, 1940); Percy Simpson, *Studies in Elizabethan Drama* (Oxford: The Clarendon Press, 1955), ch. 7; Robert Ornstein, *The Moral Vision of Jacobean Tragedy* (Madison: University of Wisconsin Press, 1960), ch. 1; Lawrence Stone, *The Crisis of the Aristocracy: 1558–1641* (Oxford: The Clarendon Press, 1965), ch. 5; Hiram Hayden, *The Counter-Renaissance,* 2nd. ed. (Gloucester, Mass.: Peter Smith, 1966), ch. 9; Elinor Bevan, "Revenge, Forgiveness, and the Gentleman," *REL* 8 (1967), 55–69; John Sibly, "The Duty of Revenge in Tudor and Stuart Drama," *REL* 8 (1967), 46–54; S. P. Zitner, "Hamlet, Duellist," *UTQ* 39 (1969), 1–18; Eleanor Prosser, *Hamlet and Revenge,* 2nd. ed. (Stanford: Stanford University Press, 1971), chs. 1–3. It is unfortunate that in Renaissance studies scholars tend to be divided into dramatic and nondramatic specialists and few who write about the contact between these types of literature. Even Fredson Bowers, whose seminal book, *Elizabethan Revenge Tragedy,* is primary reading for anyone interested in the dramatic tradition, has written an article on Book II of *The Faerie Queene* in which he fails to recognize the recurring study of revenge which shapes much of the action. See Fredson Bowers, "*The Faerie Queene,* Book II: Mordant, Ruddymane, and the Nymph's Well," in *English Studies in Honor of James Southall Wilson* (Charlottesville: University of Virginia Press, 1951), pp. 243–51.

3. "Revenge" occurs fourteen times, "wreak" ten times, in the first eight cantos of Book II. Neither word appears in the remainder of the book. See Charles G. Osgood, *A Concordance to the Poems of Edmund Spenser* (Washington, D.C., 1915).

4. *The Geneva Bible* (London, 1560). All biblical quotations come from this edition. It

has been convincingly argued that the version of the Bible most clearly used by Spenser is this one. See Naseeb Shaheen, *Biblical References in "The Faerie Queene"* (Memphis: Memphis State University Press, 1976), pp. 27–35.

5. Some discussion can be found in James Nohrnberg, *The Analogy of "The Faerie Queene"* (Princeton: Princeton University Press, 1976), pp. 357–58, 381–84 et passim. Several incisive observations, including the undeveloped recognition of Guyon as "an avenging hero" are made by Bevan, "Revenge, Forgiveness, and the Gentleman," p. 56. To my knowledge, however, no Spenserian critic has recognized the implications of her suggestions which would connect the Book of Temperance to the revenge tragedies and the tradition of revenge generally.

6. By "primitive" I do not mean to suggest that it was archaic and therefore not practiced in sixteenth-century England. The revenge play was popular on the Elizabethan and Jacobean stage precisely because this tribal code was still alive. See Bowers, *Elizabethan Revenge Tragedy*, pp. 15–20 et passim, and Stone, *The Crisis of the Aristocracy*, ch. 5.

7. Harry Berger, Jr., *The Allegorical Temper: Vision and Reality in Book II of Spenser's "Faerie Queene"* (New Haven: Yale University Press, 1957), pp. 3–38, 44–61.

8. Alastair Fowler, "The Image of Mortality: The Faerie Queene, II.i–ii," in *Essential Articles for the Study of Edmund Spenser*, ed. A. C. Hamilton (Hamden, Conn.: Archon Books, 1972), pp. 139–52; A. C. Hamilton, "A Theological Reading of *The Faerie Queene*, Book II," *ELH* 25 (1958), 155–62. Neither critic, however, is convincing in his interpretation of Amavia, Fowler variously suggesting that she is "Conscience" (p. 93), the Old Man of St. Paul's epistles (p. 98), and Nature (pp. 105–06); Hamilton that she represents "Man's former righteousness" (p. 158). It is perhaps more satisfying to see Amavia simply as the fallen Eve just as Mordant is the fallen Adam. Together they make up the "trunk" of postlapsarian mankind. Amavia's reputed innocence is advocated by herself and Guyon (and perhaps only ironically by the Palmer); Spenser himself does not say that she is innocent. If Amavia *is* Eve, however, she does not know it, having fallen from a universe protected by God into one controlled (she thinks) by fortune. It should also be noted that neither Fowler nor Hamilton questions Guyon's right to assume the role of avenger in Book II.

9. For a discussion of sixteenth-century attitudes toward ghosts, see J. Dover Wilson, *What Happens in Hamlet*, 3rd. ed. (Cambridge: Cambridge University Press, 1959), ch. 3; Keith Thomas, *Religion and the Decline of Magic: Studies in Popular Beliefs in Sixteenth- and Seventeenth-Century England* (London: Weidenfeld and Nicolson, 1971), ch. 19; Prosser, *Hamlet and Revenge*, ch. 4. In his descent into the underworld, Aeneas asks the Sibyl the reason for the gathering of souls on the banks of the Cocytus. She replies: "All this crowd thou seest is helpless and graveless; yonder warden is Charon; those whom the flood carries are the buried. Nor may he bear them o'er the dreadful banks and hoarse-voiced waters ere their bones have found a resting-place. A hundred years they roam and flit about these shores; then only are they admitted and revisit the longed-for pools." The *Aeneid*, trans. H. Rushton Fairclough, 2 vols. (London: William Heinemann, 1935), 6.325–30. When Duessa confronts Night with the state of Sans Joy, she tells the goddess that Sans Foy still lies unburied: "And now the pray of fowles in field he lyes, / Nor wayld of friends, nor laid on groning beare" (I.v.23). Moreover, Night attributes her children's ends to their fate or destiny, just as Guyon and Amavia do (I.v.25).

10. See further classical references noted by John Upton, *Var.* 2.195.

11. For a discussion of pollution as it was understood by the Greeks, see E. R. Dodds, *The Greeks and the Irrational* (Berkeley and Los Angeles: University of California Press, 1951), under the headings Miasma and Catharsis.

12. See Fowler, "The Image of Mortality," pp. 143–44.

13. The withered tree versus the fruitful tree is a commonplace metaphor for the spiritual life worked out in the Books of Holiness and Temperance. See my doctoral dissertation, "The Figure of Arthur in Spenser's *Faerie Queene:* Historical, Ethical, and Religious Studies" (University of Toronto, 1975), pp. 461–66. For a general discussion of this Christian tradition, see Robert P. Miller, "Chaucer's Pardoner, the Scriptural Eunuch, and the *Pardoner's Tale,*" in *Chaucer Criticism: The Canterbury Tales,* ed. Richard J. Schoeck and Jerome Taylor (Notre Dame: University of Notre Dame Press, 1960), pp. 221–44. Fowler has also observed, correctly I think, that canto ii, stanza 4, is structured by "legal diction that features so prominantly in the early episodes" (p. 144). I would suggest that the reason for this legal terminology is that until Arthur's rescue of Guyon in canto viii, Spenser is concerned with the old law under which all men exist. It is appropriate, therefore, to see the human predicament from a judicial perspective.

14. Traditionally revenge was portrayed as the predictable outcome of uncontrolled wrath. Thus it was a psychological problem as well as a theological problem and was to be solved not only by an acknowledgment of divine injunction but also by a rigorous tempering of the passions. Seneca's discussion of anger, *De ira,* for instance, immediately becomes a discussion of revenge. See the *Moral Essays,* trans. John W. Basore, 3 vols. (London: William Heinemann, 1970), 1.1.1–5. Christianization of the moral life, of course, did not change the nature of the passions, only the nature of human virtue. Compare with Seneca Spenser's treatment of Wrath in the procession of the Seven Deadly Sins. Cf. Phineas Fletcher, *The Purple Island,* 7.55–57; and Bowers, *Elizabethan Revenge Tragedy,* pp. 20–22.

15. This reduction of Sir Huddibras and Sans Loy to the irascible and concupiscible appetites is, of course, a simplification of the complex nature of the analysis of the passions Spenser works out in Book II, but a reduction which is acceptable, I think, in the present context. For a more detailed discussion of the passions, see James Carscallen, "The Goodly Frame of Temperance: The Metaphor of Cosmos in *The Faerie Queene,* Book II," *UTQ* 37 (1968), 136–55.

16. In *The Ruins of Rome* 24 Spenser meditates on the same problem of the origin of evil in words which Medina herself could use to these knights:

> What fell *Erynnis* with hot burning tongs,
> Did grype your hearts, with noysome rage imbew'd
> That each to other working cruell wrongs,
> Your blades in your owne bowels you embrew'd?
> Was this (ye *Romanes*) your hard destinie?
> Or some old sinne, whose vnappeased guilt
> Powr'd vengeance forth on you eternallie?
> Or brothers blood, the which at first was spilt
> Vpon your walls, that God might not endure,
> Vpon the same to set foundation sure?

17. Poisoning was considered by the Elizabethans to be the most heinous method of extracting revenge. See Bowers, *Elizabethan Revenge Tragedy,* pp. 26–28. This attitude may have made Acrasia's poisoning of Mordant even more reprehensible to Spenser's readers. In this same light we might consider Acrasia's Porter, whose corrupting "Mazer bowle of wine was set" (II.xii.49) to be offered to all visitors to the Bower.

18. Guyon's limitation in seeing the issue as only an ethical one seems pointedly rebutted by Spenser earlier in this same episode. The knight believes that Temperance is suffi-

cient in itself to overcome Furor, and yet in his own struggle with this "franticke fit" he "ouerthrew himself vnwares, and lower lay" (II.iv.8). Unknown to himself, the knight has Furor (La Primaudaye's "desire of revenge") within himself.

19. See Berger, *Allegorical Imagery*, ch. 1; and my "Figure of Arthur in Spenser's *Faerie Queene*," ch. 8. Seneca's discussion of anger in his *De ira*, a standard Renaissance text, always offers magnanimity as the remedy for the passion of revenge. Rejecting Aristotelian ethics, he argues that "you must not suppose . . . that anger contributes anything to greatness of soul [*ad magnitudinem animi*]" (1.20.1). Anger "is a puffed-up, empty thing, as far removed from greatness of soul [*magnitudine animi*] as foolhardiness is from bravery" (1.20.2). Indeed, "the really great mind, the mind that has taken the true measure of itself, fails to revenge injury only because it fails to perceive it. . . . Revenge is the confession of a hurt; no mind is truly great [*magnus animus*] that bends before injury. . . . the lofty mind [*sublimus animus*] is always calm, at rest in a quiet haven" (3.5.7–6.2). Seneca's entire discussion of mercy, *De clementia*, is a study of magnanimity also, for the two virtues are in practice synonymous. Cf. Cicero, *De officiis*, 1.25. La Primaudaye's discussion of revenge follows the standard pattern: "if we endeuor to shew forth the effects of true magnanimitie and greatnesse of hart, there is no doubt but to beare and to endure with al modestie and patience the outrages and wrongs of our enemies, is the marke of that vertue which is most absolute and perfect. . . . How greatly then ought this vertue to be accounted of, which forceth this natural lust of reuenge, bred in al liuing creatures, and how noble must the mind of that man needs be, which is able to master such a violent passion, so common to all men, thereby procuring to it selfe the name of a mild and gratious spirit, and readie to forgiue, which is proper and peculiar to the divine nature?" *The French Academie* (1586), pp. 381–82. We shall "deserue the praise of true Magnanimity, if I say, we can command our selues and all vehemencie of choler, which driueth men forward to be auenged on their enemies" (p. 383). Cf. Lodowick Bryskett, *A Discourse of Ciuill Life* (London, 1606), pp. 76–77, 232.

Guyon, of course, is capable of forgiveness for evil done *to him*, as his release of Pyrochles in canto v demonstrates. His self-assumed need to act as an agent of justice *for others*, however, in a world apparently denied divine vengeance, causes him to seek vengeance on their behalf. The problem of a world in which neither the heavens nor the state seemed prepared to act lay at the heart of many of the revenge tragedies. As Eleanor Prosser has shown, however, in no instance was this deemed justification for the hero to take vengeance into his own hands. Cf. Ornstein, *The Moral Vision of Jacobean Tragedy*, pp. 19, 22–24, for a slightly different view. Of course, on the stage the character who found himself in this predicament had been personally sinned against; he was not the agent of justice for others. Guyon's motive, therefore, may seem more honorable. However, it must stand similarly condemned because it is founded on a faulty system of metaphysics.

20. See Patrick Cullen, *Infernal Triad: The Flesh, the World, and the Devil in Spenser and Milton* (Princeton: Princeton University Press, 1974), pp. 74–76.

21. Arthur, the Palmer, and the two paynim brothers all treat Guyon as though he were dead, even though the Palmer and the Prince know that, although senseless, the knight is alive. See the Elizabethan homily, "A Sermon of Good Works Annexed unto Faith," in *Sermons, or Homilies Appointed to be Read in Churches in the Time of Queene Elizabeth of Famous Memory* (Dublin, 1821), pp. 38–40, for an explanation of this metaphoric death. There we are told at extended length that "they which glister and shine in good works, without faith in God, be like dead men" (p. 40).

22. Notice that in his discussion of the evolution of human history Guyon's metaphysics are still classical, not specifically Christian. In his description of Ruddymane's predicament, he sees him metaphorically as a "budding branch" torn from "the native tree," indi-

A Study of Revenge and Atonement in *The Faerie Queene*

cating his belief that the tree and the branch are both basically good. It is the "cruel stars" which wither man. In his conversation with Mammon, Guyon offers a comparable metaphor: "At the well head the purest streames arise: / But mucky filth his braunching armes annoyes, / And with vncomely weedes the gentle waue accloyes" (II.vii.15). Man is born good, but intemperance allows him to be corrupted by his passions. Similarly, in his Ovidian description of the ages of man, Guyon stresses the loss of the Saturnian golden age as resulting in man's exceeding the "measure" of Nature's "mean" (II.vii.16). Cause and effect are reversed from the Christian tradition: In the latter, man's intemperance *causes* his fall from a state of grace; in the former, man's intemperance is the *result* of his loss of this state. For Ovid, man "fell" from the golden age, not through any fault of his own, but because of the gods and their own revolt. Hence, we find no concept of original sin such as that found in the Christian tradition. Similarly, Guyon here omits any mention of original sin, passing over the reason for the present state of mankind, though implying through his metaphors that even today men are born spotless.

23. It can be argued that this interpretation ignores the conventions which Spenser is working with: Like a character in The *Inferno* or the emblem books, Pilate is asked who he is in order to be given a chance to reply. It is interesting though that when Tantalus reveals who he is, Guyon immediately moralizes the justice of his punishment because of his psychologically intemperate mind (II.vii.60). But, on hearing Pilate's explanation of his "sin" (as opposed to the other's "vice"), Guyon has nothing to say. And yet Pilate has committed the most heinous of sins.

24. Like Spenser in canto viii.1–2, the writer of Hebrews begins with a discussion of the angelic forces. God, he tells us, makes "the Spirits his messengers" (1.7). "Are they not all ministring spirits, sent forthe to minister, for their sakes which shalbe heires of saluation?" (1.14). Moreover, this concern of God for fallen man prompts the writer to ask Spenser's question ("O why should heauenly God to men haue such regard?" [II.viii.2]): "What is man, that thou shuldest be mindeful of him! or the sonne of man that thou woldest consider him!" (2.6).

25. Cf. St. Augustine, *De civitate Dei* 9.15. "Good angels . . . cannot mediate between miserable mortals and blessed immortals. . . . [Therefore] he chose to be in the form of a servant, and lower than the angels, that He might be our Mediator." *The City of God,* trans. Marcus Dods (New York: Random House, 1950), pp. 293–94.

26. It can be argued that Cymochles' point is simply that Guyon must have been evil or he would not have lost the battle. This, however, cannot be right because it would make Cymochles' words imply a providential, judgmental world, not a world of fortune. Cymochles here is not echoing a Christian theory of trial by battle as a method of divine justice.

27. Arthur uses the word "fortune" here in order to argue with the brothers in terms of their own metaphysics, so that his appeal is only to their reason. Only when this petition is rejected does he raise the issue of providential justice. Spenser does this to indicate that man, unless he believes that he lives in a divinely controlled world of justice, can see no reason to reject personal revenge.

28. It is true that Guyon is a knight errant in the service of Gloriana. But to see his role in Book II as an instrument of her justice and thus not motivated by personal revenge but by public responsibility and delegated authority is questionable. To see him in this light turns the study of temperance into an examination of a public, not a private, virtue. It is perhaps more satisfactory to read the story of Artegall in Book V as that of the administration of social justice. Book II, however, is essentially internal; it is a study of the proper functioning of the various capacities of the human mind. To interpret its quest as essentially external to the character of Guyon, and the lesson learned concerning vengeance as primarily social, shifts the emphasis from the theological issue explored throughout the book.

ANTOINETTE B. DAUBER

The Art of Veiling
in the Bower of Bliss

UNDENIABLY, THE Bower of Bliss is possessed of a compelling beauty. The reader, morally aware, knows that he should not allow himself to be seduced. But the powerful impression the Bower makes is not effaced when he repeats to himself, "this art is false, the nature unnatural, the sexuality corrupt."[1] And many sensitive readers find themselves not wholly able to assent to Guyon's blind act of destruction. Guyon, after all, is limited, and the virtue to which he aspires is not one we would seek out above all others. He is insensitive; he knows no love.[2] We can be fairly certain that, had he thought about it, he would have considered any art, even a Spenserian art to which we wholeheartedly consent, a threat to or a distraction from his dogged virtue. Finally, we cannot fully trust Guyon to judge art on our behalf, and, indeed, Spenser does not ask us to. For, as I will try to show, we have two champions doing battle in the Bower. As Guyon fights for temperance, stumbling along the way, slightly awkward as always, the poet himself, quietly, almost mysteriously, joins the fray in defense of his own high art. Together they help us repudiate the false and treasure the true. To enter immediately into the image I wish to pursue, Guyon's experiences allow us to see that the veils which seem to be Acrasia's favorite artistic device cover nothing worthwhile, while Spenser's counterallegory reaffirms our faith that, at its best, art mediates between man and a vision of the divine.

The Bower achieves its most characteristic effects by the use of veils. It is well known that Acrasia appears veiled and that the Palmer traps her in a net specifically forged for the occasion, but versions of veiling figure in the landscape in far more subtle ways. Genius, the official greeter, is decked with flowers, and this lavishness is redoubled in the pleasance itself, personified as Flora, whose "mother Art, as halfe in scorne / Of niggard Nature, like a pompous bride / Did decke her."[3] In the center of the Bower, such decking becomes pervasive, and nearly everything is seen through something else. In "the midst of all" stands the fountain, "Of richest substaunce, that on earth might bee, / So pure and shiny, that the siluer flood / Through euery channell running one might see" (60). The fountain is so pure that it allows the spectator to see the silvery water flowing through it. One transparency opens onto another, equally clear.[4] Adorning the fountain are

> shapes of naked boyes,
> Of which some seemd with liuely iollitee,
> To fly about, playing their wanton toyes,
> Whilest others did them selues embay in liquid ioyes. (60)

And like these bathing boys, the infamous golden ivy presents itself through a film of water:

> Low his lasciuious armes adown did creepe,
> That themselues dipping in the siluer dew,
> Their fleecy flowres they tenderly did steepe,
> Which drops of Christall seemd for wantones to weepe. (61)

And, again, the streams well from the fountain pool into a little lake, so shallow "That through the waues one might the bottom see, / All pau'd beneath with Iaspar shining bright" (62). Each of these instances of decking typifies an art that "appeared in no place." One garden object is transparently veiled by another natural substance. The artistry is all a matter of placement, the arrangements so casual that the art is almost unseen. We may assume that Guyon, unschooled in such effects, does not discern the hand of the artist and remains unaware that the landscape itself conspires to beguile him.

This setting is the appropriate showcase for the two naked damsels who also offer themselves through veils. As they frolic wantonly, "their snowy limbes, as through a vele, / So through the Christall waues appeared plaine" (64), and "their yellow heare / Christalline humour dropped downe apace" (65). Guyon is tempted to linger. The purposes and methods of the scene demand careful examination, for more than simple sexual seduction is at stake. First, we must observe that there is an abrupt suspension of allegory. Excess, who was accurately named by the moral allegorist, is followed by two nameless girls, dubbed Cissie and Flossie by the critic.[5] Lacking clear tags, like Titillation and Desire, they are not simply iconographic figures supported by a suitably allegorical background. Rather they and the setting are versions of the same thing: The elements repeat rather than complete each other. Unlike iconographic scenes which can be scanned sequentially, each new detail adding to a fuller understanding of meaning which grows at the observer's own pace, this scene offers only one clue, endlessly duplicated. The girls cannot be interpreted, only experienced, and so it is to the experience of the viewer looking at this veiled scene that we must turn.

A veil tantalizes the spectator, piques the curiosity, by swathing what lies beneath in an aura of mystery. Yet while it heightens and enhances that which it covers, it may, potentially, serve two opposite functions. It may join as well as separate, accommodate and mystify both. The clearest statement of this dual purpose comes in the description of Nature in the *Mutabilitie Cantos:*

> For, with a veile that wimpled euery where,
> Her head and face was hid, that mote to none appeare.
>
> That some doe say was so by skill deuized,
>   To hide the terror of her vncouth hew,
>   From mortall eyes that should be sore agrized;
>   For that her face did like a Lion shew,
>   That eye of wight could not indure to view:
>   But others tell that it so beautious was,
>   And round about such beames of splendor threw,
>   That it the Sunne a thousand times did pass,
> Ne could be seene, but like an image in a glass.
>
> (VII.vii.5–6)

It is the more subtle and unexpected unifying or accommodating role that defines the aesthetics of veiling in the Bower of Bliss. As the veil hovers on the linear boundary which we suppose divides an object from all that lies outside it, it embodies and expands this imaginary line, becoming as much an extension of the beholder as of the object beheld.[6] The area it fills is illusory and paradoxical, at once a metaphor for the separateness of things and a transitional zone in which they may mingle. Representing separation, it yet encourages union, by widening the space in which borders dissolve and two "others" may meet. This illusion is the province of art.

At the fountain, therefore, Guyon, who was unmoved by Phaedria, is attracted less by the blatant sexuality than by the magnetism of the veils. He responds particularly to those appeals which feed his imagination. Thus, while two lily paps displayed above the waves do, indeed, melt his heart, yet "The rest hid vnderneath, him more desirous made" (66). And when the second damsel covers her ivory body by letting down a mantle of golden hair, and so robs Guyon of a fair spectacle, "Yet that, which reft it, no lesse faire was fownd" (67). The powerfully suggestive veils seduce the eye, and Guyon, in the very act of looking, surrenders to them. Earlier on, when he had looked neither right nor left, "suffred no delight / To sincke into his sence, nor mind affect, / But passed forth, and lookt still forward right" (53), he was safe. However, once he arrives at the most dainty paradise which "It selfe doth offer to his sober eye" (58), he is willy-nilly implicated, trapped. And, properly, in calling the knight back to himself, the Palmer reserves his rebuke for "Those wandring eyes of his." If the Palmer himself escapes, he proves the rule. Protected by the allegory which labels him "reason," he is not a whole man, lacking even Guyon's rudimentary aesthetic sense. Even so, the Palmer seems not to look about. On the single occasion that we observe the direction of his gaze (69), it fixes on Guyon.

The bewildering experience Guyon undergoes at the fountain is, perhaps, best illuminated by a moving passage in *On Not Being Able to Paint,* a book by Marion Milner, the psychoanalyst and painter:

> For days my eye had wandered lost over a whole rich countryside and found nothing to rest upon, except one thing: the chance-seen glimpses of clear streams, places where the pebbly bottom showed through the water and thereby gleamed with qualities that did not show at all in the dry stones on the path. And now I remembered too that other image . . . how the thought of sand showing through the crisp froth of small waves had stayed in my mind for weeks.[7]

Like the knight, Milner wandered through the countryside and found veiled objects to be the most memorable sights. Slowly she grasps their significance. There are "moments in which one does not have to decide which is one self and which the other—moments of illusion," when outer reality is transfigured and appears to meet one's inmost dreams. Then "the eye [is] lost in a secret germination and a coloured state of grace." This arresting description recalls Guyon's response to the wet damsels (if we take "grace" as ironic, given his fall into sexual consciousness): On his "sparckling" face "secret signes" are "kindled." And in the lovely images of stanza 65, which Harry Berger finely attributes to Guyon's own awakening awareness,[8] we sense that we are witness to a colored germination:

> As that faire Starre, the messenger of morne,
> His deawy face out of the sea doth reare:
> Or as the *Cyprian* goddesse, newly borne
> Of th'Oceans fruitfull froth, did first appeare:

The Art of Veiling in the Bower of Bliss

Such seemed they, and so their yellow heare
Christalline humour dropped downe apace.
Whom such when *Guyon* saw, he drew him neare,
And somewhat gan relent his earnest pace,
His stubborne brest gan secret pleasaunce to embrace.

If these dawning images reflect the innocence of Guyon's imagination, the true stuff of his inmost dreams, they also help us to understand why he falls. The dewy-faced star and frothy goddess demonstrate Guyon's intuitive sense that that which is veiled is not for human eyes. Indeed, without considering whether the veil is intended to separate or join, he understands it to signify the presence of a power—star and goddess—which must be mediated. What Guyon, however, fails to realize is that the art of the Bower abuses the divine signification of veils. For here, the covered objects borrow false grandeur from their covering. And the nearly naked girls, their bodies glistening, blond hair dripping, ravish the knight with the illusion that he stands before celestial creatures.

If we suppose that the obvious sexual nature of the damsels' "mystery" should have invalidated them in Guyon's eyes, we need only recall two of the most conspicuous examples of veiling in our poem: great Dame Nature, already cited, and the statue of Venus in Book IV (x.40–41). In both instances, the veiling is explicitly associated with the divine sexuality of the covered goddesses, who combine "male and female, both vnder one name." The crystalline statue in the temple, especially, contrasts instructively with the imagined Cyprian goddess, as, for that matter, Scudamour's journey through the isle of Venus rehearses Guyon's trek through the Bower. But now a man, alert and discriminating, replaces the unseasoned stripling. Scudamour, recounting his adventure, observes minutely and ponders the meaning of the veil. He is certain that neither "womanish shame, / Nor any blemish" can account for it:

But for, they say, she hath both kinds in one,
Both male and female, both vnder one name:
She syre and mother is her selfe alone,
Begets and eke conceiues, ne needeth other none.
(IV.x.41)

An awesome mystery, life source, lies behind this veil. Guyon's Venus, a purged version of the debased images which surround him, is admittedly a lesser creation. Although his pristine goddess, awash with the "fruitfull" element, may hint at the maturer ideal, she springs from Guyon's youthful imagination. In context, however, she perfectly embodies the true divinity that the art of the Bower can only simulate.

Acrasia's art is founded on bad faith and is, therefore, dangerous. In her hands, the veil of allegory becomes a smokescreen, deceiving the reader into believing that genuine vision lies behind it. Instead, in her aborted metaphor, endlessly repeated, all meaning resides in the vehicle, permanently severed from a tenor. The only meaning to which the Bower aspires is fully incarnate in the physical. The artist need not struggle with stubborn materials to express an ineffable vision, for from the start her earthbound materials entirely express her idea of complete pleasure.

Indeed, in its own terms, the Bower realizes all desires it can possibly imagine. Nothing remains unexpressed, nothing transcends the objects in the garden. And so, the final spectacle must be the artist herself. Hidden until now, the only way Acrasia can represent the achievement of her art is to appear in the flesh. She is described in two justly celebrated stanzas:

> Vpon a bed of Roses she was layd,
>   As faint through heat, or dight to pleasant sin,
>   And was arayd, or rather disarayd,
>   All in a vele of silke and siluer thin,
>   That hid no whit her alablaster skin,
>   But rather shewd more white, if more might bee:
>   More subtile web *Arachne* cannot spin,
>   Nor the fine nets, which oft we wouen see
> Of scorched deaw, do not in th'aire more lightly flee.
>
> Her snowy brest was bare to readie spoyle
>   Of hungry eies, which n'ote therewith be fild,
>   And yet through languour of her late sweet toyle,
>   Few drops, more cleare then Nectar, forth distild,
>   That like pure Orient perles adowne it trild,
>   And her faire eyes sweet smyling in delight,
>   Moystened their fierie beames, with which she thrild
>   Fraile harts, yet quenched not; like starry light
> Which sparckling on the silent waues, does seeme more bright.
>   (77–78)[9]

As we would expect, she is multiply veiled: draped in thin silk, glistening with sweat, eyes filmed with moisture. But the coverings themselves steal the scene, engendering metaphors which lead us away from what lies beneath. What does lie beneath—"alablaster skin," "snowy brest" and "faire eyes"—is truncated and cold. The ultimate vision of the Bower is

embodied in a few dismembered parts, and a corresponding dismember-
ment befalls the viewer, now reduced to "hungry eies" and "fraile harts."
The veils, into which Guyon had before so raptly peered, seeking the transcendence behind them, have become blind alleys opening onto nothing,
emblems of frustration. Guyon is not moved.

Here when the vacancy of the Bower stands revealed, Spenser asserts his
own authentic poetry. In these two stanzas, he shows his awareness of the
shoddiness of Acrasia's product, and by what he reserves to himself, the
truly poetic metaphors, demonstrates the difference between his art and
hers. One sign of Spenser's presence is the figure he openly assigns to us,
the poet and his readers ("Nor the fine nets, which oft *we* wouen see").
Indeed all of the images here share the vantage point of a life outside the
Bower. The classical allusions to Arachne and nectar and the conventional
image of orient pearl remind us of the cultural bond which ties us to Spenser and excludes the Bower.[10] With this literary kinship acknowledged,
Spenser can proceed with the two images that conclude the stanzas. They
are similar and exceedingly fine:

> Nor the fine nets, which oft we wouen see
> Of scorched deaw, do not in th'aire more lightly flee.

> like starry light
> Which sparckling on the silent waues, does seeme more bright.

Neither metaphor describes a scene so much as it attempts to tease it out of
our memory, bring it to the surface, and give this buried vision adequate
articulation. Spenser places us in a position like Milner's when she recalls
the lingering veiled images and suddenly comprehends their meaning. His
deliberate reliance on the unspoken and unformed visual impressions of his
readers confirms to each of us personally the genuineness of the unbodied
vision with which he begins. But the artistic process does not end there.
Imitating Acrasia—these are, after all, vehicles the tenor of which is her
own veiled parts—Spenser shows her up. Like hers, his art work, the poetic image, will include an object and a veiling medium. But now object
and veil seem to fuse in a shimmering unity, which eclipses the casual jux-
tapositions typical of the Bower's uninspired art and mystically confirms
Spenser's truth. In the first, thin sheets of vaporous dew are seen through
the light air. But this kinetic meeting of elements cannot be arrested. As
we behold the nets, they are already scorched by the heat, and, then, before our very eyes, they disperse into the surrounding air. It is important
to insist that the drops of dew are not lost. Rather they mingle so thoroughly with the surrounding medium that only molecular vision can dis-

cern them. The second image also involves light and water, only they have reversed their roles, and now water is the medium. But here again the elements join in the wink of an eye, and a new unity, starlight-on-the-waves, is born, before we have a chance to sort them out. Thomas Roche's comment on a parallel image in Book IV is apposite: "The two rivers are described as that curious state where sunlight and waves become nothing and everything all at once, where things are just about to become ideas—the realm of mythic vision."[11]

It can hardly be accidental that the Bower is designed to prevent such a sight. The pool is deliberately shaded:

> And all the margent round about was set,
>   With shady Laurell trees, thence to defend
>   The sunny beames, which on the billowes bet,
>   And those which therein bathed, mote offend.   (63)

Neither Acrasia nor her cohorts wish to be disturbed by a true art which speaks a higher meaning. And if Acrasia blocks out intimations of transcendence in order to substitute her own false gods, Guyon, too, may prefer to remain undisturbed, but for other reasons. For his virtue depends on a vigilance so unwavering, it can never become second nature or automatic. It demands that opposing inclinations always be held in balance. But art, as Acrasia well knew, can be profoundly unbalancing. The loss of self to which it leads, even that moment of supreme illusion in the face of a true art, may disrupt the knight's virtuous concentration. Those less devoted to temperance will, perhaps, accede to the temptations of art, but, as our canto plainly teaches, they then run the risk of yielding to an unscrupulous artist.

Indeed some readers have feared lest Spenser himself fall into this trap, especially when he stops to admire the Jason and Medea gate.[12] The gate, however, affords Spenser his best opportunity to champion a true art. For his open admiration is problematic only if we assign the gate to Acrasia, and the evidence points elsewhere. The classical theme and the harsh depiction of the torments of love bespeak a consciousness superior to that admitted within the Bower. Why would the arch-seductress advertise love's anguish at her very doorstep? Alternatively interpreted, the portal celebrates love's triumph. But this view, too, represents a consciousness higher than the somnolent wishfulfillment of the Bower proper.

The stylistic evidence against Acrasia's authorship is even more compelling. Framed of ivory, colored with paint, this gate cannot be the work

of an artist whose materials elsewhere are the found objects of the garden.
The exquisite craftsmanship which shapes the medium to the vision—

> Ye might haue seene the frothy billowes fry
> Vnder the ship, as thorough them she went,
> That seemd the waues were into yuory,
> Or yuory into the waues were sent   (45)

—surely exceeds the skills of one whose vision never transcends her earthen
materials and who relies on slick juxtaposition for her most artistic effects.

This gate, the work of an unknown artist, was made for the threshold
between the real and the illusory. Like its uncertain message, its function
appears cloudy. Too frail to be a true barrier, it marks the boundary, sym-
bolizing the transitional space where dreams are born. In short, it stands
for the principle of veiling:

> Goodly it was enclosed round about,
>   Aswell their entred guestes to keepe within,
>   As those vnruly beasts to hold without;
>   Yet was the fence thercof but weake and thin;
>
>   .   .   .   .
>
> And eke the gate was wrought of substaunce light,
> Rather for pleasure, then for battery or fight.   (43)

The veil, as fence, emerges as a strictly structural element. Its privileged
status to mediate between the eyes of the viewer and the (divine) object beyond, which, as we have seen, Acrasia ruthlessly exploits, is excluded here
from the start. The veil is drained of all divine signification. Entered guests
and unruly beasts, ranged on opposite sides of the fence, remain equally
unholy, and neither side achieves an unearned mystique. Honest and disin-
terested, the gate stands in opposition to the many veils of the Bower. Indeed, we might speculate that this particular version of this particular
myth was chosen for the gate, because it includes both divine fleece and
poisoned gown, the one veil trailing clouds of glory, the other abusing the
trust of the innocent Creusa. And so the poles of veiling are defined at the
outset.

This interpretation of the gate, as a neutral introduction to a device
which in the Bower will become debased, is cast in doubt by the attitude
of Temperance and Reason toward it. That the knight and his companion
march by, unmindful of its beauty, is what we have learned to expect of

them and their self-protective virtue. Spenser, however, prefers to mystify their indifference and slander the gate, rather than admit openly that the art which he loves may be in conflict with the virtue he respects. He, therefore, briefly associates the gate with the corruption of the Bower and names Wisdom and Temperance as its sole conquerors: "Nought feard their force, that fortilage to win, / But wisedomes powre, and temper-aunces might, / By which the mightiest things efforced bin" (43). In truth no special powers are needed to triumph over the "weake and thin" fence. But Spenser sacrifices both the gate and his own integrity, making himself appear to admire an art he knows to be tainted, in order not to foreclose entirely the possibility of an alliance between temperance and art.

Within the artful Bower, needless to say, such an alliance is devoutly to be shunned. Guyon and the Palmer decline throughout to become enmeshed in the aesthetic debate. They offer their final answer to the enchantress's deceitful veils at the Bower's last stand. The Palmer forges a net solely for the use at hand, "A subtile net, which onely for the same / The skilfull Palmer formally did frame" (81). He thoroughly de-aestheticizes the veil, now solid and opaque, emptied of all paradox, the agent only of separation. Acrasia resorts to her arts in vain, for now the imagination is immune to the spectacle of a woman in a net; its power to bind us is lost.

Spenser, however, not the Palmer, has the last word. For the proem to Book III, following immediately on the destruction of the Bower, openly deals with veiling. If we read it as a companion piece to the proem of Guyon's book, the two together form a frame for our discussion. Both address Elizabeth and assure her that she is the divine inspiration of *The Faerie Queene*. Here, then, the issue of a visionary art, of which Acrasia's Bower afforded no examples at all and Spenser's art in the Bower but weak glimmers, can be raised. The two ethereal images of light and water, which we ascribed to Spenser, hinted at divinity: The first, in its evocation of infinite extension, of complete indestructibility, of a fire which does not consume; the second, in its portrayal of a bright darkness, light falling on black waves and, to our poor eyes, seeming the brighter for it.[13] The proems confront transcendence directly:

> And thou, O fairest Princesse vnder sky,
> In this faire mirrhour maist behold thy face,
> And thine owne realmes in lond of Faery,
> And in this antique Image thy great auncestry.
>
> The which O pardon me thus to enfold
> In couert vele, and wrap in shadowes light,

That feeble eyes your glory may behold,
Which else could not endure those beames bright,
But would be dazled with exceeding light.   (II.Pr.4–5)

How then shall I, Apprentice of the skill,
That whylome in diuinest wits did raine,
Presume so high to stretch mine humble quill?
Yet now my lucklesse lot doth me constraine
Hereto perforce. But O dred Soueraine
Thus farre forth pardon, sith that choicest wit
Cannot your glorious pourtraict figure plaine
That I in colourd showes may shadow it,
And antique praises vnto present persons fit.   (III.Pr.3)

The first proem is bouyant, the speaker self-confident. He begs pardon for
shrouding his sovereign in "shadowes light," but, he confides, his feeble
audience could not endure her true grandeur. The whole proem is a good-
humored attack on readers so untrained, so literal-minded, that they dismiss Faery Land as a "painted forgery," because they cannot find it on a
map. The condescension implicit in the veiling seems justified.

Self-doubt replaces condescension in the second proem. The poet turns
inward and questions his own ability to make art, a result, perhaps, of his
confrontation with Acrasia's. For now he knows that art is both difficult
and dangerous, and his complacent account of sheathing his queen in veils
for the reader's sake suddenly seems self-deluded. The shadows that obscure his portrait are now seen as flaws, vestiges of his struggle to fuse imperfect materials with ineffable vision. He worries that Elizabeth's divine
chastity may elude translation—"If pourtrayd it might be by any liuing
art"—and he broods lest his medium fail him: "For fear through want of
words her excellence to marre." In the midst of this self-conscious reas-
sessment, there is evidence of one lesson learned, the proper use of the veil.
As screen, in the first proem, the veil realized only half its potential. In
Acrasia's Bower it realized the other half, metamorphosing into a filmy
negligee and attempting to seduce the same weak reader. But, as Spenser
sees, these two functions need not be mutually exclusive. A light veil can
reduce the glare and draw the eye. Thus, when in the following stanza of
the proem to Book III, the poet cites one work of art as truly perfect, his
appreciation incorporates new insights:

But if in liuing colours, and right hew,
Your selfe you couet to see pictured,

ANTOINETTE B. DAUBER

> Who can it doe more liuely, or more trew,
> Then that sweet verse, with *Nectar* sprinckeled,
> In which a gracious seruant pictured
> His *Cynthia,* his heauens fairest light?   (III.Pr.4)

The nectar-sprinkled medium reminds us of the "nectar" on Acrasia's breast, but here it veils, in both senses, "heauens fairest light."

This fearless poaching in Acrasia's preserve foreshadows the bold way in which the poet's avowed response to Ralegh's poem reenacts Guyon's fall:

> That with his melting sweetnesse rauished,
> And with the wonder of her beames bright,
> My senses lulled are in slomber of delight.   (III.Pr.4)

In this collage of forbidden emotions, the poet bravely conjures up Guyon's melting heart and Verdant "a slombering." He has not forgotten the threat of the enchantress and the lesson of temperance, but to the rapturous participant in transcendent art, their claims are no more than telltale debris carried along on an overflowing fountain of bliss.

Hebrew University, Jerusalem

NOTES

1. It was C. S. Lewis who first made this admonition. See *The Allegory of Love: A Study in Medieval Tradition* (1936; rpt. Oxford: Oxford University Press, 1958), pp. 324–33.

2. Isabel G. MacCaffrey's superb book, *Spenser's Allegory: The Anatomy of Imagination* (Princeton: Princeton University Press, 1976), portrays Guyon as limited in these and other ways and suggests that much of what Spenser reveals in the course of Book II takes place over his hero's head.

3. *Spenser's "Faerie Queene,"* ed. J. C. Smith (Oxford: Clarendon Press, 1909), II.xii.50. Subsequent citations appearing in the text will refer to Book II, canto xii, unless otherwise noted.

4. John B. Bender, *Spenser and Literary Pictorialism* (Princeton: Princeton University Press, 1972), pp. 175–97, discusses many of the same images from the perspective of Spenser's art, not Acrasia's.

5. Lewis, *Allegory of Love,* p. 331.

6. Cf. Leonardo da Vinci's speculations on "nothingness," in *The Notebooks,* trans. and ed. Edward Macurdy (London, 1954), pp. 73–74, quoted by Rosalie L. Colie, *Para-*

doxia Epidemica: The Renaissance Tradition of Paradox (Princeton: Princeton University Press, 1966), p. 293:

> A mere surface is the common boundary of two things that are in contact; thus the surface of water does not form part of the water nor consequently does it form part of the atmosphere, nor are any other bodies interposed between them. What is it therefore that divides the atmosphere from the water? It is necessary that there should be a common boundary which is neither air nor water but is without substance.

7. *On Not Being Able to Paint,* 2nd ed. (New York: International Universities Press, 1957), pp. 30–31.

8. *The Allegorical Temper: Vision and Reality in Book II of Spenser's "Faerie Queene"* (New Haven: Yale University Press, 1957), pp. 218–19.

9. Bender analyzes these stanzas as instances of "focusing," *Spenser and Literary Pictorialism,* pp. 41–43.

10. It seems fair to say that the classical references in the Bower are almost exclusively the product of an imagination alien to it. Two apparent exceptions confirm the rule. The Jason and Medea gate, as we shall discuss below, is not part of Acrasia's art. Genius, the porter, whom we the readers might take to be the classical god Adgistes, is expressly dissociated from him.

11. Thomas P. Roche, Jr., *The Kindly Flame: A Study of the Third and Fourth Books of Spenser's "Faerie Queene"* (Princeton: Princeton University Press, 1964), p. 183. For a more detailed account of how Spenser's two images intimate divinity, see below.

12. See Berger, *Allegorical Temper,* p. 222 ff. and MacCaffrey, *Spenser's Allegory,* pp. 244–47, for important discussions of the gate.

13. Cf. Geoffrey H. Hartman, "Adam on the Grass with Balsamum," in *Beyond Formalism: Literary Essays, 1958-1970* (New Haven: Yale University Press, 1970), p. 136.

MAREN-SOFIE RØSTVIG

Canto Structure
in Tasso and Spenser

*A*UGUSTINE MUST serve as my point of departure, since my concern here is with a concept of unity which the Renaissance itself often referred back to certain works by Augustine. As I have explained elsewhere, Augustine derived the principle of unity in a work of art from the unity he attributed to the interrelated patterns of creation and redemption—patterns he defined as numbers held in time or space.[1] It is these spatial and temporal patterns the artist should embody in his own work, as Augustine explains in the *De libero arbitrio* 2.16. And in the *De vera religione* Augustine defines the nature of the unity which invests a work with beauty: It is a matter of arranging parts either in a symmetrical pattern, or in what he calls a "graded arrangement."[2] A graded arrangement embodies one of the ratios that secure harmony, most notably the diapason, 2:1. Augustine discovers this ratio in the structures of the two works of creation and redemption as an expression of their harmony, and this circumstance warns us not to neglect graded arrangements in favor of symmetrical ones. Augustine's concept of unity in a work of art embraces both.

If we look beyond Augustine to his biblical proof passages, we find certain Old Testament statements bearing on the harmony of God's creation: God created everything "in number, weight, and measure" (Wisd. of Sol. 11.20; Vulg. 11.21); he ordered everything sweetly (*suaviter;* Wisd. of Sol. 8.1). Passages like these were supposed to provide insight into God's method of creation as defined in the structural terms employed by Augustine. To such Old Testament passages should be added the significant apostolic statement, in Romans 1.20, that the invisible world may be understood by studying that which is visible. A juxtaposition of this statement with Wisdom of Solomon 11.20 is the clue which informs us that the emphasis is on an underlying pattern. It is a study of *pattern* which brings illumination, whether the abstract order or pattern be in God's work of creation, in the providentially ordered course of human history, or in a work of art. In each case it is the pattern which mediates between our world of sense and time, and that of the Deity.

We find Augustine's argument, and his biblical proof passages, in Landino's preface to his widely disseminated edition of Dante.[3] We should read this preface in the context established by *De vera religione,* where Augustine used his rhetorical powers to the full in order to present a poetically moving account of the soul's turning toward God in love through a contemplation of Unity or Beauty. It is this Unity we must try to perceive as we ponder the shows and "phantasms" of this world, including those which have been created by artists. Unless we consider them in this manner they will be as unreal as painted banquets, while conversely they will feed the mind if they make us perceive that Wisdom which orders everything *suaviter.* What spectacle can be more wonderful than that of the incorporeal power which creates and rules our corporeal world? And what more beautiful than its ordering and adorning of this material world?[4] So far Augustine. When Landino states in his preface that the poet works like the Deity who *disposes all creatures,* that is, the *visible* and *invisible world* which is his work, in *number, measure,* and *weight,* the phrases I have italicized paraphrase Wisdom of Solomon 8.1 and 11.20 and Romans 1.20. It is important to recognize not only the religious or philosophical import of this juxtaposition, but also its implications for Renaissance literary theory. When Landino touches on the divine fury of the poet he makes direct use of Romans 1.20 to support his view that the images of harmony which we perceive on earth through our senses enable us to ascend to a contemplation of heavenly things. This is one of Augustine's favorite arguments, but Landino invokes Plato, who posits that this harmony is of two kinds: "One consists in the eternal mind of the Deity, and the second in the order and in the movements of the heavenly bodies, from which a pleasing concord arises." The soul fed on these harmonies before birth, and while on earth it seeks to regain them, one method being to imitate the heavenly harmonies in "measured verses" describing "divine significances" so that the mind is fed, as it were, with heavenly ambrosia.[5]

Landino cites Augustine's basic metaphor when he writes that God is the greatest poet and the world his poem, and that poets, too, should order everything in number, weight, and measure. However, we move closer to Spenser on considering the importance of this very metaphor in the critical works of Torquato Tasso. Tasso's exposition of the similarity between cosmic unity and the unity of an epic poem is perhaps sufficiently familiar, but its import has not been fully understood. It should be taken quite literally. Tasso's frequent references to Augustine prove his indebtedness, and I would particularly draw attention to his extensive quotation from the concluding peroration of Augustine's *De vera religione.*[6] Since Augustine's theory of unity rests on classical number lore as subsumed under divine revelation, it is significant that Tasso relates Plato's numerical account of creation in the *Timaeus* to poetry in a passage in his *Discourses on the Heroic Poem*—a passage which his modern editor finds puzzling.[7] In it he states that he prefers an eight-line stanza because of the mathematical properties of the number 8, and his brief list of these properties summarizes book 1, chapters 5–6 of Macrobius' *Commentary on the Dream of Scipio*.[8] A comparison is enough to establish the connection, but let it be added that Tasso refers to Macrobius' famous treatise in his *Discourses on the Heroic Poem* and elsewhere.[9] The passages in Macrobius present a detailed analysis of Plato's numerical account of creation, an account where symbolic numbers and symbolic ratios exist in symbiotic fusion. Fusion or coexistence is the norm and not the exception, as one will discover on studying, for example, Augustine's comments on the symbolic import of the six days of creation or of the 150 psalms.[10]

This must suffice as a brief sketch of the theoretical basis for the structural attitude to poetic unity in the Renaissance. The structures I shall discuss here are primarily textual ones, as readers already familiar with the so-called numerological approach will realize. (This term, by the way, is an unfortunate one—it is both inadequate and misleading. I would recommend that it be abandoned in favor of *topomorphical*.)[11] However, before I approach the subject of canto structure in Tasso and Spenser, I must explain that my analytical method will include a consideration of verbal repetitions as a possible clue to textual structure. The traditional analytical method bears almost entirely on the contents. One observes, for example, that a certain event or episode occupies a certain number of stanzas in a given canto, that a canto usually contains several such episodes, and that there may be introductory and concluding stanzas which function as frames. If the segments that constitute a canto should form a pattern which may be seen as symbolic, the structure should be referred to as conceptual. The point I wish to make here is that such conceptual structures often are accompanied by verbal manipulations in the form of carefully balanced patterns of repetition. What the structures are intended to convey, or how they are supposed to function, will always be open to discussion, but the reality of their presence cannot be doubted when they are underlined by pointed rhetorical devices.

Curiously little attention has been paid to the surface verbal texture of Renaissance poetry, except by critics interested in rhetoric or style. That verbal patterning may create *meaning* has not been adequately considered. In an essay on circular structure in Marvell, I have shown that a reiteration of key words may signpost textual structures of significance to our understanding both of the contents and of the unity of the poem where they occur.[12] Let me mention one example of attention to verbal structure. In

Samuel Daniel's *The Complaint of Rosamond* (1592), seven stanzas (44–50) present Rosamond's psychomachia when tempted to become the king's mistress. Thematic analysis suffices to ascertain the presence of this structure within the poem as a whole, but when he reaches stanza 50, the poet creates a circular pattern by repeating, in inverse order, no less than four of the rhyme words used in the opening stanza. Similar patterns of balanced repetition abound in the poems included in Daniel's *A Panegyrike . . . Also Certaine Epistles. With a Defence of Ryme* (1603). Before we can understand Daniel's famous *Defence of Ryme,* therefore, we must study his technique of placing the same group of words in rhyme position at carefully calculated points within the frame of a poem or a segment. When poetry is considered in architectural terms as a building made according to a preconceived plan (in the manner suggested by Exodus 25.40 and Hebrews 8.5),[13] a poem resolves itself into a set of positions where the required links are established by distributing themes, events, and possibly also certain key words according to a master plan. Once we have studied the structural techniques that Daniel shared with Spenser and a number of contemporary and later poets, we realize that his reply to Campion's advocacy of classical quantitative meters hinges on his clever reinterpretation of Augustine's definition of unity as order and proportion: The harmonious proportions established by long and short syllables may be invested in the textual structure of a poem, so that rhymed stanzaic verse is a distinct improvement even in this respect.

The points most frequently linked by means of verbal repetition are the beginning and the end, the beginning and the middle, and the middle and the end. (The actual practice, however, is more complex than this simple formula would seem to suggest.) Readers skilled in rhetoric will recognize the similarity between these large-scale patterns and the figures known as *epanalepsis* and *epanados. Epanalepsis* occurs when what Abraham Fraunce calls the "same sound" links the beginning and the end of a sentence, while *epanados* links either the beginning and the middle, or the middle and the end.[14] This pattern of linking was the concern also of Augustine in the *De musica* 6. Since the soul loves equality *(aequalitas)* and order, it dislikes an arrangement where the preceding units are *not* linked to the middle, or where those in the middle are *not* linked to those that follow.[15] Augustine puts his proposition in general terms: Ordered linking establishes beauty or harmony, and so ordered linking must prevail in the metrical pattern, or the temporal rhythm. It is exactly this argument which permits Augustine to refer to the universe as God's poem. Within a poem, ordered linking may be achieved by arranging themes, events, and key words in the manner of an *epanalepsis* or an *epanados,* or both. The principle is valid at all levels: that of a single segment, a single canto, or the epic as a whole. (And in God's poem of the world we similarly observe the same principle in the structure of the universe, in that of society, and in man.)

For the sake of brevity I must exclude from consideration the verbal patterns we find in Tasso's *Gerusalemme liberata* (1581), but one point must nevertheless be made: When Tasso repeats a rhyme word, he places it *within* the line. The polysyllabic character of Tasso's rhyme words must be one reason why he as a rule avoided repetition in rhyme position, but Fairfax's translation adopts the English custom, which is so much more emphatic than the more discreet Italian practice.

A short survey of the total structure of Tasso's epic will be useful, since a similar survey cannot be made of *The Faerie Queene*. Tasso's epic contains 1917 stanzas distributed into twenty books in such a manner that the textual center consists of the first 19 stanzas of Canto 11, preceded and followed by 949 stanzas. The second half, then, is longer than the first by 19 stanzas, and these stanzas present a self-contained episode of such a character that it functions as a unifying nexus for the entire epic action. Its placement at the textual center must therefore have been the result of conscious choice. This segment (11.1–19) describes the day set aside by Godfrey and his army to celebrate mass on Mount Olivet before the assault on the walls of Jerusalem. Through the elevation of the host on the mountain where Christ suffered, heaven and earth are united, and earthly power is derived from heaven above (11.1). After mass, the "warlike companies" are dismissed with the pregnant word *Itene* (rendered by Fairfax: "You servants of the Lord depart"), and their new condition is indicated by the phrase "le squadre pie" ("the pious hosts"). This relates the middle to the beginning: "Canto l'arme pietose" (Fairfax: "The sacred armies . . . I sing"). This is the moment when the arms become truly *pietose* or sacred, and this sacred character is honored as the poem ends, when Godfrey hangs up his arms in the temple (20.144). The segment is itself carefully structured, central accent falling on the twice-repeated reference to the mountain which was supposed to be at the center of the earth (one exegete argued that the heavenly Jerusalem was right above it): "Monte che da l'olive il nome prende: / Monte per sacra fama al mondo noto" ("Mountain which takes its name from the olive tree, Mountain known to the world for its sacred fame" 11.10). This is how Tasso aligns the structure of his epic with that of the world and of sacred history. At the heart of each is a celebration of union between God and man, a union that turns carnal man into spiritual man, possessed of power from above.

A web of thematic, phrasal, and verbal patterns forge the nine stanzas which precede and follow stanza 11.10 into a mirror of the "triplicati giri" formed by the procession.[16] To use Spenser's phrase, the stanzas are arranged in "trinall triplicities" (*FQ* I.xii.39). Tasso repeats this arrangement when he describes Godfrey's vision of the "sacred hosts of heav'n" at 18.96: "A battaile round of squadrons three they shew, / And all by threes those squadrons ranged were." The structural alignments show that harmony prevails when God is honored as the head.

Around this unifying nexus the events which precede and follow in the poem as a whole are carefully balanced. As Tasso himself puts it in his discourses on the heroic poem, certain events must answer to, or correspond with, other events. The link between cantos may be an event or a theme, or both. When Canto 3 begins, the crusaders see the walls of Jerusalem for the first time, and they achieve their entry as Canto 18 draws to its end. The link between Cantos 8 and 13 is the theme of pacification: After Rinaldo's departure Godfrey prevents internal strife (8), and Godfrey again pacifies his troops when his prayers for rain are answered (13). The technique of linking resembles the type/antitype relationship between an Old Testament event and its inner significance as revealed in the life of Christ: There must be differences as well as similarities. Cantos 9 and 12 illustrate this point with unusual clarity. In both cantos pagan forces attack during the hours of darkness: Soliman attacks the Christians asleep in their tents in Canto 9, and in Canto 12 Clorinda leaves Jerusalem at night to set fire to the wooden tower. To protect herself, she dons black armour. In Canto 9 Satanic spirits are present on the field of battle, thus reinforcing the general sense of darkness; in Canto 12 the spiritual darkness which surrounds Clorinda is that of paganism. In Canto 9 the victory falls to the Christians after God has sent Michael to purify the earth from the presence of the spirits of hell, and in Canto 12 Clorinda is purified from paganism when she requests baptism on the point of death. When Tancred performs the rite, he sees to his horror that he has slain the woman he loved, and his subsequent agony is such that he feels invaded by all the powers of hell ("still my hell within myself I bear" 12.77). However, the hermit Peter, acting as a "good shepherd ought" (12.85), warns him that his suffering is divine chastisement which should be accepted as proffered grace; Tancred listens and obeys, and so is purified from the "hell within." On examining the similarity between these two cantos, we are made to spot differences of the greatest importance: In the one case it is the earth which is purified from the presence of evil spirits, in the other the microcosmos of man. This must suffice as a brief indication of the way in which the relationship between the two halves of Tasso's epic resembles that between the Old Testament and the New.

In poems of some length, an overall pattern of recessed symmetry may coexist with graded arrangements, or symmetry may be avoided alto-gether in favor of ratios. This is true of single cantos as of an epic as a whole. Books I and II of *The Faerie Queene,* for example, are organized in a sequence of eight plus four cantos, or the ratio 2:1. This ratio occurs with considerable frequency in the cantos of Book II, devoted as it is to the Temperance which secures harmony in the individual as in the body poli-tic. Finally let it be noted that in individual cantos symmetry need not en-tail linking: A balanced pattern may derive quite simply from the number of stanzas given to the narrative segments that compose a canto.

When trying to assess the various structural possibilities in a given canto, patterns of verbal repetition will indicate points of emphasis. Let me illus-trate this by analyzing two narrative segments in *The Faerie Queene,* Book I.[17] Canto iii is the first to focus on Una, and the first important event is her meeting with the lion and their stay in Corceca's house. Stanzas 10–21 constitute a narrative segment framed by the first stanza and the last, both of which describe how she passes on, always seeking "her wandring knight." Within this frame the first five stanzas describe the entry into Corceca's house, and the last five the killing of Kirkrapine as he tries to force an entry during the hours of the night. The verbal links between stanzas 10/21 and 11/20 are unusually emphatic, as a diagram of verbal repetitions will indicate (see fig. 1; parentheses indicate words occurring within the line). Stanza 15 is climactic both formally and thematically. In-tensity is engendered by a rhyme scheme with two elements only, the *a* and *c* rhymes being fused. This is a deviation from the established norm re-served by Spenser for special occasions. What is important is the picture of Una lamenting the loss of her knight during the hours of the night, in strong contrast to the ostentatious "painefull pennance" of Corceca as de-scribed in the preceding stanza, and even more so to the "whoredome" of

FIGURE 1. *The Faerie Queen* I.iii.10–21.

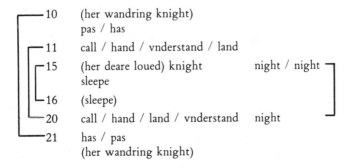

Abessa as described in the stanzas that follow. If Corceca illustrates "the superstition, which fosters a particular kind of faithlessness," Una displays a living faith which engenders a love that suffers all.[18] If this were an Aristotelian paradigm of too much, a golden mean, and too little, the third term must represent a total lack of faith, and this is certainly displayed by Abessa and Kirkrapine. One purpose served by this segment, therefore, must be to underline the nature of true faith by contrasting it with blind superstition and with atheism. This nature is displayed at the center, in stanza 15, and in the framing stanzas showing Una traveling on with a heart and will as firm as her faith. This emblematic picture recalls a similarly emblematic representation of Redcrosse as the embodiment of the golden mean with regard to action: He sticks to one clear path ("Ne euer would to any by-way bend"), and so he passes forward "with God to frend" (I.i.28). This stanza incidentally holds the textual center of its canto, twenty-seven stanzas preceding and following. And at the halfway point of each twenty-seven-stanza sequence we find the logically related pictures of rashness (I.i.14) and sloth (I.i.42).

Since Aristotle's concept of virtue as a mean between related extremes clearly invited structural embodiment, it seems reasonable to assume that Spenser's famous phrase about the twelve virtues "as Aristotle hath deuised" may bear more on method than on specific virtues. These structural implications were sufficiently familiar in the Renaissance for Pietro Bongo, canon in the cathedral church at Bergamo, to take Aristotle's definition of virtue as the point of departure for a long chapter, "De numero III," in his handbook on biblical number symbolism.[19] Bongo explains that 3 represents Justice and the highest perfection and, as it were, virtue itself, since virtue is a mean between extremes. Because the mean compels the extremes toward the center, 3 may be seen as a circle where Unity holds the middle as the center. Three is thus the number that represents the beginning of all order.[20]

The second segment I wish to discuss before considering a single canto as a whole tells the story of the escape from the Castle of Pride (I.v.45–53). Duessa returns to the castle to find Redcrosse gone, and a flashback narrative then relates the dwarf's discovery of the "wretched thrals" in the dungeon. The main body of the segment lists the proud tyrants who have fallen from their high estate (47–51), and the escape itself occupies the last two stanzas. A circular effect is scored by means of identical rhyme words repeated in inverse sequence (see fig. 2). Although the pictures of the "wretched thrals" in the dungeon and of the carcases presented in the opening and concluding stanzas seem sufficiently graphic, such was apparently the pull of the center that stanza 49 must turn aside from the task of

FIGURE 2. *The Faerie Queen* I.v.45–53.

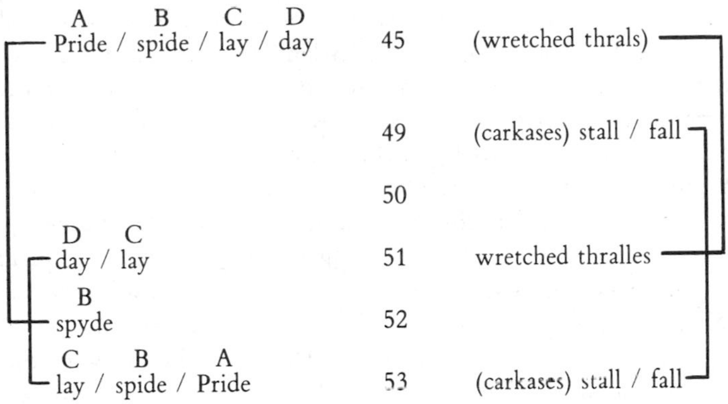

```
  A      B     C    D
  Pride / spide / lay / day        45        (wretched thrals)

                                   49        (carkases) stall / fall

                                   50

  D    C
  day / lay                        51        wretched thralles
    B
  spyde                            52
  C     B      A
  lay / spide / Pride              53        (carkases) stall / fall
```

listing the victims to convey yet a third description capable of forming a structural midpoint. When we reach the last stanza (see fig. 3) a sense of climax is engendered in part by the large number of verbal repetitions, in part because the stanza is itself balanced around its center line. Thus the penultimate line echoes the second, but in reverse sequence: "corses . . . Lay-stall" become "donghill . . . dead carkases." The only example of a repetition of the same word is the use of *Pride* to link the center to the climactic last line.

But it is time to turn from segments to entire cantos, and the cantos selected are Tasso's *Gerusalemme liberata* 15 and *The Faerie Queene* II.x. Spenser's chronicle canto is sufficiently self-contained to be presented in isolation, and another point in its favor is that it contains such a splendid example of linking, through rhyme, of widely separated stanzas where I would argue that the linking serves a specifically numerical purpose.

FIGURE 3. *The Faerie Queen* I.v.53.

```
Scarse could he footing find in that fowle way,
     For many corses, like a great Lay-stall
     Of murdred men which therein strowed lay,
     Without remorse, or decent funerall:
     Which all through that great Princesse pride did fall
     And came to shamefull end. And them beside
     Forth ryding vnderneath the castell wall,
     A donghill of dead carkases he spide,
The dreadfull spectacle of that sad house of Pride.
```

In Tasso's Canto 15 a journey is undertaken, with divine assistance, to rescue Rinaldo from his unworthy pursuit of love in Armida's delightful bower on one of the Fortunate Islands. The journey by sea from Palestine through the Mediterranean into the Atlantic requires forty-four stanzas, while the remaining twenty-two describe the ascent of a steep mountain. (The rescue itself occurs in Canto 16, when Rinaldo leaves the island to return to the siege of Jerusalem.) But the canto structure has more refinements than the 2:1 ratio created by the division into forty-four and twenty-two stanzas: The first forty-four stanzas on the journey (undertaken in a magic vessel guided by an angelic spirit) break into equal halves as the boat passes through the Strait of Gilbraltar, and when we are halfway through the canto as a whole (stanza 33) we are told that the travelers are halfway between the rising and the setting sun. This is when they first spy the mountain which is their goal. The intricate "providential" design of this canto may be compressed into the following formula:

$$
\begin{array}{ccc}
44 & : & 22 \\
\overline{22-11} & \overline{-11-22} \\
33 & : & 33
\end{array}
$$

The ratio 2:1 occurs three times, at the same time that there is an *aequalitas* structure based on the number of redemption, 33. As we shall see, the structures in Spenser's chronicle canto are remarkably similar. And just as Canto 15 precedes the successful invasion of Armida's bower, Spenser's chronicle precedes the destruction of Acrasia's Armida-like Bower of Bliss. Finally, Tasso's canto is itself in part historical, since the description of the long sea voyage contains historical information bearing on the countries they pass by.

Spenser's chronicle canto consists of sixty-six stanzas on Briton kings (studied by Arthur) and seven on the lineage of the Elfin Emperors (read by Guyon), framed by three introductory stanzas and one concluding stanza. The sixty-six stanzas divide into equal halves: thirty-three on Brutus and his progeny, and thirty-three on the generations from the English Numa, Donwallo.

That the chronicle should be taken to begin with stanza 4 is supported by a study of the verbal texture. As shown in figures 4 and 5, stanza 4 is linked with stanzas 61–69, while the first three stanzas have a double circular pattern, one formed by all three stanzas, and another by the first

Canto Structure in Tasso and Spenser

Figure 4. *The Faerie Queen* II.x.1–4.

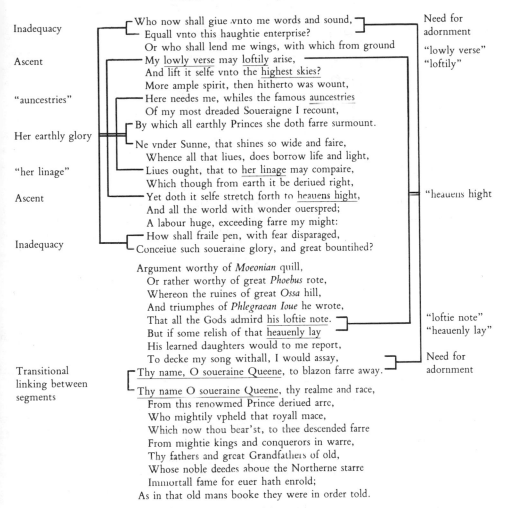

Inadequacy	Need for adornment
Ascent	"lowly verse" "loftily"
"auncestries"	
Her earthly glory	
"her linage"	
Ascent	"heauens hight"
Inadequacy	
	"loftie note" "heauenly lay"
	Need for adornment
Transitional linking between segments	

Who now shall giue vnto me words and sound,
Equall vnto this haughtie enterprise?
Or who shall lend me wings, with which from ground
My lowly verse may loftily arise,
And lift it selfe vnto the highest skies?
More ample spirit, then hitherto was wount,
Here needes me, whiles the famous auncestries
Of my most dreaded Soueraigne I recount,
By which all earthly Princes she doth farre surmount.

Ne vnder Sunne, that shines so wide and faire,
Whence all that liues, does borrow life and light,
Liues ought, that to her linage may compaire,
Which though from earth it be deriued right,
Yet doth it selfe stretch forth to heauens hight,
And all the world with wonder ouerspred;
A labour huge, exceeding farre my might:
How shall fraile pen, with fear disparaged,
Conceiue such soueraine glory, and great bountihed?

Argument worthy of *Moeonian* quill,
Or rather worthy of great *Phoebus* rote,
Whereon the ruines of great *Ossa* hill,
And triumphes of *Phlegraean Ioue* he wrote,
That all the Gods admird his loftie note.
But if some relish of that heauenly lay
His learned daughters would to me report,
To decke my song withall, I would assay,
Thy name, O soueraine Queene, to blazon farre away.

Thy name O soueraine Queene, thy realme and race,
From this renowmed Prince deriued arre,
Who mightily vpheld that royall mace,
Which now thou bear'st, to thee descended farre
From mightie kings and conquerors in warre,
Thy fathers and great Grandfathers of old,
Whose noble deedes aboue the Northerne starre
Immortall fame for euer hath enrold;
As in that old mans booke they were in order told.

two. The circular patterns are created by means of a careful positioning of words, phrases, and themes; at the center of the two-stanza structure the Queen is presented as supreme under the sun, far surmounting "all earthly Princes," while the connection of her lineage with "heauens hight" holds the center of the three-stanza structure. The homage to the royal lineage in stanza 2 is, in fact, an assertion that it has achieved the transition to the liberated Jerusalem that Augustine contrasts with the earthly city in *De*

FIGURE 5. Verbal links in *The Faerie Queen* II.x.4–69.

```
          A      B      C
    4     arre / farre / warre


          a      b      c
   61     deare / land / hand

          C      B      b      A      c
   65     warre / farre / land / arre / hand

          b      a      c
   69     land / deare / hand
```

civitate Dei. This means that the introductory three stanzas connect with the concluding seven-stanza segment on the lineage of the Elfin Emperors, as it is the essence of both to have achieved the kind of perfection that Augustine associates with the heavenly city (the liberated Jerusalem) in contrast to the city dedicated to this world. The homage at the center of stanza 2 is appropriately framed by descriptions of ascent (of the "lowly verse" to "highest skies") and descent (of the "heauenly lay" to the earthly poet). Although stanzas 1–3 are based on Ariosto's *Orlando furioso* 3.1–3, where we find the same textual structures, Spenser has added touches of his own to make the pattern even richer and more complex. Thus it is Spenser's invention that each stanza concludes climactically with a reference to the "dreaded Soueraine," her "soueraine glory," and the "soueraine Queene." Then, too, Spenser has strengthened the links between stanzas 1 and 2, while in the case of the three-stanza structure it is Ariosto who stresses this pattern most strongly. Thus Ariosto's second stanza has a beautifully balanced pattern honoring Bradamante's lineage, the "gloriosa stirpe o in pace o in guerra" ("glorious lineage, both in peace and war").

The verbal linking between stanzas 3 and 4 would seem to suggest that stanza 4 is part of the introduction, but this is not so. It is on the contrary Spenser's practice (and Tasso's) to link the end of one segment to the beginning of the next, as if to smooth over the point of transition. A good example is found in *The Faerie Queene* II.i.1–8, a passage which sets the stage for what follows. That the beginning and the end of this passage are linked by the rhymes "guile" and "wile" in stanza 1 and "wile" and "guile" in stanza 8 supports the impression that this is a segment. When the action instigated by Archimago's guile begins in stanza 9, the first line repeats the last line in the preceding stanza: "Vouchsafe to stay your steed for humble misers sake" leads on to: "He stayd his steed for humble misers sake," and we are off on another adventure. Similarly Spenser uses the terminal climax of II.x.3 as the point of departure for his chronicle—a story which is "in order told." The nature of this order is set out in figures 6 and 7, where the analysis is in terms of thematic or narrative developments.

Figure 6 shows the division of II.x into halves of equal length. The nation which was redeemed from a state resembling chaos by the arrival of Brutus returns to this condition in stanza 36: "Here ended *Brutus* sacred progenie . . . Through discord . . . Thenceforth this Realme was into factions rent . . . That in the end was left no moniment / Of *Brutus*." The beginning of the second cycle (37–39) is emphasized by letting the opening line of the first three stanzas employ the same formula beginning with "then": "Then vp arose a man of matchlesse might," "Then made he head against his enimies", and "Then made he sacred lawes."

Figure 7 shows the subdivision of each half into groups of eleven and twenty-two stanzas each, so that the same ratio prevails here, and the same numbers, as in Tasso's Canto 15. The diagram indicates the nature of the events responsible for the patterning: In one case, for example, an invasion is successfully resisted (stanza 15), in another it is not (stanza 48). Since the most important events will be located at the center, one observes with some surprise that a pattern has emerged which stresses all the positive achievements beginning with the arrival of Brutus (stanza 9) and concluding with the renewal of the realm and the marriage that produced the second Constantine (stanza 58–59).[21] Figure 7 similarly shows that central accent falls on the great positive events in the life of the nation: Stanza 20 praises the first woman ruler, and stanza 53 tells the story of the bringing of the gospel to England. When the two are related, what emerges is indirect homage to Elizabeth as protector of the faith.

FIGURE 6. *The Faerie Queen* II.x.

Stanza total	Stanza number	
33	4	Britain originally a savage country civilized by Brutus.
	20	Praise of the first woman ruler.
	36	End of "*Brutus* sacred progenie."
33	37	A new beginning.
	53	The gospel brought to England.
	69	The history is left unfinished. Praise of one's native land.

FIGURE 7. *The Faerie Queen* II.x.

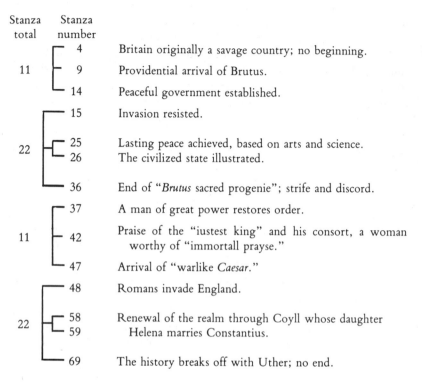

Stanza total	Stanza number	
	4	Britain originally a savage country; no beginning.
11	9	Providential arrival of Brutus.
	14	Peaceful government established.
	15	Invasion resisted.
22	25	Lasting peace achieved, based on arts and science.
	26	The civilized state illustrated.
	36	End of "*Brutus* sacred progenie"; strife and discord.
	37	A man of great power restores order.
11	42	Praise of the "iustest king" and his consort, a woman worthy of "immortall prayse."
	47	Arrival of "warlike *Caesar*."
	48	Romans invade England.
22	58	Renewal of the realm through Coyll whose daughter
	59	Helena marries Constantius.
	69	The history breaks off with Uther; no end.

The textual structures indicated here directly contradict the impression that the course of history is a meaningless sequence of war and peace, chaos and order. The emphasis is unambiguously on the happy events, and the moment that we perceive the hidden, harmonious pattern we are compelled to realize that its source must be in God.

The first subdivision or segment of the canto (4–14) has a symmetrical structure focused on the providential arrival of Brutus. Since the subject is the unification of the country under Brutus, recessed symmetry around a unifying nexus is the appropriate structural image. A thematic analysis yields the diagram shown as figure 8. The bestowal of names recalls Adam, and Genesis 6.4–5 comes to mind as we read about the daughters who "companying with feends and filthy Sprights . . . brought forth Giants and such dreadfull wights" (stanza 8).[22] The invasion, which inaugurates the next phase (in stanza 15), is compared to the Flood of Noah, so that scriptural allusions are explicit as well as oblique. The most important direct allusion is, of course, the reference to the incarnation in stanza 50,

FIGURE 8. *The Faerie Queen* II.x.4–14.

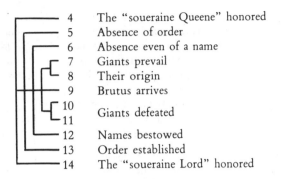

4	The "soueraine Queene" honored
5	Absence of order
6	Absence even of a name
7	Giants prevail
8	Their origin
9	Brutus arrives
10 11	Giants defeated
12	Names bestowed
13	Order established
14	The "soueraine Lord" honored

so that an alignment with sacred history is there in the text itself. Since the second half-cycle (37–69) refers to the "thrise eleuen descents" (II.x.45) from the English Numa, Donwallo, this statement should perhaps alert us to the possibility of an alignment between stanzas and generations. The narrative which takes us from the arrival of Brutus to the incarnation requires forty-two stanzas, so that this number may be taken to represent the three-times-fourteen generations from Abraham to Christ as listed in Matthew 1. The traditional gloss on this genealogy and on the numbers it contains is too extensive to be quoted here, but let me at least adduce one statement about the symbolism invested in the sum total. It was taken to denote a spiritual road leading to Christ through the pilgrimage of this life.[23]

Before a structural symbolism of this kind can be credited, more is needed than just symbolic appropriateness, however striking, and Spenser provides what is needed in two ways. He works oblique allusions to Old Testament patriarchs and kings into his narrative, and, most importantly, he has forged such strong structural and thematic links between stanzas 9 and 50 that they must be seen as the beginning and the end of a cycle. These links are shown in figure 9. The three identical rhyme words repeated in inverse order also establish a linkage through the theme they help to express. It is as the result of "fatall error" that Brutus arrives in England to redeem the inhabitants from their beastly state, and the incarnation is of course the supreme act of heavenly grace to purge "the guilt of sinfull crime" from "wretched *Adams* line." A different kind of verbal link is found in the repetition of the rhyme word "line" in the third position respectively from the end and the beginning of the two stanzas, and an additional point of interest is that the phrase "old *Assaracs* line" (9.7) is not perfectly integrated with the rhyme scheme of the stanza. It is, in fact, one

FIGURE 9. *The Faerie Queen* II.x.9 and II.x.50.

They held this land, and with their filthinesse		
Polluted this same gentle soyle long time:	time	A
That their own mother loathd their beastlinesse,		
And gan abhorre her broods vnkindly crime,	crime	B
All were they borne of her owne natiue slime,	slime	C
Vntill that *Brutus* anciently deriu'd		
From royall stocke of old *Assaracs* line, ◄	no	
Driuen by fatall error, here arriu'd,	rhyme	
And them of their vniust possession depriu'd.		
Next him *Tenantius* raigned, then *Kimbeline,*		
What time th'eternall Lord in fleshly slime	slime	C
Enwombed was, from wretched *Adams* line ◄		
To purge away the guilt of sinfull crime:	crime	B
O ioyous memorie of happy time,	time	A
That heauenly grace so plenteously displayd;		
(O too high ditty for my simple rime.)		
Soone after this the *Romanes* him warrayd;		
For that their tribute he refusd to be let payd.		

of a limited number of unrhymed lines in *The Faerie Queene.*[24] The lack of perfection built into stanza 9 in this manner may be taken to express the imperfect character of all merely human acts of redemption; the achievement of Brutus belongs within the context of the line of Assaracus, a king associated with the earthly cities of Troy and Rome, while Christ is the "eternall Lord" who assumed mortal flesh to purge the guilt from "wretched *Adams* line." The perfect integration of this phrase within the rhyme scheme of stanza 50 expresses the perfect character of the scheme for our redemption, imperfectly foreshadowed by Brutus in stanza 9. As in the *Jerusalem Delivered,* then, the linking of parts may on occasion resemble the traditional biblical linking between Old Testament types and corresponding events in the life of Christ, the antitype.

To the Old Testament allusions already identified may be added the following. The fourteenth stanza from stanza 9 describes a ruler who resembles Jacob in his fertility (Genesis 28.13–15): "An happie man in his first dayes he was, / And happie father of faire progeny" (II.x.22). While Jacob had twelve sons associated with the twelve tribes (and, by extension, with the months and the signs of the zodiac), this ruler had as many children as the year has weeks. The twenty-eighth stanza-generation (II.x.36) coincides with the break between the two thirty-three-stanza cycles, and the description of the end of the line of Brutus and the total destruction of all monuments invokes the biblical description of the total destruction of Jerusalem with the end of the twenty-eighth generation after Abraham. The new beginning marked in the twenty-ninth stanza-generation with the appearance of the strong man who gave sacred laws revealed to him "in vision" as "some men say" (II.x.39) could correspond to Daniel and the emergence from the Babylonian yoke. However, Matthew stresses the role of David, since Christ is "the son of David, the son of Abraham" (Matthew 1.1), so that the parallel may be with David rather than Daniel. This would permit stanza 42 to refer to Solomon and the Queen of Sheba in its description of the king who was the "iustest man," and of the queen "worthy of immortall prayse." If so, then the chronological pattern cannot be an exact one in terms of stanza-generations as listed by Matthew. Perhaps one should not press the alignment too much: What is certain is that once readers are alerted to the scriptural allusions, they draw the desired conclusion that England, too, has been providentially guided since the beginning of history in such a manner as to lead the nation to the one true God upheld by the one true ruler.

The double pattern set out in figure 10 may seem complex, but cannot have been difficult to invent. The basic choice must have been to place the decisive break between stanzas 36 and 37; from this break thirty-three stanzas reach out in each direction in the chronicle proper, while the sacred line extends twenty-eight stanzas back to stanza 9 and fourteen forward to stanza 50, thus establishing yet another occurrence of the ratio 2:1.

The linking between stanzas 9 and 50 is the most striking example of linking through the repetition of identical rhyme words, but it is certainly not the only one. Figure 11 shows further interesting examples, all of which coincide with the chronological patterns. One observes that the rhyme words function as thematic key concepts whose importance is strengthened by the reiteration. The three rhymes connecting stanzas 42 and 59 ("dayes," "prayse," "layes" repeated as "prayse," "dayes," "layes") are equidistant from stanza 50, so that the incarnation falls midway between the two. And stanza 42 describes the "woman worthy of immortall prayse" deemed by many to "haue beene of the *Fayes*," and a woman is again featured in stanza 59, where Helena, daughter of Coyll, marries Constantius (and becomes the mother of the famous second Constantine). This praise of women rulers may glance in the direction of Elizabeth, but it may also connect with the Queen of Heaven, whose son secured immortal life for fallen man. The two great conquerors—the second Brute and Caesar—are honored in stanzas which share the triple rhymes "name," "fame," "conquered" (stanzas 23 and 47). Both are seen solely as conquerors: "warlike *Caesar*" was prompted by ambition to conquer

FIGURE 10. Sacred and profane history aligned.

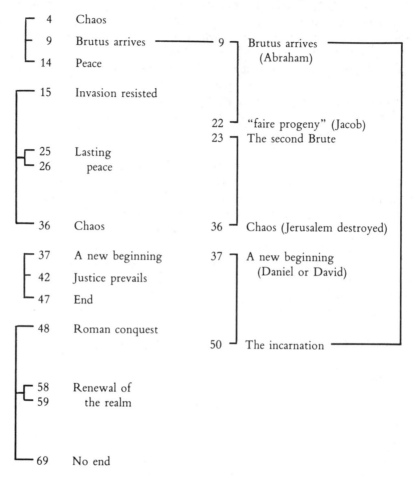

Britain, "O hideous hunger of dominion" (47.9), and this sentiment is repeated in the stanza that holds the middle: "But O, the greedy thirst of royall crowne" (35.1). This recognition of man's basic urge for power and dominion pinpoints the reason for the dismal pattern of never-ending war and internal strife and discord. No sooner has "constant peace" been established (34.4) than the hunger reasserts itself, and total chaos results (36). This particular structure, therefore, enacts the pattern of earthly glory: The peace which the earthly "city" can establish must needs be of short duration.

Canto Structure in Tasso and Spenser

FIGURE 11. Patterns of reiterated rhyme words.

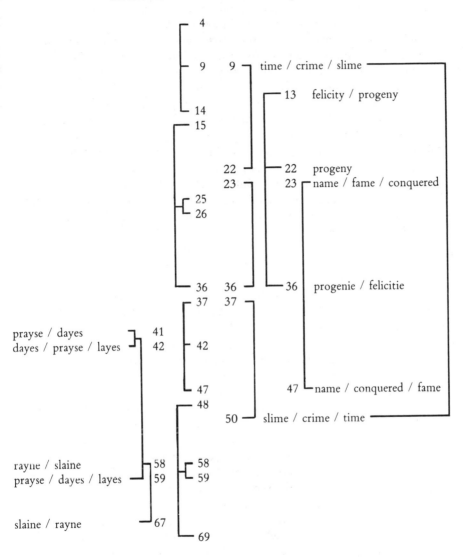

The society established by the "Elfin Emperours" (Argument) retains its peaceful state and hence must be taken to represent what Augustine calls the liberated Jerusalem, or the state toward which we should endeavor to move. The seven stanzas of this chronicle should be divided into two on the creation of Elfe and Fay, and five on the history. (Because 5 holds the middle of the numbers from 1 to 9 it was taken to represent Justice.) Of these five stanzas, the central one summarizes the history of the "seuen hundred Princes, which maintaynd / With mightie deedes their sundry gouernments" so that they may serve as "most famous moniments, / And braue ensample" to "kings and states imperiall" (74). In the chronicle of Briton kings we meet the same number in the stanza that concludes the first half: "*Brutus* sacred progenie" reigned for "seuen hundred yeares," but only to see chaos replace order so that "in the end was left no moniment / Of *Brutus,* nor of Britons glory auncient" (36). Stanzas II.x.36 and 74 share the same number and the same rhyme ("moniments"), but the contrast is stronger than the similarity. It is in the nature of the line descending from Elfe and Fay to *maintain* their government, while the line stemming from Brutus must suffer constant change from peace to war and back again. I take the symbolic import of the numbers 7 and 700 to be fullness of time, the fullness that is a measure of the completeness of the providential design for each lineage.[25]

A Christian epic cannot present a picture of the course of history as chaotic. The chronicle may be "a large-scale representation of the 'image of mortalitie,' of human nature struggling vainly to subdue its own bestial and savage instincts," but it is impossible to agree that "the slime in which we are generated claims us inexorably."[26] The importance of the stanza on the incarnation follows from our perception of its position within a flow of stanzas that imitate, or enact, the course of history. It is, in a way, appropriate that the birth of Christ should seem *either* an obscure *or* an all-important event depending on the reader's choice of perspective. To the careless observer the chronicle seems as chaotic as life itself, and the incarnation a curiously casual and unrelated event; however, the evidence of highest order is there for everyone to see who looks in the right direction and in the right manner, as illustrated by Augustine's analysis of human history in the *De civitate Dei.* He posits two branches of the human race, one stemming from Cain and the other from Adam through the son (Seth) born to replace Abel. Augustine traces these lines with great care, and he is particularly concerned to arrive at numbers possessed of an appropriate symbolism.[27] One branch is "made up of those who live according to man, the other of those who live according to God. I speak of these branches also allegorically as two cities, that is, two societies of human beings" (*De civ. Dei* 15.1). Each individual, and man as a race, must begin with "the inferior," but this should lead on to the "superior, toward which we may advance as we move forward and in which we may abide when we have reached it." The earthly city is always divided against itself: "there are wars and battles; there is pursuit of victories that either cut lives val and Renaissance chronicles, see Antonia Gransden, "Silent Meanings in Ranulf Higden's *Polychronicon* and in Thomas Elmham's *Liber metricus de Henrico Quinto*," *Medium Aevum* 46 (1977), 231–40.

26. Madelon S. Gohlke, "Embattled Allegory: Book II of *The Faerie Queene*," *ELR*, 8 (1978), 131.

27. Thus the number of generations from Cain to the Flood must be eleven, since it is the number of transgression. "On the other hand, in the line extending from Adam through Seth down to Noah we find the number ten, which is the number of law." *The City of God* 15.20. See The Loeb Classical Library: Saint Augustine, *The City of God Against the Pagans*, vol. 4 (Cambridge, Mass.: Harvard University Press, 1966), p. 535.

28. See the thesis by Marianne Brown, " 'Finely framed, and strongly trussed vp together': A Structural Approach to Edmund Spenser's *The Shepheardes Calender*" (University of Oslo, 1978).

29. Considerations of space have prevented me from including Tasso's Canto 17, where Rinaldo studies the history of his own ancestors. Cantos 14–17 of the *Gerusalemme liberata* constitute a substructure with a clear beginning, middle, and end, and it is difficult to detach parts from the whole without distorting the perspective. Canto 15 is unique only in its brevity, Tasso's average canto length being around one hundred. I shall present a full-length study of Tasso's epic in a forthcoming book.

short or at any rate are short-lived. . . . For it will not be able to rule lastingly over those whom it was able to subjugate victoriously" (15.4). Lasting peace belongs only in the superior state, where due order is observed in loving good things in a good way. "Hence, in my opinion, a short and true definition of virtue is 'a due ordering of love' " (15.22).

By way of conclusion let me quote Milton's words on the order which informs all God's works in space and time as shown in the "Mystical dance" performed by the angels in heaven: "mazes intricate, / Eccentric, intervolved, yet regular / Then most, when most irregular they seem" (*PL* 5.622–24).

The analysis submitted here will carry more conviction when seen as but one of many similar examples of Spenser's manipulation of canto structure. Another point which must be borne in mind is that even canto x cannot be adequately considered without relating it to the group of four cantos of which it is a part, that is cantos ix–xii. Although Spenser's canto structures require the same structural approach as Tasso's, and although we may trace identical structures in both, Spenser must by no means be taken to have learnt the art of shaping cantos from Tasso. The *Gerusalemme liberata* was published in 1581, and an analysis of *The Shepheardes Calender* along these lines shows that Spenser already mastered the art of imposing unity on highly varied subject matter by means of the techniques illustrated here.[28] What my analysis shows is, quite simply, that Spenser read Tasso as one master craftsman would read another, and that Tasso would seem to have inspired Spenser's choice of structure for the chronicle of Briton kings.[29] If this is what happened, then the elaborations on the basic pattern are Spenser's own invention, and these elaborations transform an apparently chaotic history into a mirror of heavenly grace. This makes it highly appropriate that it is Arthur who studies these chronicles, while it is the champion of Temperance, Guyon, who admires the harmony established and maintained by the Elfin line. It is for Arthur to discover the pattern of grace.

University of Oslo

NOTES

1. "Ars Aeterna: Renaissance Poetics and Theories of Divine Creation," in *Chaos and Form*, ed. Kenneth McRobbie (Winnipeg: University of Manitoba Press, 1972), pp. 101–19.

2. See "Ars Aeterna" for a fuller exposition. The passage in the *De vera religione* 30.55 may be translated as follows: "In all the arts that which pleases is harmony *[convenientia]*, which alone invests the whole with unity and beauty. This harmony requires equality and unity *[aequalitatem unitatemque]* either through the resemblance of symmetrically placed parts, or through the graded arrangement of unequal parts."

3. I have used the edition published at Venice in 1564. My quotations are from a translation into English by Roy Tommy Eriksen, as yet available in manuscript only.

4. I have paraphrased passages from sections 30.55; 31.58 and 51.100. The available English translation by J. H. S. Burleigh is deplorably unreliable with regard to terminology, so that the precision of Augustine's argument is blurred. St. Augustine, *Of True Religion* (Chicago: Henry Regnery Company, 1964). For a reliable Latin-French edition, see *Oeuvres de Saint Augustin,* vol. 8 (Paris: Desclée de Brouwer et Cie, 1951).

5. Landino's argument suggests influence from the Hermetic dialogues, but one must bear in mind that the Renaissance "Platonists" were, in fact, syncretists like Augustine. They subordinated Plato and Hermes to Moses, or to an original divine revelation.

6. See the last paragraph in the first book "Del giudizio sovra la Gerusalemme . . . Libri Due," *Opere* (Venice, 1735), vol. 4, p. 335 f. Yet another reference to the *De vera religione* occurs in the second book, in Tasso's discussion of imitation (4.341). Tasso's frequently quoted statement on the similarity between poetic and cosmic unity is located in his *Discourses on the Heroic Poem,* trans. M. Cavalchini and Irene Samuel (Oxford: Oxford University Press, 1973), p. 78: "the art of composing a poem resembles the plan of the universe, which is composed of contraries, as that of music is." (Cf. Augustine, *De civ. Dei* 11.18, where the reference is to chronological as well as spatial patterns, and to the rhetorical use of antitheses.) This observation is relevant to the technique of linking, which is in terms of parallels or contrasts. Tasso's clearest statement about linking is that episodes and descriptions "should be so combined that each concerns the other, corresponds to the other, and so depends on the other . . . that removing any one part or changing its place would destroy the whole" (ibid., p. 7).

7. Samuel, *Discourses,* p. xxxiii. For the passage, see p. 201.

8. Macrobius, *Commentary on the Dream of Scipio,* trans. William Harris Stahl (New York: Columbia University Press, 1966), pp. 94–117.

9. For example in his prose defence of his epic (see note 6).

10. See Augustine, *De Trinitate* 4, and his sermon on Psalm 150. I discuss the role of symbolic numbers and ratios in "Structure as Prophecy: The Influence of Biblical Exegesis Upon Theories of Literary Structure," *Silent Poetry,* ed. Alastair Fowler (London: Routledge & Kegan Paul, 1970), pp. 32–72.

11. I am indebted to Roy Tommy Eriksen for this useful term, which he explains in a thesis on the connection between rhetorical schemes and thematic structures. See "The Forme of Faustus Fortunes: A Structural and Thematic Analysis of Christopher Marlowe's *The Tragicall Historie of Doctor Faustus* (1616)" (University of Oslo, 1980). A topomorphical approach investigates the relationship between literary themes (or *topoi*) and textual units.

12. "In ordine di ruota: Circular Structure in 'The unfortunate Lover' and 'Upon Appleton House'," in *Tercentenary Essays in Honor of Andrew Marvell,* ed. Kenneth Friedenreich (Hamden, Conn.: The Shoe String Press, Inc., 1978), pp. 245–67. See also "A Frame of Words: On the Craftsmanship of Samuel Daniel," *ES* 60 (1979), 122–37.

13. Moses was told to build the tabernacle according to the pattern shown to him on the mountain, glossed as the pattern of the universe. According to Hebrews 8.5 this pattern was a "shadow of heavenly things," and this was the interpretation given to the structure which informs the cosmos.

14. Abraham Fraunce, *The Arcadian Rhetorike* (1588; rpt. Menston: The Scolar Press, 1969), book I, chs. 22–23.

15. *De musica* 6.14.47. It is noteworthy that this discussion of ordered linking is followed by an extended consideration of the way in which the virtue of Temperance assists in the task of linking man to the heavenly city rather than the earthly. The context which Augustine establishes here (6.15.49–17.59) seems to me relevant to the interpretation of *FQ* II.ix–xii, as I hope to explain elsewhere.

16. I must acknowledge my indebtedness here to Roy Tommy Eriksen, whose analysis of Tasso's text has been of great assistance.

17. All quotations are from *The Faerie Queene,* ed. J. C. Smith (Oxford: The Clarendon Press, 1909).

18. Spenser, *The Faerie Queene,* ed. Thomas P. Roche, Jr., . . . (Harmondsworth: Penguin Books, 1978), p. 1084 (note on I.iii.18.4).

19. Bongo seems to have spent his whole life in Bergamo, where he was born and where he died on 24 September 1601. The frequency with which his learned compilation of the symbolism connected with numbers *(Numerorum mysteria)* was reprinted testifies to its popularity. The dates of the first edition (in two parts) are 1583 and 1584; later expanded editions appeared in 1585, 1590, 1591, 1599, 1614, and 1618. The book was authorized by the Roman Catholic church, and it should be listed among the popular handbooks of the Renaissance, not among its esoterica. D. W. Smith, *Rara arithmetica* (Boston: Ginn & Co., 1908) believes that a Frenchman—also a canon—wrote the first treatise solely concerned with number symbolism: Jodocus Clichtoveus, *De mysticae numerorum significatione opusculum: eorum presertim qui in sacris litteris vsitati habentur spirituale[m] ipsorum designatione succincte elucidans* (Paris, 1513). Clichtoveus was educated at the Sorbonne and became a canon of Saint-Jean, Chartres. I mention these facts here in an attempt to demystify the subject of number symbolism. It belongs within the precincts of the church. It is a pleasing thought that Tasso may have known Bongo: Tasso's family, too, lived in Bergamo. Could it have been Tasso who inspired Bongo to include so much material from the poets in the later editions?

20. This definition could serve as a gloss on the events in Medina's castle.

21. See Joy Mulligan, "The British Constantine: An English Historical Myth," *JMRS* 8 (1978), 257–79.

22. On the giants see Augustine, *De civ. Dei* 15.9, 23. Spenser's account of the giants is entirely in keeping with the traditional view of the first age in human history. See Jean Céard, "La querelle des géants et la jeunesse du monde," *JMRS* 8 (1978), 37–76.

23. See Bongo's *Numerorum mysteria* on the number 42.

24. Single unrhymed lines can be found in Chapman, Ben Jonson, George Herbert, Henry Vaughan, and John Dryden, and their function will be indicated by the context. This is only one of several kinds of deviation from the established norm which may be employed to achieve special effects. One finds the occasional unrhymed line (or a violation of the established rhyme scheme) also in *The Shepheardes Calender,* and I take the famous astronomical error in "November" (when the sun is said to be in Pisces, which is the sign for February) to be such a deviation from an established pattern.

25. For an interesting structural analysis based on the numbers 7 and 9, see Jerry Leath Mills, "Spenser and the Numbers of History: A Note on the British and Elfin Chronicles in *The Faerie Queene,*" *PQ,* 55 (1976), 281–87. I had finished my own essay before reading the same author's thoughtful study, "Prudence, History, and the Prince in *The Faerie Queene,* Book II," *HLQ,* 41 (1978), 83–101. As Mills puts it, "The superficial moral confusion of the history is a challenge to Arthur's prudence, and he must find in it patterns to inform the conduct of his present affairs" (p. 90). For the use of number symbolism in late medie-